Rick Steves' PARIS 2000

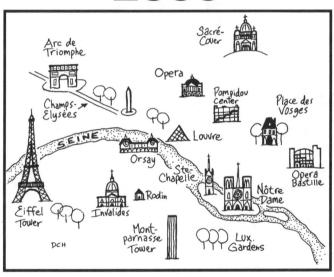

by Rick Steves, Steve Smith, and Gene Openshaw

John Muir Publications
Santa Fe, New Mexico

Other JMP travel guidebooks by Rick Steves
Europe 101: History and Art for the Traveler (with Gene Openshaw)
Rick Steves' Europe Through the Back Door
Rick Steves' Mona Winks (with Gene Openshaw)
Rick Steves' Best of Europe
Rick Steves' France, Belgium & the Netherlands (with Steve Smith)
Rick Steves' Germany, Austria & Switzerland
Rick Steves' Great Britain & Ireland
Rick Steves' Italy
Rick Steves' London (with Gene Openshaw)
Rick Steves' Postcards from Europe
Rick Steves' Rome (with Gene Openshaw)
Rick Steves' Scandinavia
Rick Steves' Spain & Portugal
Asia Through the Back Door (with Bob Effertz)
Rick Steves' Phrase Books: German, Italian, French,
   Spanish/Portuguese, and French/Italian/German

John Muir Publications, P.O. Box 613, Santa Fe, NM 87504
Copyright © 2000, 1999 by Europe Through the Back Door
Cover copyright © 2000, 1999 by John Muir Publications
All rights reserved.

Printed in the United States of America. Second printing April 2000.

Portions of this book were originally published in *Rick Steves' Mona Winks*
© 1998, 1996, 1993, 1988 by Rick Steves and Gene Openshaw and in *Rick Steves'*
France, Belgium & the Netherlands © 2000, 1999, 1998, 1997, 1996 by Rick Steves and
Steve Smith.

ISBN 1-56261-524-6
ISSN 1522-3299

For the latest on Rick's lectures, guidebooks, tours, and public television series,
contact Europe Through the Back Door, Box 2009, Edmonds, WA 98020,
tel. 425/771-8303, fax 425/771-0833, www.ricksteves.com, or e-mail:
rick@ricksteves.com.

Europe Through the Back Door Editor: Risa Laib
John Muir Publications Editors: Laurel Gladden Gillespie, Krista Lyons-Gould,
   Donna Leverenz
Production & Typesetting: Kathleen Sparkes, White Hart Design
Cover and Interior Design: Janine Lehmann
Maps: David C. Hoerlein
Photography: pp. 64, 67, 125: David C. Hoerlein, p. 206: Janine Lehmann,
   all others Rick Steves
Printer: Publishers Press
Front cover photo: Tour Eiffel; Paris, France; copyright © Blaine Harrington III

Distributed to the book trade by Publishers Group West,
Berkeley, California

CONTENTS
paris

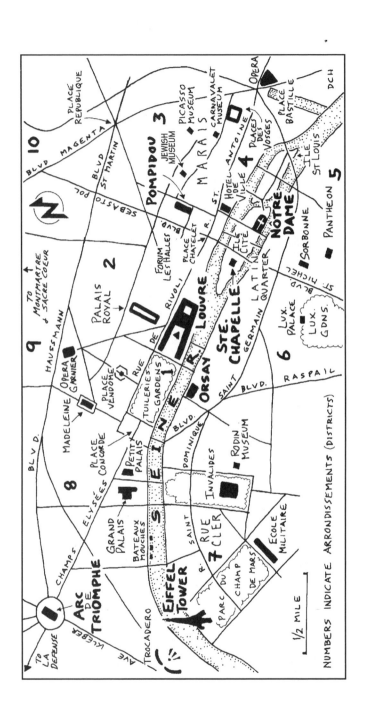

NUMBERS INDICATE ARRONDISSEMENTS (DISTRICTS)

1/2 MILE

INTRODUCTION

Paris—the City of Light—has been a beacon of culture for centuries. As a world capital for art, fashion, food, literature, and ideas, it stands as a symbol of all of the fine things that human civilization can offer. Come prepared to celebrate rather than judge the cultural differences, to capture the romance and joie de vivre that Paris exudes. Here, lovers of beauty can indulge themselves without looking ridiculous.

Paris offers sweeping boulevards, sleepy parks, world-class art galleries, chatty crêpe stands, Napoleon's body, sleek shopping malls, the Eiffel Tower, and people watching from outdoor cafés. Climb Notre-Dame and elevator up the Eiffel Tower, cruise the Seine and the Champs-Élysées, and master the Louvre and Orsay museums. Save some after-dark energy for one of the world's most romantic cities.

Sip decaf with Deconstructionists in a street-side café. Step into an Impressionist painting in a tree-lined park. Endure a rude waiter in the same restaurants that once insulted other visitors, from van Gogh and Picasso to Hemingway and Gershwin to Milan Kundera and Woody Allen.

This Information Is Accurate and Up-to-Date

This book is updated every year. Most publishers of guidebooks that cover a city from top to bottom can afford an update only every two or three years. Since this book is selective, covering only the places we think make the top week or two in and around Paris, we can update it each summer. Even with an annual update, things change. But if you're traveling with the current edition of this book, we guarantee you're using the most up-to-date information available. This book will help you have an inexpensive, hassle-free trip. Use this year's edition. Saving a few bucks by traveling on old information is not smart. If you're packing an old book, you'll learn the seriousness of your mistake ... in Paris. Your trip costs at least $10 per waking hour. Your time is valuable. This guidebook saves lots of time.

Welcome to Our Paris City Guide

This book is organized in the following way:

Paris Orientation includes tourist information, public transportation basics, and easy-to-read maps. The "Planning Your Time" section offers a suggested schedule with thoughts on how to best use your limited time.

Sights provides a succinct overview of Paris' most important sights, arranged by neighborhood, with ratings: ▲▲▲—Don't miss; ▲▲—Try hard to see; ▲—Worthwhile if you can make it; No rating—Worth knowing about.

The **Walks** cover five of Paris' most enjoyable neighborhoods: Historic Paris (Notre-Dame and Sainte-Chapelle), Champs-Élysées, Marais, Rue Cler (near the Eiffel Tower), and Montmartre.

The **Self-Guided Museum Tours** take you through Paris' six most interesting museums: Louvre, Orsay, Rodin, Cluny, Napoleon's Tomb, and Versailles.

Day Trips recommends nearby sights, ranging from châteaus to Monet's Giverny to Disneyland Paris.

Sleeping in Paris is a guide to our favorite budget hotels in three cozy neighborhoods, with orientation tips geared to make you feel at home.

Eating in Paris offers good-value restaurants ranging from inexpensive eateries to splurges, arranged by neighborhood, with a special section on Grand Cafés.

Paris with Children includes our top 10 recommendations to keep your kids (and you) happy in Paris.

Shopping in Paris helps you shop painlessly and enjoyably, without letting it overwhelm your vacation or ruin your budget.

Paris at Night is a guide to entertainment and evening fun, with music, bus tours, and river cruises, plus information on how to easily translate *Pariscope* magazine, the weekly entertainment guide.

Transportation Connections covers connections by train and plane, with detailed information on Paris' two airports and six train stations, laying the groundwork for your smooth arrival and departure.

The **Appendix** includes a Paris history, a climate chart, telephone tips, French survival phrases, and a handy almanac of resources.

Throughout the book, when you see a ✪ in a listing, it

means that the sight is covered in much more depth in one of our walks or self-guided tours—a page number will tell you just where to look to find more information.

Browse through this book and choose your favorite sights. Then have a *fantastique* trip! You'll become your own guide with our self-guided walks and museum tours. Traveling like a temporary local, you'll get the absolute most out of every mile, minute, and dollar. You won't waste time on mediocre sights because, unlike other guidebooks, we cover only the best. Since lousy, expensive hotels are a major financial pitfall, we've worked hard to assemble the best accommodations values. And, as you explore the city we know and love, we're happy you'll be meeting some of our favorite Parisian people.

Trip Costs

Five components make up your trip costs: airfare, surface transportation, room and board, sightseeing/entertainment, and shopping/miscellany.

Airfare: Don't try to sort through the mess. Find and use a good travel agent. A basic round-trip U.S.A.–Paris flight costs $700 to $1,100, depending on where you fly from and when.

Surface Transportation: For a typical one-week visit, allow about $50 for Métro tickets and a couple of day trips. Add an additional $100 if you opt for taxi rides to and from the airport (or save money by taking a shuttle express, airport bus, or the RER).

Room and Board: You can thrive in Paris on $70 a day per person for room and board. A $70-a-day budget allows $10 for lunch, $15 for dinner, and $45 for lodging (based on two people splitting the cost of a $90 double room that includes breakfast). That's doable. Students and tightwads do it on $40 ($20 per bed, $15–20 for meals and snacks). But budget sleeping and eating require aggressive utilization of the skills and information covered in this book (and in much greater depth in *Rick Steves' Europe Through the Back Door*).

Sightseeing and Entertainment: You want the Paris Museum Pass, which covers most sights in Paris. (For more information, see Sights chapter.) You'll pay about $30 for a three-day pass and $45 for a five-day pass. Without a museum pass, figure $6 to $8 per major sight (e.g., Louvre-$8, Rodin-$6), $4 for minor ones (climbing church towers), and $25 for bus tours and splurge experiences (concerts in Sainte-Chapelle). An overall average of $15 a day works for most. Don't skimp here. After all, this category directly powers most of the experiences all the other expenses are designed to make possible.

Shopping and Miscellany: Figure $3 per ice-cream cone,

coffee, or soft drink. Shopping can vary in cost from nearly nothing to a small fortune. Good budget travelers find that this category has little to do with assembling a trip full of lifelong and wonderful memories.

Exchange Rate

We've priced things in this book in the local currency:

6F (French francs) = about $1.

To convert French prices to dollars, divide by six (350F = about $60).

Prices, Times, and Discounts

The prices in this book, as well as the hours and telephone numbers, are accurate as of late 1999. Europe is always changing, and we know you'll understand that this, like any other guidebook, starts to yellow even before it's printed.

In Europe—and in this book—you'll be using the 24-hour clock. After 12 noon, keep going—13:00, 14:00, and so on. For anything over 12, subtract 12 and add p.m. (for example, 14:00 is 2:00 p.m.).

This book lists peak-season hours for sightseeing attractions. Off-season, expect generally shorter hours and more lunchtime breaks.

While discounts for sights and transportation are not listed in this book, seniors (60 and over), students (with International Student Identification Cards), and youths (under 18) often get big discounts—but only by asking.

When to Go

Late spring and fall are best for weather but are the most crowded. Summers are generally hot and dry; look for the rare room with air-conditioning if you wilt in the heat. Hotels are easy in the summer, and while many French businesses close in August, the traveler hardly notices. Paris makes a great winter getaway. Airfares are cheap and the city feels lively but not particularly touristy. The only problem—weather—is fixed by dressing correctly. Expect cold and rain but no snow.

Red Tape and Business Hours

You need a passport but no visa or shots to travel in France. Many small markets, *boulangeries* (bakeries), and the like are open Sunday mornings until noon. On Mondays many businesses are closed until 14:00, and often all day. Saturdays are like weekdays.

PTT (Postal, Telegraph, and Telephone) offices' hours vary, though most are open weekdays from 8:00 to 19:00 and Saturdays from 8:00 to 12:00. Stamps are also sold at the *tabac* (tobacco shop). It costs 4.40F to mail a postcard to the United States.

Banking

Bring your ATM, credit, or debit card, along with traveler's checks in dollars.

The best and easiest way to get cash in French francs is to use the omnipresent French bank machines (always open, lower fees, quick processing); you'll need a four-digit PIN (numbers only, no letters) with your Visa or MasterCard. Some ATM bankcards will work at some banks, though Visa and MasterCard are more reliable. Before you go, verify with your bank that your card will work. Bring two different cards or two copies of the same card; demagnetization seems to be a common problem. "Cash machine" in French is *distributeur automatique des billets*, or D.A.B. (day-ah-bay).

Regular banks have the best rates for cashing traveler's checks. For a large exchange, it pays to compare rates and fees. The Bank of France (Banque de France) usually offers the best rates. Banking hours vary, though most are open Tuesday through Friday 9:00 to 16:30. Some branches are open Saturday morning, and many are closed on Monday.

Post offices, train stations, and tourist offices usually change money if you can't get to a bank. Post offices (which take cash or American Express checks) give a good rate, have longer hours, and charge no fee.

Just like at home, credit (or debit) cards work easily at larger hotels, restaurants, and shops. Smaller businesses prefer payment in local currency. Smart travelers function with hard local cash.

If using traveler's checks, don't be petty about changing money. The greatest avoidable money-changing expense is having to waste time every few days returning to a bank. Change 10 days' or two weeks' worth of money, get big bills, stuff it in your money belt, and travel!

The Language Barrier

You've no doubt heard that the French are "mean and cold and refuse to speak English." This is an out-of-date preconception that's going the same way as the "Ugly American." The French are as friendly as any other people; Parisians are no more disagreeable than New Yorkers. And, without any doubt, the French speak more English than Americans speak French. Be reasonable in your expectations: Small-town French postal clerks are every bit as speedy, cheery, and multilingual as ours are back home.

With an understanding of French culture, you're less likely to misinterpret the French people. The French take great pride in their culture, clinging to their belief in cultural superiority despite the fact that they're no longer a world superpower. Let's face it, it's tough to keep on smiling when you've been crushed by a Big Mac, lashed by Levis, and drowned in instant coffee. To the French, Americans must seem a lot like Ross Perot in a good mood. The French are cold only if you decide to see them that way. Look for friendliness and give them the benefit of the doubt. The cultural fine points, not rugged Yankee individualism, are respected here.

Communication difficulties in France are exaggerated. To hurdle the language barrier, bring a small English/French dictionary, a phrase book (look for ours), a menu reader, and a good supply of patience. If you learn only six phrases, learn and use these: *bonjour* (good day), *pardon* (pardon me), *s'il vous plaît* (please), *merci* (thank you), *au revoir* (good-bye), and *Comment trouvez-vous mon haleine?* (how's my breath?). The French place great importance on politeness.

The French are language perfectionists—they take their language (and other languages) seriously. Often, they speak more English than they let on. This isn't a tourist-baiting tactic but timidity on their part to speak another language less than fluently. Start any conversation with *"Bonjour, Madame/Monsieur. Parlez-vous anglais?"* and hope they speak more English than you speak French. In transactions, a small notepad and pen minimize misunderstandings about prices; have vendors write down the price.

Travel Smart

Reread this book as you travel. Buy a phone card and use it for reservations and confirmations. Enjoy the friendliness of the local people. Ask questions. Most locals are eager to point you in their idea of the right direction. Wear your money belt and see simplicity as a virtue. Those who expect to travel smart, do. Plan ahead for banking, laundry, post office chores, and picnics. Mix intense and relaxed periods. Every trip (and every traveler) needs at least a few slack days. Pace yourself. Assume you will return.

As you read through this book, note the days when sights are closed. Sundays have pros and cons, as they do for travelers in the U.S.A. (special events and weekly markets, limited hours, shops and banks closed, limited public transportation, no rush hours). Saturdays are virtually weekdays. Popular places are even more popular on weekends and inundated on three-day weekends (most common in May).

French Tourist Offices in the U.S.A.

France's national tourist offices in the United States are a wealth of information. Before your trip, request any specific information you may want (such as city maps and schedules of upcoming festivals).

French Tourist Offices: For general information, call 410/286-8310 or write to the nearest office: 444 Madison Ave., 16th floor, New York, NY 10022; 676 N. Michigan Ave., #600, Chicago, IL 60611; 9454 Wilshire Blvd., #715, Beverly Hills, CA 90212; www.francetourism.com. For the latest on Paris, visit www.pariscope.fr.

Recommended Guidebooks

For most travelers, this book is all you need. But if you'd like more information, you may want to buy an additional guidebook. The Michelin Green Guide, which is somewhat scholarly, and the more readable *Paris Access* guide are both well researched. If you'll be traveling elsewhere in France, consider *Rick Steves' France, Belgium & the Netherlands.*

Rick Steves' Books and Videos

Rick Steves' Europe Through the Back Door 2000 (John Muir Publications, 2000) gives you budget travel tips on minimizing jet lag, packing light, planning your itinerary, traveling by car or train, finding budget beds without reservations, changing money, avoiding rip-offs, outsmarting thieves, hurdling the language barrier, staying healthy, taking great photographs, using your bidet, and lots more. The book also includes chapters on 34 of Rick's favorite "Back Doors."

Rick Steves' Country Guides are a series of seven guidebooks covering the Best of Europe; France, Belgium, and the Netherlands; Great Britain and Ireland; Italy; Spain and Portugal; Scandinavia; and Germany, Austria, and Switzerland. All are updated annually and come out in January.

Rick Steves' City Guides, updated annually, include this book and *Rick Steves' London* and *Rome*. With the sleek Eurostar train, London is now just three hours from Paris. Consider combining the two cities (and books) for a great visit.

Europe 101: History and Art for the Traveler (co-written with Gene Openshaw, John Muir Publications, 1996) gives you the story of Europe's people, history, and art. Written for smart people who were sleeping in their history and art classes before they knew they were going to Europe, *101* carbonates Europe's sights.

Rick Steves' Mona Winks (also co-written with Gene Openshaw, John Muir Publications, 1998) gives you fun, easy-to-follow, self-guided tours of Europe's top 20 museums. All of the *Mona Winks* chapters on Paris are included in this Paris guidebook. But if you'd like similar coverage for the great museums in London, Amsterdam, Venice, Florence, and Rome, *Mona*'s for you.

Rick Steves' French Phrase Book & Dictionary (John Muir Publications, 1999) gives you the words and survival phrases you'll need while traveling in Paris.

My television series, *Travels in Europe with Rick Steves*, has 13 brand-new shows for 2000, including a show on Paris. Of my 52 original episodes, three cover Paris and six half-hour shows cover other parts of France. These air throughout the country on local public-television stations and the Travel Channel. They are also available as information-packed videotapes, along with my two-hour slide-show lecture on France (call 425/771-8303 for our free newsletter/catalog).

Rick Steves' Postcards from Europe (John Muir Publications, 1999), my autobiographical book, packs 25 years of travel anecdotes and insights into the ultimate 3,000-mile European adventure. Through my guidebooks, I share my favorite European discoveries with you. *Postcards* introduces you to my favorite European friends.

Maps
The maps in this book, drawn by Dave Hoerlein, are concise and simple. Dave, who is well traveled in Paris, designed these maps to help you orient quickly and get to where you want to go painlessly. Once in Paris, simply pick up the free Paris map at your hotel and you're ready to travel.

Transportation
Transportation concerns within Paris are limited to the subway, buses, and taxis, all covered extensively in the Orientation chapter. If you have a car, stow it. You don't want to drive in Paris. For all the specifics on transportation throughout France by train or car, see *Rick Steves' France, Belgium & the Netherlands 2000*.

Telephones and Mail
Make local and long-distance calls from the public phones on the street. An efficient card-operated system has replaced coin-operated public phones in Paris. Phone cards are a breeze to use. Buy a phone card *(une télécarte)*, available at any post office, train station, and most newsstands and tobacco shops *(tabac* in France). There are two denominations of phone cards in France: *une petite* costs 49F; *une grande* is 98F. When you use the card, simply take the phone off the hook, insert the card, and wait for a dial tone. The price of the call (local or international) is automatically deducted. Buy a card at the beginning of your

trip and use it for hotel reservations, calling tourist information offices, and phoning home.

France's newest phone card (KOSMOS) is not inserted into the phone but allows you to dial from the comfort of your hotel (or anywhere) and charge the call to the card for lower rates than with a *télécarte*. It's simple to use, instructions are provided in English, and the card is sold wherever *télécartes* are sold. And while the per-minute rates are cheaper than a *télécarte*, it's slower to use (more digits to dial), so local calls are more quickly made with a *télécarte* from a phone booth.

U.S.A. Direct services are no longer a good value. While it's psychologically comforting to dial an AT&T, MCI, or Sprint access number and get an operator in Atlanta, this will now double your per-minute costs for calls from Paris to the U.S.A. (and some hotels will charge a fee for calling-card calls). The cheapest way to phone home is to use a KOSMOS card or a French *télécarte*. You can make a very quick call for as little as 50 cents.

France has a dial-direct 10-digit telephone system. There are no area codes. To call to or from anywhere in France, including Paris, you dial the 10 numbers directly. All Paris numbers start with 01. If you encounter any old eight-digit numbers, add that prefix.

To dial out of France, you must start your call with its international code: 00. To call France from another country, start with the international access code of the country you're calling from (00 for most European countries and 011 from America or Canada), dial France's country code (33), then drop the initial 0 of the 10-digit local number and dial the remaining nine digits. For example, the number of our favorite hotel in Paris is 01 47 05 49 15. To call it from home, dial 011-33-1 47 05 49 15. For a listing of international access codes and country codes, see the Appendix. Paris time is six/nine hours ahead of the east/west coast of the U.S.A.

Mail: To arrange for mail delivery, reserve a few hotels along your route in advance and give their addresses to friends, or use American Express Company's mail services (available to anyone who has at least one Amex traveler's check). Allow 10 days for a letter to arrive. Phoning is so easy that we've dispensed with mail stops altogether.

Sleeping

A comfortable hotel in Paris costs less than a comparable hotel in London or in most major U.S. cities. It's a great hotel city. Still, you should reserve in advance to secure the best hotel for you. We like places that are clean, small, central, traditional, inexpensive, friendly, and not listed in other guidebooks. Most places we list have at least five of these seven virtues.

Paris Hotels

In this book, the price for a double room will normally range from
$40 (very simple, toilet and shower down the hall) to $150 (maximum plumbing and more), with most clustering around $80. A
triple and a double are often the same room, with a small double
bed and a sliver single, so a third person sleeps very cheaply. Most
hotels have a few singles, triples, and quads. While groups sleep
cheap, traveling alone can be expensive—a single room usually
costs about the same as a double. Hotels cannot legally allow more
in the room than that shown on their price list.

French receptionists are often reluctant to mention the
cheaper rooms. Study the room price list posted at the desk.
Understand it. You'll save about $15 on the average if you get a
room with a "shower down the hall" rather than in your room;
ask for a room without a shower (*sans douche*) rather than with a
shower (*avec douche*). A room with a bathtub (*salle de bain*) costs $5
to $10 more than a room with a shower. A double bed (*grand lit*) is
$5 to $10 cheaper than twins (*deux petits lits*). Hotels are inclined to
give you a room with a tub (which the French prefer). If you prefer
a double bed and a shower, you'll need to ask for it, and you'll save
up to $20. If you'll take twins or a double, ask for a *chambre pour
deux* (room for two) to avoid being needlessly turned away.

The French have a simple hotel rating system (zero through
four stars) depending on the amenities offered. We like the one-
or two-star hotels. More than two stars gets you expensive and
unnecessary amenities. Unclassified hotels (no stars) can be bar-
gains or depressing dumps. You'll almost always have the option
of breakfast at your hotel, which is pleasant and convenient, but—
at 25F to 50F—often double the price of the corner café. While
hotels hope you'll spring for their breakfast, this is optional unless
otherwise noted.

Rooms are safe. Still, keep cameras and money out of sight.
Towels aren't routinely replaced every day; drip-dry and conserve.
If that French Lincoln-log pillow isn't your idea of comfort,
American-style pillows (and extra blankets) are usually in the
closet or available on request. To get a pillow, ask for "*Un oreiller,
s'il vous plaît*" (un oar-ray-yay, see-voo-play). And if you're planning to visit Paris in the summer, the extra expense of an air-
conditioned room can be money well spent.

Making Reservations

Reserve ahead for Paris, the sooner the better. May, June, September, and October are the busiest months. We've taken great
pains to list telephone numbers with long-distance instructions
(see "Telephones and Mail," above, and the Appendix). Use the

Sleep Code

To give maximum information with a minimum of space, we use these codes to describe accommodations listed in this book. Prices listed are per room, not per person.

S = Single room (or price for one person in a double)
D = Double or Twin (French double beds can be very small)
T = Triple (generally a double bed with a single)
Q = Quad (usually two double beds)
b = Private bathroom with toilet and shower or tub
t = Private toilet only (the shower is down the hall)
s = Private shower or tub only (the toilet is down the hall)
CC = Accepts credit cards (**V** = Visa, **M** = MasterCard, **A**= American Express). If CC isn't mentioned, assume you'll have to pay cash.
* = French hotel rating system, ranging from zero to four stars.

According to this code, a couple staying at a "Db-450F, CC:V" hotel would pay a total of 450 French francs (or about $75) for a double room with a private bathroom. The hotel accepts Visa or French cash in payment.

telephone and convenient telephone cards. Most hotels listed are accustomed to English-only speakers. A hotel receptionist will trust you and hold a room until 16:00 without a deposit, though some will ask for a credit-card number. Honor (or cancel by phone) your reservations. Long distance is cheap and easy from public phone booths. Don't let these people down—we promised you'd call and cancel if for some reason you won't show up. Don't needlessly confirm rooms through the tourist office; they'll take a commission.

To reserve from home, call, fax, e-mail, or write the hotel. E-mail is preferred when possible. Phone and fax costs are reasonable, and simple English is usually fine. To fax, use the fax form in the Appendix (online at www.ricksteves.com/reservation). If you're writing, add the zip code and confirm the need and method for a deposit. A two-night stay in August would be "2 nights, 16/8/00 to 18/8/00"—Europeans write the date day/month/year, and European hotel jargon uses your day of departure. You'll often receive a letter back requesting one night's deposit. A credit card will usually be accepted as a deposit, though you may need to send a signed traveler's check or a bank draft in the local currency.

If your credit card is the deposit, you can pay with your card or cash when you arrive. If you don't show up, you'll be billed for one night. Reconfirm your reservations a day in advance for safety.

Hostels
Parisian hostels charge about $18 per bed. Some require a hostel membership; the best don't. Get a hostel card before you go if you need one. Travelers of any age are welcome if they don't mind dorm-style accommodations and meeting other travelers. Travelers without a hostel card can generally spend the night for a small extra "one-night membership" fee. Cheap meals are sometimes available, and kitchen facilities are usually provided for do-it-yourselfers.

Apartments
It's easy, though not necessarily cheaper, to rent a furnished apartment in Paris. Consider this option if you're either traveling with a family or staying two weeks or longer. For listings, see the end of the Sleeping chapter.

Eating in France
The French eat long and well. Relaxed lunches, three-hour dinners, and endless hours sitting in outdoor cafés are the norm. They have a legislated 35-hour workweek and a self-imposed 36-hour eat-week. The French spend much of their five annual weeks of paid vacation at *la table*. Local cafés, cuisine, and wines become a highlight of any French adventure—sightseeing for your palate. Even if the rest of you is sleeping in cheap hotels, let your taste buds travel first-class in Paris. (They can go coach in England.) You can eat well without going broke, but choose carefully— you're just as likely to blow a small fortune on a mediocre meal as you are to dine wonderfully for $15.

Restaurants
If you want the menu, ask for *la carte* (and order à la carte like the locals do); if you ask for the *menu*, you'll get a fixed-price meal. This no-brainer *menu* offers three or four courses, generally a good value: You get your choice of soup, appetizer, or salad (*entrée*); your choice of three or four main courses (*plat principal*) with vegetables; plus a cheese course and/or a choice of desserts. Service is included, but wine or drinks are generally extra.

In France an entrée is the first course and *le plat* is the main course. *Le plat* or *le plat du jour* (plate of the day) is the main course with vegetables (usually 50–70F). For a light, healthy, fast, and inexpensive option in a pricey restaurant, the various salads are 40F to 50F well spent. Soft drinks and beer cost 8F to 20F

($1.50–4), and a bottle or carafe of house wine—which is invariably good enough for Rick and Gene, if not always Steve—costs 30F to 70F ($6–14). Service is always included. To get a waiter's or waitress' attention, simply say, *"S'il vous plaît"* (please). To alienate the same person, snap your fingers and say, *"Garçon."*

Café Culture

French cafés (or *brasseries*) provide reasonable light meals and a refuge from museum and church overload. They are carefully positioned viewpoints from which to watch the river of local life flow by. It's easier for the novice to sit and feel comfortable in a café when you know the system.

Check the price list first. Prices, which must be posted prominently, vary wildly between cafés. Cafés charge different prices for the same drink depending upon where you want to be seated. Prices are posted: *comptoir* (counter/bar) and the more expensive *salle* (seated).

Your waiter probably won't overwhelm you with friendliness. Notice how hard they work. They almost never stop. Cozying up to clients (French or foreign) is probably the last thing on their minds.

The standard menu items are the Croque Monsieur (grilled cheese sandwich) and Croque Madame (Monsieur with a fried egg on top). The *salade composée* (com-po-zay) is a hearty chef's salad. Sandwiches are least expensive but plain unless you buy them at the *boulangerie* (bakery). To get more than a piece of ham (*jambon*) on a baguette, order a sandwich *jambon-crudité* (crew-dee-tay), which means garnished with lettuce, tomatoes, cucumbers, and so on. Omelettes come lonely on a plate with a basket of bread. The *plat du jour* (daily special) is your fast, hearty 50F to 60F hot plate. Regardless of what you order, bread is free; to get more, just hold up your bread basket and ask, *"Encore, s'il vous plaît."*

To order coffee, here is the lingo:
- *un express* (uh nex-press) = shot of espresso
- *une noisette* (oon nwah-zette) = shot of espresso with a shot of milk
- *café au lait* (kah-fay oh lay) = coffee with lots of milk; also called *un grand crème* (uh grahn krem = big) or *un petit crème* (uh puh-tee krem = average)
- *un café allongé* (uh kah-fay al-own-zhay) = cup of coffee, closest to American style
- *un décaffine* (uh day-kah-fee-nay) = decaf, and can modify any of the above drinks

Note: By law the waiter must give you a glass of tap water with your coffee if you request it; ask for *"un verre d'eau"* (uh vayre dough).

House wine at the bar is cheap (5–10F per glass, cheapest by the *pichet*, or pitcher), and the local beer is cheaper on tap (*une pression*) than in the bottle (*bouteille*). While prices include service, tip, and tax, it's polite to round up for a drink or meal well served (e.g., if your bill was 24F, leave 25F).

Breakfast

Petit déjeuner (peh-tee day-zhu-nay) is typically *café au lait* (coffee with hot milk), hot chocolate, or tea; a roll with butter and marmalade; and a croissant. Don't expect much variety for breakfast, but the bread is fresh and the coffee is great. While available at your hotel (25–50F), breakfasts are cheaper at the corner café. It's entirely acceptable to buy a croissant or roll at a nearby bakery and eat it with your cup of coffee (no refills) at a café. Some hotels offer a *petit-déjeuner* buffet (about 50F) with cereals, yogurt, cheeses, fruit, and breads. If the morning urge for an egg gets the best of you, drop into a café and order *une omelette* or *oeufs sur le plat* (fried eggs). You could also buy or bring plastic bowls and spoons from home, buy a box of French cereal and a small box of milk, and eat in your room before heading out for coffee. We carry fruit and a package of *Vache Qui Rit* (Laughing Cow) cheese to supplement the morning jelly.

Lunch

For lunch—*déjeuner* (day-zhuh-nay)—we picnic or munch a take-away *boulangerie* sandwich.

French picnics can be first-class affairs and adventures in high cuisine. Be daring. Try the smelly cheeses, ugly pâtés, sissy quiches, and minuscule yogurts. Local shopkeepers are accustomed to selling small quantities of produce. Try the tasty salads to go and ask for *une fourchette en plastique* (a plastic fork).

Gather supplies early; you'll probably visit several small stores to assemble a complete meal, and many close at noon. Look for a *boulangerie* (bakery), a *crémerie* (cheeses), a *charcuterie* (deli items, meats, and pâtés), an *épicerie* or *alimentation* (small grocery with veggies, drinks, and so on), and a *pâtisserie* (delicious pastries). For the best picnic shopping in Paris, try the rue Cler neighborhood; take the Rue Cler Walk (see page 68), and shop as you go.

Local *supermarchés* offer less color and cost, more efficiency, and adequate quality. Department stores often have supermarkets in the basement.

If not picnicking, look for food stands and bakeries selling take-out sandwiches and drinks, or *crêperies* or *brasseries* for fast and easy sit-down restaurant food. *Brasseries* are cafés serving basic fare such as omelettes, chicken, and fries, as well as simple sandwiches and hearty salads. Look for their *plat du jour* (daily special).

Many French restaurants offer good value, three- to five-course menus at lunch only. The same menu is often 40F more at dinner. For more tips, see "Café Culture," above.

Dinner

For *dîner* (dee-nay), choose restaurants filled with locals, not places with big neon signs boasting, "We Speak English." Consider your hotelier's opinion. If the menu (*la carte*) isn't posted outside, move along. Also look for set-price menus and restaurants serving regional specialities. Ask the waiter for help deciphering *la carte*. Go with his or her recommendations and anything *de la maison* (of the house). Galloping gourmets should bring a menu translator; the Marling Menu Master is excellent. Remember, if you ask for a menu, you'll get a meal (*la carte* is the list of what's cooking), and if you ask for an entrée, you'll get a first course (soup, salad, or appetizer). The wines are often listed in a separate *carte des vins*. Tipping (*pourboire*) is unnecessary, though if you enjoyed the service, it's polite to leave a few francs.

Drinks

In stores, unrefrigerated soft drinks and beer are one-third the price of cold drinks. Milk and boxed fruit juice are the cheapest drinks. Avoid buying drinks-to-go at street-side stands; you'll find them far cheaper in a shop. Try to keep a water bottle with you. Water quenches your thirst better and cheaper than anything you'll find in a store or café. We drink tap water throughout France.

The French often order bottled water with their meal (*eau minérale*, oh mee-nay-rahl). If you'd prefer a free pitcher of tap water, ask for *une carafe d'eau*. Otherwise, you may unwittingly buy bottled water. When ordering a beer at a café or restaurant, ask for *une pression* or *un demi* (draft beer), which is cheaper than bottled. When ordering table wine at a café or restaurant, ask for a pitcher (*un pichet*, pee-shay), again cheaper than a bottle. If all you want is a glass of wine, ask for *un verre de vin*. You could drink away your children's inheritance if you're not careful. The most famous wines are the most expensive, while lesser-known taste-alikes remain a bargain. If you like brandy, try a *marc* (regional brandy, e.g., *marc de Bourgogne*) or Armagnac, cognac's cheaper twin brother. Pastis, the standard apéritif, is a sweet anise or licorice drink that comes on the rocks with a glass of water. Cut it to taste with lots of water. France's best beer is Alsatian; try Krônenburg or the heavier Pelfort. *Une panache* (pan-a-shay) is a very refreshing French shandy (7-Up and beer). For a fun, bright, nonalcoholic drink, order *un diabolo menthe* (7-Up with mint syrup). The ice cubes melted after the last Yankee tour group left.

Stranger in a Strange Land

We travel all the way to Europe to enjoy differences—to become temporary locals. You'll experience frustrations. Certain truths that we find "God given" or "self evident," like cold beer, ice in drinks, bottomless cups of coffee, hot showers, body odor smelling bad, and bigger being better, are suddenly not so true. One of the benefits of travel is the eye-opening realization that there are logical, civil, and even better alternatives. Paris is an understandably proud city. To enjoy its people you need to celebrate the differences. A willingness to go local ensures that you'll enjoy a full dose of Parisian hospitality.

Back Door Manners

While updating our guidebooks, we hear over and over again that our readers are considerate and fun to have as guests. Thank you for traveling as temporary locals who are sensitive to the culture. It's fun to follow you in our travels.

France Tours by Rick Steves and Steve Smith

At Europe Through the Back Door, we organize and lead one-week tours of Paris and longer tours covering the highlights of France, including Paris. The Paris tours take place in January and November, when crowds and airfare are at their lowest, and are limited to 20 people. Our France tours depart each year from April through October, are limited to 26 people per group, and have two guides and big buses with lots of empty seats. For details on how to travel with us, call 425/771-8303 or check www.ricksteves.com.

Send Us a Postcard, Drop Us a Line

If you enjoy a successful trip with the help of this book and would like to share your discoveries, please fill out and send the survey at the end of this book to Europe Through the Back Door, Box 2009, Edmonds, WA 98020. We personally read and value all feedback. Thanks in advance—it helps a lot.

For our latest travel information, tap into our Web site: www.ricksteves.com. To check for any updates to this book, visit www.ricksteves.com/update. Our e-mail address is rick @ricksteves.com. Anyone is welcome to request a free issue of our Back Door quarterly newsletter.

Judging from all the positive feedback and happy postcards we receive from travelers who have used this book, it's safe to assume you're on your way to a great, affordable vacation—with the finesse of an independent, experienced traveler.

From this point, "we" (your co-authors) will shed our respective egos and become "I."

Thanks, and bon voyage!

BACK DOOR TRAVEL PHILOSOPHY
As Taught in *Rick Steves' Europe Through the Back Door*

Travel is intensified living—maximum thrills per minute and one of the last great sources of legal adventure. Travel is freedom. It's recess, and we need it.

Experiencing the real Europe requires catching it by surprise, going casual... "Through the Back Door."

Affording travel is a matter of priorities. (Make do with the old car.) You can travel—simply, safely, and comfortably—anywhere in Europe for $70 a day plus transportation costs. In many ways, spending more money only builds a thicker wall between you and what you came to see. Europe is a cultural carnival, and, time after time, you'll find that its best acts are free and the best seats are the cheap ones.

A tight budget forces you to travel close to the ground, meeting and communicating with the people, not relying on service with a purchased smile. Never sacrifice sleep, nutrition, safety, or cleanliness in the name of budget. Simply enjoy the local-style alternatives to expensive hotels and restaurants.

Extroverts have more fun. If your trip is low on magic moments, kick yourself and make things happen. If you don't enjoy a place, maybe you don't know enough about it. Seek the truth. Recognize tourist traps. Give a culture the benefit of your open mind. See things as different but not better or worse. Any culture has much to share.

Of course, travel, like the world, is a series of hills and valleys. Be fanatically positive and militantly optimistic. If something's not to your liking, change your liking. Travel is addicting. It can make you a happier American, as well as a citizen of the world. Our Earth is home to 6 billion equally important people. It's humbling to travel and find that people don't envy Americans. They like us, but, with all due respect, they wouldn't trade passports.

Globe-trotting destroys ethnocentricity. It helps you understand and appreciate different cultures. Travel changes people. It broadens perspectives and teaches new ways to measure quality of life. Many travelers toss aside their hometown blinders. Their prized souvenirs are the strands of different cultures they decide to knit into their own character. The world is a cultural yarn shop. And Back Door Travelers are weaving the ultimate tapestry. Come on, join in!

ORIENTATION

Many people fall in love with Paris. Some see the essentials and flee, overwhelmed by the huge city. With the proper approach and a good orientation, you'll fall head over heels for Europe's capital city.

This orientation to the City of Lights will illuminate your trip. The day plans—for visits of one to seven days—will help you prioritize the many sights. You'll tap into Paris' information sources for current events. Most important, you'll learn to navigate Paris by Métro, bus, taxi, or foot. For most travelers, the key to the city is a Métro ticket.

Planning Your Time

Paris in One, Two, or Three Days
If you have only one day, just do Day One; for two days, do the first two days.

Day 1
Morning: Follow Historic Paris Walk, featuring Île de la Cité, Notre-Dame, Latin Quarter, and Sainte-Chapelle.
Afternoon: Tour Louvre Museum.
Evening: Cruise Seine River or take illuminated Paris by Night bus tour.

Day 2
Morning: Follow Champs-Élysées Walk, from Arc de Triomphe down the grand Champs-Élysées boulevard to Tuileries Gardens.
Midday: Tour Orsay Museum.
Afternoon: Catch RER from Orsay to Versailles. To avoid crowds, see the park first and the palace late.
Evening: Enjoy Trocadero scene and twilight ride up Eiffel Tower.

Day 3
Morning: Follow Marais Walk.
Afternoon: Tour Rodin Museum, then Napoleon's Tomb.
Evening: Take Montmartre Walk, featuring Sacré-Coeur.

Paris in Four to Seven Days without Going In-Seine

Day 1
Morning: Follow Historic Paris Walk, featuring Île de la Cité, Notre-Dame, Latin Quarter, and Sainte-Chapelle.
Afternoon: Sit in a café and go shopping.
Evening: Cruise Seine River or take illuminated Paris by Night bus tour.

Day 2
Morning: Tour Louvre Museum.
Afternoon: Follow Champs-Élysées Walk, from Arc de Triomphe down the grand Champs-Élysées boulevard to Tuileries Gardens.
Evening: Take Montmartre Walk, featuring Sacré-Coeur.

Day 3
Morning: Take Rue Cler Walk.
Midday: Tour Orsay Museum.
Afternoon: Catch RER from Orsay to Versailles. To avoid crowds, see the park first and the palace late.

Day 4
Morning: Follow Marais Walk.
Afternoon: Tour Rodin Museum, then Napoleon's Tomb.
Evening: Enjoy Trocadero scene and twilight ride up Eiffel Tower.

Day 5, 6, and 7
Choose from:
Shopping and cafés
Montmartre and Sacré-Coeur (by day)
Picasso, Cluny, Marmottan, or Jewish History museums
Day trip to Chartres
Day trip to Vaux-le-Vicomte and Fontainebleau
Day trip to Disneyland Paris
Evening: Night bus or boat tour (whichever you have yet to do)

Paris: A Verbal Map

Paris is split in half by the Seine River, divided into 20 *arrondissements* (proud and independent governmental jurisdictions), and

Daily Reminder

Monday: These museums—Orsay, Rodin, Marmottan, Montmartre, and Versailles—are closed today; the Louvre is more crowded because of this but the Richelieu wing stays open until 21:45. Many small stores don't open until 14:00. Some restaurants close on Monday. It's discount night at most cinemas.

Tuesday: Many museums are closed today, including the Louvre, Picasso, and Cluny, as well as the châteaus of Chantilly and Fontainebleau. Versailles and the Orsay are particularly busy today.

Wednesday: All sights are open, the Louvre until 21:45. The weekly *Pariscope* magazine comes out today. School is out, so many child-related activities are open (and busy).

Thursday: All sights are open, and department stores are open late. Vaux-le-Vicomte hosts candlelight visits (May–Oct).

Friday: All sights are open. Afternoon trains and roads leaving Paris are crowded; TGV reservation fees are higher.

Saturdays: All sights are open. There are candlelight visits of Vaux-le-Vicomte (May–Oct); otherwise avoid weekend crowds at area châteaus. Paris department stores are busy.

Sunday: Some museums are two-thirds price all day (Louvre, Orsay, Cluny, and Picasso). The fountains run at Versailles. The Marais is the place to window shop and café hop; many of Paris' stores are closed on Sunday, but, as this is the Jewish Quarter, it bustles. Look for organ concerts at St. Sulpice and possibly other churches. The American Church offers a free evening concert (18:00).

circled by a ring-road freeway (the *périphérique*). You'll find Paris easier to negotiate if you know which side of the river you're on, which *arrondissement* you're in, and which subway (Métro) stop you're closest to. If you're north of the river (the top half of any city map), you're on the Right Bank (*rive droite*). If you're south of it, you're on the Left Bank (*rive gauche*).

Arrondissements are numbered, starting at Notre-Dame (ground zero) and moving in a clockwise spiral out to the ring road. The last two digits in a Parisian zip code are the *arrondissement* number, and the notation for the Métro stop is "Mo." In Parisian jargon, Napoleon's tomb is on *la rive gauche* (the Left Bank) in the *7ème* (7th *arrondissement*), zip code 75007,

Mo: Invalides. Paris
Métro stops are used as
a standard aid in giving
directions, even for
those not using the
Métro. As you're track-
ing down addresses,
these definitions will
help: *place* (square), *rue*
(road), and *pont*
(bridge).

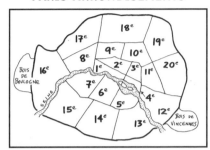

PARIS ARRONDISEMENTS

Arrival in Paris

For a comprehensive rundown on Paris' six train stations and two
airports, see the Transportation Connections chapter page 200.

Tourist Information

Avoid the Paris tourist offices—long lines, short information, and
a 5F charge for maps. This book, the *Pariscope* magazine (described
below), and one of the freebie maps available at any hotel are all
you need. The main tourist office is at 127 avenue des Champs-
Élysées (daily 9:00–20:00, tel. 08 36 68 31 12, or 01 49 52 53 10),
but the tourist offices at the Louvre, Eiffel Tower, and Gare de
Lyon are less busy (daily 8:00–20:00). For a complete list of
museum hours and scheduled English museum tours, pick up the
free *Musées, Monuments Historiques, et Expositions* booklet from any
museum.

Pariscope: The *Pariscope* weekly magazine (or one of its
clones, 3F at any newsstand) lists museum hours, art exhibits, concerts, music festivals, plays, movies, and nightclubs. See "Tour of
Pariscope" on page 196.

Maps: While Paris is littered with free maps, they don't show
all the streets. You may want the huge Michelin #10 map of Paris.
For an extended stay, we prefer the pocket-size and street-indexed
Paris Practique (40F).

Bookstores: There are many English-language bookstores
in Paris where you can pick up guidebooks (for nearly double
their American price). A few are: Shakespeare & Company (daily
12:00–24:00, lots of used travel books, 37 rue de la Boucherie,
across the river from Notre-Dame), W. H. Smith (248 rue de
Rivoli, Mo: Concorde, tel. 01 44 77 88 99), and Brentanos (37
avenue de L'Opéra, Mo: Opéra, tel. 01 42 61 52 50).

American Church: The American Church is a nerve center
for the American émigré community. It distributes a free, handy,
and insightful monthly English-language newspaper, called the

PARIS OVERVIEW

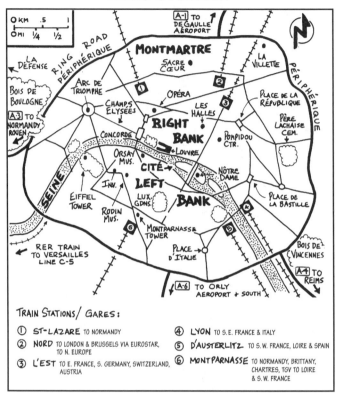

0 KM .5
0 MI 1/4 1/2

LA DÉFENSE
RING ROAD PÉRIPHÉRIQUE
PÉRIPHÉRIQUE
MONTMARTRE
SACRE CŒUR
LA VILLETTE
BOIS DE BOULOGNE
ARC DE TRIOMPHE
OPÉRA
❶
❷
❸
PLACE DE LA RÉPUBLIQUE
A-1 TO DE GAULLE AÉROPORT
CHAMPS ELYSÉES
LES HALLES
PÈRE LACHAISE CEM.
A-3 TO NORMANDY ROUEN
RIGHT BANK
CONCORDE
+LOUVRE
POMPIDOU CTR.
ORSAY MUS.
CITÉ
NÔTRE DAME
SEINE
INV.
LEFT BANK
❹
PLACE DE LA BASTILLE
EIFFEL TOWER
LUX. GDNS.
RODIN MUS.
❻
MONTPARNASSE TOWER
❺
PLACE D'ITALIE
BOIS DE VINCENNES
RER TRAIN TO VERSAILLES LINE C-5
A-6 TO ORLY AEROPORT + SOUTH
A-4 TO REIMS

TRAIN STATIONS / GARES:

① ST-LAZARE TO NORMANDY

② NORD TO LONDON & BRUSSELS VIA EUROSTAR, TO N. EUROPE

③ L'EST TO E. FRANCE, S. GERMANY, SWITZERLAND, AUSTRIA

④ LYON TO S.E. FRANCE & ITALY

⑤ D'AUSTERLITZ TO S.W. FRANCE, LOIRE & SPAIN

⑥ MONTPARNASSE TO NORMANDY, BRITTANY, CHARTRES, TGV TO LOIRE & S.W. FRANCE

Free Voice, with useful reviews of concerts, plays, and current events (available at around 200 locations in Paris), and an advertisement paper called *France—U.S.A. Contacts*, full of useful information for those looking for work or long-term housing. The church faces the river between the Eiffel Tower and Orsay Museum (65 quai d'Orsay, Mo: Invalides, tel. 01 40 62 05 00).

Helpful Hints

Theft Alert: Use your money belt and never carry a wallet in your back pocket or a purse over your shoulder. Thieves thrive in tourist areas and the Métro (at stations and in subway cars).

Paris Museum Pass: This worthwhile pass, covering most sights in Paris, is available at major Métro stations, tourist offices, and museums. For detailed information, see page 27.

Toilets: Carry small change for pay toilets, or walk into any outdoor café like you own the place and find the toilet in the back. Remember, the toilets in museums are free and generally the best you'll find. Modern super-sanitary street booths provide both relief and a memory.

Getting around Paris

By Métro: Europe's best subway is divided into two systems—the Métro (puddle-jumping everywhere in Paris) and the RER (which makes giant speedy leaps around town and connects suburban destinations). You'll be using the Métro for almost all your trips.

In Paris you're never more than a 10-minute walk from a Métro station. One ticket takes you anywhere in the system with unlimited transfers. Save 40 percent by buying a *carnet* (car-nay) of 10 tickets for 54F at any Métro station (a single ticket is 8F). Métro tickets work on city buses, though one ticket cannot be used as a transfer between subway and bus.

The *Mobilis* ticket (pron: moh-bee-lee) allows unlimited travel for a single day on all bus and Métro lines (30F). If you're staying longer, the *Carte Orange* (pron: kart oh-rahnzh) pass gives you free run of the bus and Métro system for one week (80F, ask for the *Carte Orange Coupon Vert*, supply a photo) or a month (280F, ask for the *Carte Orange Coupon Orange*, supply a photo). These pass prices cover only central Paris; you can pay more for passes covering regional destinations (e.g., Versailles). The weekly pass begins Monday and ends Sunday, and the monthly pass begins the first day of the month and ends the last day of that month, so midweek or midmonth purchases are generally not worthwhile. All passes can be purchased at any Métro station (most have photo booths).

To get to your destination, determine which "Mo" stop is closest to it and which line or lines will get you there. The lines have numbers, but they're best known by their direction or end-of-the-line stop. (For example, the La Defense/Château de Vincennes line runs between La Defense in the west and Vincennes in the east.)

Once in the Métro station, you'll see blue-and-white signs directing you to the train going in your direction (e.g., "direction: La Defense"). Insert your ticket in the automatic turnstile, pass through, and reclaim and keep your ticket until you exit the system. Fare inspectors regularly check for cheaters and accept absolutely no excuses from anyone. I repeat, keep that ticket.

Transfers are free and can be made wherever lines cross. When you transfer, look for the orange *correspondence* (connections) signs when you exit your first train, then follow the proper direction sign.

Before you *sortie* (exit), check the helpful *plan du quartier* (map of the neighborhood) to get your bearings, locate your

Key Words for the Métro and RER

- *direction* (dee-rek-see-ohn): direction
- *correspondance* (kor-res-pohn-dahns): transfer
- *sortie* (sor-tee): exit
- *carnet* (kar-nay): cheap set of 10 tickets
- *Pardon, madame/monsieur* (par-dohn, mah-dahm/mes-yur): Excuse me, lady/bud.
- *Je descend* (juh day-sahn): I'm getting off.
- *Donnez-moi mon porte-monnaie!*: Give me back my wallet!

destination, and decide which *sortie* you want. At stops with several *sorties*, you can save lots of walking by choosing the best exit.

Thieves spend their days in the Métro. Be on guard. For example, a pocket picked as you pass through a turnstile leaves you on the wrong side and the thief strolling away. Any jostle or commotion (especially when boarding or leaving trains) is likely the sign of a thief or team of thieves in action. Paris is most dangerous late at night.

Paris has a huge homeless population and over 11 percent unemployment; expect a warm Métro welcome by panhandlers, musicians, and those selling magazines produced by the homeless community.

By RER: The RER (Réseau Express Régionale, air-ay-air) is the suburban train system, indicated by thick lines on your subway map and identified by letters A, B, C, and so on. The RER works like the Métro but is speedier (if it serves your destination directly) because it makes only a few stops within the city. One Métro ticket is all you need for RER rides within Paris. You can transfer between the Métro and RER systems with the same ticket. Unlike the Métro, you need to insert your ticket in a turnstile to exit the RER system. To travel outside the city (to Versailles or the airport, for example), you'll need to buy a separate, more expensive ticket at the station window before boarding; make sure your stop is served by checking the signs over the train platform (not all trains serve all stops).

By City Bus: The trickier bus system is worth figuring out. Métro tickets are good on both bus and Métro, though you can't use the same ticket to transfer between the two systems. One ticket gets you anywhere in central Paris, but if you leave the city center (shown as section 1 on the diagram on board the bus), you must validate a second ticket. While the Métro shuts down about 00:30, some buses continue much later. Schedules are posted at bus stops. Handy bus system maps (*plan des autobus*) are available in any Métro station and are provided in your *Paris Practique* map book if you invest (40F).

Big system maps, posted at each bus and Métro stop, display the routes. Individual route diagrams show the exact routes of the lines serving that stop. Major stops are painted on the side of each bus. Enter through the front doors. Punch your Métro ticket in the machine behind the driver, or pay the higher cash fare. Get off the bus using the rear door. Even if you're not certain you've figured it out, do some joyriding (outside of rush hour). Lines #24, #63, and #69 are Paris' most scenic routes and make a great intro- duction to the city. Bus #69 is particularly handy, running between the Eiffel Tower, rue Cler (recommended hotels), Orsay, Louvre, Marais (recommended hotels), and Père Lachaise Cemetery. The most handy bus routes are listed for each hotel area recommended (see the Sleeping chapter, on page 166).

By Taxi: Parisian taxis are almost reasonable. A 10-minute ride costs about 50F (versus 5.5F to get anywhere in town on the Métro). You can try waving one down, but it's easier to ask for the nearest taxi stand (*Où est une station de taxi?*; oo ay oon stah-see- ohn duh taxi) or ask your hotel to call for you. Higher rates are charged at night from 22:00 to 6:30, all day Sunday, and to either airport. If you call from your hotel, the meter starts as soon as the call is received. Taxis are tough to find on Friday and Saturday night, especially after the Métro closes (around 00:30).

By Foot: Be careful! Parisian drivers are notorious for ignor- ing pedestrians. Never assume you have the right of way, even in a crosswalk. When crossing a street, keep your pace constant and don't stop suddenly. Drivers carefully calculate your speed and will miss you, providing you don't alter your route or pace.

Organized Tours of Paris

Bus Tours: Paris Vision offers handy bus tours of Paris, day and night (advertised in hotel lobbies); their "Illuminated Paris" tour is far more interesting and is explained on page 198. A better day- time bus tour for most is the "hop-on, hop-off" double-decker bus service called **Open Deck Tours**, offering three different routes covering most of the important sights in Paris (the Paris Grand Tour is the best to start with). Use these buses to connect the major sights (with a running commentary) and get a good city orientation tour at the same time. Buy your tickets from the driver (1-day ticket-135F, 2-day ticket-150F, 2 buses/hrly about 10:00–18:00, you can hop off at various sights, then catch a later bus). You'll see these bright yellow topless double-decker buses all over town—pick one up at the first important sight you visit, or start your tour at the Eiffel Tower stop (the first street on the nonriver side of the tower).

Boat Tours: Several companies offer one-hour boat cruises on the Seine (by far best at night). The huge, mass-production **Bateaux-Mouches** boats depart every 30 minutes from pont de l'Alma's right bank and are convenient to rue Cler hotels (daily 10:00–23:00, 40F, 20F under age 14, useless taped explanations in six languages and tour groups by the dozens, tel. 01 42 25 96 10). The much smaller and more intimate **Vedettes de pont Neuf** depart only once an hour from the center of the pont Neuf but come with a live guide giving explanations in French and English only and are convenient to Marais and Contrescarpe hotels (50F, 25F under age 14, tel. 01 46 33 98 38). From April to October, **Bateau-Bus** operates boats on the Seine, connecting six key stops about every 25 minutes: Eiffel Tower, Orsay/place de la Concorde, Louvre, Notre-Dame, Hôtel de Ville, and St. Germain-des-Prés. Pick up their schedule at any stop (or tourist office) and use them as a scenic alternative to the Métro. Tickets are available for single trips (20F), one day (60F), and two days (90F). Boats run from 10:00 to 19:00, until 22:00 in summer.

Walking Tours: Paris Walking Tours offers a variety of excellent two-hour walks nearly daily for 60F (tel. 01 48 09 21 40, fax 01 42 43 75 51, http://ParisWalkingtours.com). They focus on the Marais, Luxembourg Gardens, Opéra Garnier, Montmartre, and Hemingway's Paris. Call ahead a day or two to learn their schedule and starting point. No reservations are required. These are thoughtfully prepared, humorous, and relaxing walking tours led by British or American guides. Don't hesitate to stand close to the guide to hear. For Lost Generation fans, **Paris Literary Promenades** takes you through areas once popular with literary giants from Joyce to Beckett to Hemingway (60F, 2 hours, tours depart from place de l'Odeon daily except Wed at 14:30 and 19:00, late May to mid-Oct, tel. 01 48 07 80 72 or cellular 06 03 27 73 52). You can also hire a Parisian as your personal guide. Arnaud Servignat (tel. 01 42 57 03 35, fax 01 42 62 68 62, e-mail: arnotour@cybercable.fr) and Marianne Siegler (tel. 01 42 52 32 51) are licensed local guides who freelance for individuals and families ($150/4 hrs, $250/day).

Bike Tours: Bullfrog Bike Tours will show you Paris on two wheels at a relaxed pace (120F, 3–4-hour tours in English at 11:00 and 15:30, May–mid-Sept, no bikes or reservations needed, meet at fountain on avenue Joseph, 100 yards from the Eiffel Tower in Champ de Mars park, http://BullfrogBikes.com, e-mail: bullfrogbikes@hotmail.com, cellular 06 09 98 08 60).

PARIS
SIGHTS

These sights are arranged by neighborhood for handy sight-seeing. When you see a ✪ in a listing, it means the sight is covered in much more depth in one of our walks or self-guided tours.

The Paris Museum Pass: All of the sights listed in this chapter are covered by a Paris Museum Pass, except for the Eiffel Tower, Montparnasse Tower, Marmottan Museum, new Jewish Art and History Museum, Jeu de Paume Exhibition Hall, and the ladies of Pigalle.

In Paris there are two classes of sightseers: those with a museum pass and those who stand in line. Serious sightseers save time and money by getting this pass. Sold at museums, main Métro stations, and tourist offices, it pays for itself in two admissions and gets you into sights with no lining up (one day-80F, three consecutive days-160F, five consecutive days-240F; no discounts for youth). You can buy one on any day at any sight where it's valid. The pass is not activated until the first time you use it (you enter the date on the pass).

Included sights (and admission prices without the pass) you're likely to visit: Louvre (45F), Orsay (40F), Sainte-Chapelle (32F), Arc de Triomphe (40F), Napoleon's Tomb (38F), Carnavalet Museum (35F), Conciergerie (32F), Sewer Tour (25F), Cluny Museum (38F), Notre-Dame towers (35F) and crypt (32F), L'Orangerie (closed), Picasso Museum (30F), Rodin Museum (28F), and the elevator to the top of the Grand Arche de La Defense (43F). Outside Paris, the pass covers the Palace of Versailles (45F) and its Grand Trianon (25F) and Château Chantilly (39F). Tally it up—but remember, an advantage of the pass is that you skip to the front of all lines, saving hours of waiting in the summer (though everyone must pass through the slow-moving metal detector lines). If buying a pass at a museum with a long line, skip to the front and find the sales window. And with the pass, you'll pop painlessly into sights that you're walking by (even for a few minutes) that might otherwise not be worth the expense (e.g., Notre-Dame crypt, Conciergerie, Victor Hugo's House). The free museum and monuments directory that comes with your pass lists the latest hours, phone numbers, and specifics on what kids pay. The cutoff age for free entry varies from 5 to 18. Most major, serious art museums let young people under 18 in for free. For some reason, anyone over age five has to pay to tour the sewers.

Museum Tips: The Louvre and many other museums are closed on Tuesday. The Orsay, Rodin, Marmottan, and Versailles are closed Monday. Most museums offer reduced prices but have shorter hours on Sunday. Many sights stop admitting people 30 to 60 minutes before they close, and many begin closing rooms 45 minutes before the actual closing time. For the fewest crowds, visit very early, at lunch, or very late. Most museums have slightly shorter hours October through March. French holidays can really mess up your sightseeing plans (Jan 1, May 1, May 8, Jul 14, Nov 1, Nov 11, and Dec 25). The best Impressionist art museums are the Orsay and Marmottan (described below; also see our self-guided tour of the Orsay; note that L'Orangerie, another Impressionist museum, is closed for renovation).

Paris Museums near the Tuileries Gardens

The newly renovated Tuileries Gardens were once the private property of kings and queens. Paris' grandest public park links these museums: Louvre, Jeu de Paume, and the Orsay.

▲▲▲**Louvre**—This is Europe's oldest, biggest, greatest, and possibly most crowded museum. It's packed with Greek and Roman masterpieces, medieval jewels, Michelangelo statues, and paintings by the greatest artists from the Renaissance to the Romantics (mid-1800s).

Cost: 45F, 26F after 15:00 and on Sun, free on first Sun of month and for those under 18, covered by museum pass.

Hours: Wed–Mon 9:00–18:00, closed Tue, all wings open Wed until 21:45, Richelieu Wing (only) until 21:45 on Mon. Closed Jan 1, Easter, May 1, Nov 1, and Dec 25. Tel. 01 40 20 53 17 or 01 40 20 51 51 for recorded information.

Location: At Palais Royal/Musée du Louvre Métro stop. The old Louvre Métro stop called Louvre Rivoli no longer goes to the Louvre. ✪ See Louvre Tour on page 79.

▲**L'Orangerie**—Closed until 2001.

Jeu de Paume—This one-time home to the Impressionist art collection now located in Musée d'Orsay hosts rotating exhibits of top contemporary artists (38F, Tue 12:00–21:30, Wed–Fri 12:00–19:00,

— MUSEUMS NEAR TUILERIES GARDENS —

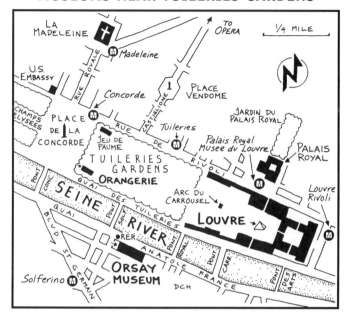

Sat–Sun 10:00–19:00, closed Mon, on place de la Concorde, just inside Tuileries Garden on rue de Rivoli side, Mo: Concorde).

▲▲▲**Orsay Museum**—This is Paris' 19th-century-art museum (actually, art from 1848–1914), including Europe's greatest collection of Impressionist works.

Cost: 40F, 27F for the young and old, under 18 free. English language tours usually run daily except Sun at 11:30, cost 38F, take 90 min, and are also available on audiotape. Tel. 01 40 49 48 48.

Hours: Tue–Sat 10:00–18:00, Thu until 21:45, Sun 9:00–18:00, closed Mon. Jun 20–Sept 20, museum opens at 9:00. Last entrance is 45 min before closing.

Location: Directly at the RER-C stop called Musée d'Orsay; the nearest Métro stop is Solferino, three blocks south of the Orsay. From the Louvre, it's a 15-minute walk downstream to the Orsay. ✪ See Orsay Tour on page 98.

Historic Core of Paris: Notre-Dame, Sainte-Chapelle, and More

✪ All of these sights are covered in detail in the Historic Paris Walk on page 39. Only the essentials are listed here.

▲▲**Notre-Dame Cathedral**—The 700-year-old cathedral is packed with history and tourists. Walk all around the outside, study its sculpture and windows, eavesdrop on guides, and take in a mass. Sunday masses are at 8:00, 8:45, 10:00, 11:30, 12:30, and 18:30. (Free, daily 8:00–18:45; treasury-15F, daily 9:30–17:30; ask about the free English tours, normally Wed and Thu at noon and Sat at 14:30; Mo: Cité, Hôtel de Ville, or St. Michel; clean 2.70F toilets in front of church near Charlemagne's statue.) ✪ See page 39.

Church Tower: Climb to the top for a great gargoyle's-eye view of the city. You get 400 steps for only 35F (entrance on outside, north tower open 9:30–17:30, closed at lunch and earlier off-season).

Crypt: The archaeological crypt is a worthwhile 15-minute stop with your museum pass (32F, 50F with Notre-Dame's tower, daily 10:00–18:00, closes at 17:00 Oct–Apr, enter 100 yards in front of church). You'll see Roman ruins, trace the street plan of the medieval village, and see diagrams of how the earliest Paris grew and grew, all thoughtfully explained in English.

▲▲**Deportation Memorial (Mémorial de la Déportation)**— This memorial to the 200,000 French victims of the Nazi concentration camps draws you into their experience. (Free, Mon–Fri 8:30–21:45, Sat–Sun and holidays from 9:00, sometimes closes 12:00–14:00, shorter hours off-season, east tip of the island near Île St. Louis, behind Notre-Dame, Mo: Cité.) ✪ See page 45.

Île St. Louis—This island behind Notre-Dame is known for its restaurants (see the Eating chapter), great Bertillon ice cream (31 rue St. Louis en l'Île), and shops (along rue St. Louis en l'Île). ✪ See page 45.

Cité "Métropolitain" Stop and Flower Market—On place Louis Lepine, between Notre-Dame and Sainte-Chapelle, you'll find a turn-of-the-century subway entrance and a flower market (that chirps with a bird market on Sunday).

▲▲▲**Sainte-Chapelle**—The triumph of Gothic church architecture is a cathedral of glass like no other. It was speedily built from 1242 to 1248 by St. Louis IX to house the supposed Crown of Thorns (32F, daily 9:30–18:30, off-season 10:00–16:30, Mo: Cité, call 01 48 01 91 35 for concert information). ✪ See page 50.

▲**Conciergerie**—Marie Antoinette was imprisoned here, as were 2,600 others on the way to the guillotine (32F, daily 9:30–18:30, 10:00–17:00 in winter, good English descriptions). ✪ See page 54.

▲**Samaritaine Department Store Viewpoint**—For a great, free viewpoint, take the elevator to the ninth floor and walk to the 11th-floor rooftop panorama (daily 9:30–19:00, reasonably priced café on 10th-floor terrace, supermarket in basement, Mo: Pont Neuf, tel. 01 40 41 20 20). ✪ See page 194.

Southwest Paris: Eiffel Tower Neighborhood

▲▲▲**Eiffel Tower**—It's crowded and expensive but worth the trouble. Go early (by 9:15) or late in the day (after 18:00) to avoid most crowds; weekends are worst. Pilier Nord (the north pillar) has the biggest elevator and, therefore, the fastest-moving line.

The Tower is 1,000 feet tall (six inches taller in hot weather), covers 2.5 acres, and requires 50 tons of paint. Its 7,000 tons of metal are spread out so well at the base that it's no heavier per square inch than a linebacker on tiptoes. Visitors to Paris may find Mona Lisa to be less than expected, but the Eiffel Tower rarely disappoints, even in an era of skyscrapers.

Built a hundred years after the French Revolution (and in the midst of an Industrial one), the Tower served no function but to impress. Bridge-builder Gustave Eiffel won the contest for the 1889 Centennial World's Fair by beating out such rival proposals as a giant guillotine. To a generation hooked on technology, the Tower was the marvel of the age, a symbol of progress and of man's ingenuity. To others it was a cloned-sheep monstrosity. The writer Maupassant routinely ate lunch in the Tower just so he wouldn't have to look at it.

Delicate and graceful when seen from afar, it's massive—even a bit scary—from close up. You don't appreciate the size until you walk toward it; like a mountain, it seems so close but takes forever to reach. There are three observation platforms, at 200, 400, and 900 feet; the higher you go, the more you pay. Each requires a separate elevator (and a line), so plan on at least 90 minutes if you want to go to the top and back. The view from the 400-foot-high second level is plenty.

Begin at the first floor, read the informative signs (in English) describing the major monuments, see the entertaining free movie on the history of the Tower, and consider a drink overlooking all of Paris at the café or at the reasonable restaurant Altitude 95 (decent 110F meals until 20:00 and Paris' best view bar). Take the elevator to the second floor for even greater views. As you ascend through the metal beams, imagine being a worker, perched high above nothing, riveting this giant erector set together. On top, all of Paris lies before you, with a panorama guide. On a good day, you can see for 40 miles.

Cost and Hours: It costs 21F to go to the first level, 43F to the second, and 60F to go all the way for the 1,000-foot view (not covered by museum pass). On a budget? You can climb the stairs to the second level for only 15F (summers daily 9:00–24:00, off-season 9:30–23:00, Mo: Trocadero, RER: Champ de Mars, tel. 01 44 11 23 23).

The best place to view the Tower is from Trocadero square to

SOUTHWEST PARIS: EIFFEL TOWER NEIGHBORHOOD

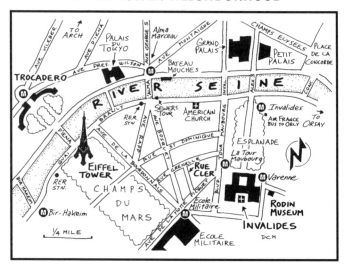

the north (a 10-minute walk across the river, and a happening scene at night). Consider arriving at the Trocadero Métro stop, then walking toward the Tower. Another great viewpoint is the long, grassy field, le Champ de Mars, to the south (after about 20:00 the gendarmes look the other way as Parisians stretch out or picnic on the grass). However impressive it may be by day, it's an awesome thing to see at twilight, when the Tower becomes engorged with light, and virile Paris lies back and lets night be on top.

▲**Paris Sewer Tour (Égouts)**—This quick and easy visit takes you along a few hundred yards of underground water tunnel lined with interesting displays, well described in English, explaining the evolution of the world's longest sewer system. (If you lined up Paris' sewers, they would reach beyond Istanbul.) Don't miss the slide show, the fine WCs just beyond the gift shop, and the occasional tours in English (25F, Sat–Wed 11:00–17:00, closed Thu–Fri, where pont de l'Alma hits the Left Bank, tel. 01 47 05 10 29).

▲▲**Napoleon's Tomb and Les Invalides Army Museum**— The emperor lies majestically dead inside several coffins under a grand dome—a goose-bumping pilgrimage for historians. Napoleon is surrounded by the tombs of other French war heroes and Europe's greatest military museum, in the Hôtel des Invalides. The restored dome glitters with 26 pounds of gold (38F, daily

10:00–17:45, closes off-season at 16:45, Mo: La Tour Maubourg or Varennes, tel. 01 44 42 37 67). ✪ See Napoleon's Tomb Tour on page 132.

▲▲**Rodin Museum**—This user-friendly museum is filled with passionate works by the greatest sculptor since Michelangelo. See *The Kiss, The Thinker, The Gates of Hell*, and many more (28F, 18F on Sun, 5F for gardens only, which may be Paris' best deal as many works are well displayed in the beautiful gardens; Tue–Sun 9:30–17:45, closed Mon and at 17:00 off-season, 77 rue de Varennes, Mo: Varennes, near Napoleon's Tomb, tel. 01 44 18 61 10). ✪ See Rodin Museum Tour on page 124.

▲▲**Marmottan**—In this private, intimate, less-visited museum you'll find more than 100 paintings by Claude Monet (thanks to his son Michel), including the *Impressions of a Sunrise* painting that gave the movement its start and name (40F, Tue–Sun 10:00–17:00, closed Mon, not covered by museum pass, 2 rue Louis Boilly, Mo: La Muette, follow museum signs 6 blocks through park to museum, tel. 01 42 24 07 02). Combine this fine museum with a stroll down one of Paris' most pleasant shopping streets, the rue de Passy (from La Muette Métro stop).

Southeast Paris: Latin Quarter

✪ The Historic Paris Walk, on page 39, dips into the Latin Quarter.

▲**Latin Quarter**—This Left Bank neighborhood, just opposite Notre-Dame, was a center of Roman Paris. But the Latin Quarter's touristic fame relates to its intriguing artsy, bohemian character. This was perhaps Europe's leading university district in the Middle Ages, when Latin was the language of higher education. The neighborhood's main boulevards (St. Michel and St. Germain) are lined with cafés—once the haunts of great poets and philosophers, now the hangout of tired tourists. While still youthful and artsy, the area has become a tourist ghetto filled with cheap north African eateries.

▲**Cluny Museum (Musée National du Moyen Age)**—This treasure trove of medieval art fills the old Roman baths, offering close-up looks at stained glass, Notre-Dame carvings, fine goldsmithing and jewelry, and rooms of tapestries—the best of which is the exquisite *Lady with the Unicorn* (38F, 28F on Sun, Wed–Mon 9:15–17:45, closed Tue, near the corner of boulevards St. Michel and St. Germain, Mo: Cluny, tel. 01 53 73 78 00). ✪ See Cluny Museum Tour on page 137.

St. Germain-des-Près—A church was first built on this site in A.D. 452. The church you see today was constructed in 1163. The area around the church hops at night with fire-eaters, mimes, and scads of artists (Mo: St. Germain-des-Près).

—— SOUTHEAST PARIS: LATIN QUARTER ——

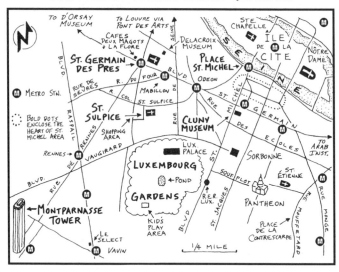

▲St. Sulpice Organ Concert—For pipe-organ enthusiasts, this is a delight. The Grand-Orgue at St. Sulpice has a rich history, with a line of 12 world-class organists (including Widor and Dupre) going back 300 years. Widor started the tradition of opening the loft to visitors after the 10:30 service on Sundays. Daniel Roth continues to welcome guests in three languages while playing five keyboards at once. The 10:30 Sunday mass is followed by a 25-minute recital at 11:40. If you're lucky, at noon the small unmarked door will open (left of entry as you face the rear), and visitors scamper like 16th notes up spiral stairs to a world of 7,000 pipes, where they can watch the master perform the next mass, friends warming his bench, and a committee scrambling to pull and push the 102 stops (Mo: St. Sulpice or Mabillon).

▲Luxembourg Gardens—Paris' most beautiful, interesting, and enjoyable garden/park/recreational area is a great place to watch Parisians at rest and play. (See the Paris with Children chapter, page 190.) These private gardens are property of the French Senate (housed in the château) and have special rules governing their use (e.g., where cards can be played, where dogs can be walked, where joggers can run, when and where music can be played). The brilliant flower plantings are completely changed three times a year, and the boxed trees are brought out of the *orangerie* in May. Challenge the card and chess players to a game (near the tennis courts), or find a

free chair near the main pond and take a breather. Notice any
pigeons? A poor Ernest Hemingway used to hand-hunt (read:
strangle) them here. Paris Walks offers a good tour of the park
(see "Organized Tours," page 25). The grand neoclassical-domed
Panthéon, now a mausoleum housing the tombs of several great
Frenchmen, is a block away and is only worth entering if you have
a museum pass. The historic cafés of Montparnasse are a few blocks
from the far right (or southwest) corner exit of the park (rue Vavin,
see "Les Grands Cafés de Paris" on page 187). The park is open
until dusk (Mo: Odéon, RER: Luxembourg). If you enjoy the
Luxembourg Gardens and want to see more, visit the more elegant
Parc Monceau (Mo: Monceau) and the colorful Jardin des Plantes
(Mo: Jussieu or Gare d'Austerlitz, RER: Luxembourg).

▲**Montparnasse Tower**—This 59-floor superscraper—it's cheaper
and easier to get to the top of this than the Eiffel Tower—offers
one of Paris' best views, since the Eiffel Tower is in it and the
Montparnasse Tower isn't. Buy the photo guide to the city, then
go to the rooftop and orient yourself (46F, daily in summer 9:30–
23:30, off-season 10:00–22:00, disappointing after dark, entrance
on rue l'Arrivé, Mo: Montparnasse). This is an efficient stop when
combined with a day trip to Chartres, which begins at the Montparnasse train station.

Northwest Paris: Champs-Élysées, Arc de Triomphe, and Beyond

✪ Take the Champs-Élysées Walk, on page 57, for a pleasant
downhill stroll connecting the sights from the enduring Arc de
Triomphe to the historic place de la Concorde.

▲▲**Champs-Élysées**—This famous boulevard is Paris' backbone,
with the greatest concentration of traffic. From the Arc de
Triomphe down the Champs-Élysées, all of France seems to
converge on place de la Concorde, the city's largest square.
While the boulevard has become a bit Americanized, a walk here
is a must. Take the Métro to the Arc de Triomphe (Mo: Étoile)
and saunter down the Champs-Élysées (Métro stops every few
blocks: Étoile, George V, FDR). ✪ See page 57.

▲▲▲**Arc de Triomphe**—Napoleon had the magnificent Arc de
Triomphe commissioned to commemorate his victory at the Battle
of Austerlitz. There's no triumphal arch bigger (50 meters high,
40 meters wide). An elevator and a spiral staircase lead to a cute
museum about the arch and a grand view from the top, even after
dark (40F, daily 9:30–23:00, Oct–May daily 9:30–22:00, Mo: Étoile,
use underpass to reach arch, tel. 01 43 80 31 31). ✪ See page 57.

▲**Grande Arche de La Defense**—The centerpiece of Paris' ambi-
tious skyscraper complex (La Defense) is the Grande Arche. Built to

celebrate the 200th anniversary of the 1789 French Revolution, the place is big—38 floors on more than 200 acres. It holds offices for 30,000 people. Notre-Dame Cathedral could fit under its arch. The La Defense complex is an interesting study in 1960s land-use planning. Over 100,000 workers commute here daily, directing lots of business and development away from downtown and allowing central Paris to retain its more elegant feel. This makes sense to most Parisians, regardless of whatever else they feel about this controversial complex. You'll enjoy city views from the Arche elevator (43F includes a film on its construction and art exhibits, daily 10:00–19:00, RER or Mo: La Defense, follow signs to Grande Arche, or get off one stop earlier at Esplanade de la Defense and walk through the interesting business complex, tel. 01 49 07 27 57).

Northeast Paris: Marais Neighborhood and More

✪ To connect the sights with a fun, fact-filled stroll leading from place de la Bastille to the Pompidou Center, take the Marais Walk on page 64.

▲▲**Pompidou Center**—Europe's greatest collection of far-out modern art, the Musée National d'Art Moderne, is housed on the top floor of this newly renovated and colorful exoskeletal building. Once ahead of its time, this 20th-century art (remember that century?) has been waiting for the world to catch up with it. After so many Madonnas and Children, a piano smashed to bits and glued to the wall is refreshing. The center and its square are lively, with lots of people, street theater, and activity inside and out—a perpetual street fair. Ride the escalator for a great city view from the café terrace on top and don't miss the free exhibits on the ground floor (50F Tue–Fri 10:00–17:30, Sat–Sun and most hoildays 10:00–19:00, closed Mon, Mo: Rambuteau, tel. 01 44 78 12 33). Kids of any age enjoy the fun, colorful fountain (called *Homage to Stravinsky*) next to the Pompidou Center.

▲▲**Museum of Art and History of Judaism (Hotel d'Aignan)**—This remarkable new museum, located in a beautifully restored Marais mansion, tells the story of Judaism throughout Europe from the Roman destruction of Jerusalem to the theft of famous artworks during World War II. Helpful audiophones and many English explanations make this an enjoyable history lesson (red numbers on small signs indicate the number you should press on your audiophone, then press the play button). Move along at your own speed. The museum illustrates the cultural unity maintained by this continually dispersed population. You'll learn about the history of Jewish traditions from Bar Mitzvahs to menorahs and see exquisite traditional costumes and objects around which daily life revolved. Don't miss the explanation of "the Dreyfus affair," a major event in early

1900 French politics. You'll also see photographs of and paintings by famous Jewish artists, including Chagall, Modigliani, and Soutine. The small section devoted to the deportation of Jews from Paris is moving (40F, not covered by museum pass, Mon–Fri 11:00–18:00, Sun 10:00–18:00, closed Sat, 71 rue du Temple, tel. 01 53 01 86 53).

▲**Picasso Museum (Hôtel Salé)**—This is the world's largest collection of Pablo Picasso's paintings, sculptures, sketches, and ceramics, and includes his personal collection of Impressionist art. It's well explained in English and worth ▲▲▲ if you're a fan (30F, Wed–Mon 9:30–18:00, closed Tue, 5 rue Thorigny, Mo: St. Paul or Chemin Vert, tel. 01 42 71 25 21).

▲**Carnavalet Museum**—The tumultuous history of Paris is well displayed in this converted Marais mansion. Unfortunately, explanations are in French only, but many displays are fairly self-explanatory. You'll see paintings of Parisian scenes, French Revolution paraphernalia, old Parisian store signs, a small guillotine, a model of 16th-century Île de la Cité (notice the bridge houses), and rooms full of 15th-century Parisian furniture. The medieval rooms and Revolution rooms are the most interesting (35F, Tue–Sun 10:00–17:00, closed Mon, 23 rue de Sévigné, Mo: St Paul, tel. 01 42 72 21 13).

Victor Hugo's House—France's literary giant lived in this house on place des Vosges from 1832 to 1848. Inside are posters advertising theater productions of his works, paintings of some of his most famous character creations, and a few furnished rooms (22F, Tue–Sun 10:00–17:40, closed Mon, 6 place des Vosges).

Promenade Plantée Park—This three-kilometer narrow garden walk, once a train track and now a joy, runs from place de la Bastille (Mo: Bastille) along Avenue Daumesnil to Saint-Mandé (Mo: Michel Bizot). Part of the park is elevated. At times you'll walk along the street till you pick up the next segment. From place de la Bastille, take avenue Daumesnil (past Opéra building) to the intersection with avenue Ledru Rollin; walk up the stairs and through the gate (free, hours vary with season, open roughly 8:00–20:00).

▲**Père Lachaise Cemetery**—Littered with the tombstones of many of the city's most illustrious dead, this is your best one-stop look at the fascinating, romantic world of "permanent Parisians." The place is confusing, but maps will direct you to the graves of Chopin, Molière, Edith Piaf, Oscar Wilde, Gertrude Stein, Heloise, Abelard, and even American rock star Jim Morrison (who died in Paris). In section 92, a series of statues memorializing World War II makes the French war experience a bit more real (helpful 10F maps at flower store near entry, across street from Métro stop, closes at dusk, Mo: Père Lachaise or bus #69).

North Paris: Montmartre

✪ Connect the sights with the Montmartre Walk on page 73.

▲▲**Sacré-Coeur and Montmartre**—This Byzantine-looking church, while only 130 years old, is impressive (daily until 23:00). One block from the church, the place du Tertre was the haunt of Toulouse-Lautrec and the original bohemians. Today it's mobbed by tourists and unoriginal bohemians, but it's still fun. Take the Métro to the Anvers stop (one Métro ticket buys your way up the funicular and avoids the stairs) or the closer but less scenic Abbesses stop. A taxi to the top of the hill saves time and sweat.

Pigalle—Paris' red-light district, the infamous "Pig Alley," is at the foot of Butte Montmartre. *Ooh la la.* It's more shocking than dangerous. Walk from place Pigalle to place Blanche teasing desperate barkers and fast-talking temptresses. In bars a 1,000F bottle of cheap champagne comes with a friend. Stick to the bigger streets, hang on to your wallet, and exercise good judgment. Cancan can cost a fortune, as can con artists in topless bars. After dark, countless tour buses line the streets, reminding us that tour guides make big bucks by bringing their groups to touristic night-clubs like the famous Moulin Rouge (Mo: Pigalle or Abbesses).

Disappointments *de* Paris

Here are a few negatives to help you manage your limited time:

La Madeleine is a big, stark, neoclassical church with a post-card facade and a postbox interior. The famous aristocratic deli behind the church, Fauchon, is elegant, but so are many others handier to your hotel.

Paris' **Panthéon** (nothing like Rome's) is another stark neo-classical edifice, filled with mortal remains of great Frenchmen who mean little to the average American tourist.

The old **Opéra Garnier** has a great Chagall-painted ceiling but is in a pedestrian-mean area. Don't go to American Express (behind the Opéra) just to change money. You'll get a better rate at many other banks.

The **Bastille** is Paris' most famous nonsight. The square is there, but confused tourists look everywhere and can't find the famous prison of Revolution fame. The building's gone and the square is good only as a jumping-off point for the Marais Walk (see page 73) or Promenade Plantée Park (see "Northeast Paris," above).

And the **Latin Quarter** is a frail shadow of its characteristic self. It's more Tunisian, Greek, and Woolworth's than old-time Paris. The café life that turned on Hemingway and endeared boul' Miche and boulevard St. Germain to so many poets is also trampled by modern commercialism.

HISTORIC PARIS
WALK

From Notre-Dame to Sainte-Chapelle

4 paris

Paris has been the capital of Europe for centuries. We'll start where it did, on the Île de la Cité, with forays onto both the Left and Right Banks, on a walk that laces together the story of Paris: Roman, medieval, the Revolution, café society, the literary scene of the '20s, and the modern world. Allow four hours to do this three-mile walk justice.

Orientation

All sights that charge admission are covered by the Paris Museum Pass, which for many is a great time- and money-saver.

Notre-Dame: Free, daily 8:00–18:45; treasury-15F, daily 9:30–17:30; Sunday mass at 8:00, 8:45, 10:00, 11:30, 12:30, and 18:30. Leaflet with church schedule at booth inside entrance. Ask about free English tours, normally Wed and Thu at 12:00 and Sat at 14:30. The tower climb takes 400 steps and 35F—expensive but worth it for the gargoyle's-eye view of the cathedral, Seine, and city (daily 9:00–17:30, off-season closes earlier and during lunch).

Notre-Dame Archeological Crypt: 32F, 50F with Notre-Dame's tower, daily 10:00–18:00, closes at 17:00 Oct–Apr, entry 100 yards in front of the cathedral.

Deportation Memorial: Free, Mon–Fri 8:30–21:45, Sat–Sun and holidays from 9:00, sometimes closes 12:00–14:00, shorter hours off-season.

Sainte-Chapelle: 32F, daily 9:30–18:30, off-season 10:00–16:30.

Conciergerie: 32F, daily 9:30–18:30, off-season 10:00–17:00.

NOTRE-DAME

• *Start at the Notre-Dame Cathedral on the island in the River Seine, the physical and historic bull's-eye of your Paris map (closest Métro stops are Cité, Hôtel de Ville, and St. Michel, each requiring a short walk).*

ÎLE DE LA CITÉ

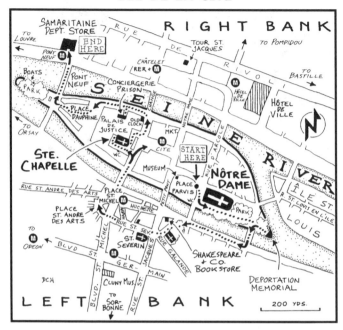

On the square in front of the cathedral, stand far enough back to take in the whole facade. Look at the circular window in the center.

For centuries, the main figure in the Christian "pantheon" has been the goddess Mary, the mother of Jesus. Common people pray to her directly in times of trouble to gain comfort and to ask her to convince God to be compassionate with them. The church is dedicated to "Our Lady" (Notre Dame), and there she is, cradling God, right in the heart of the facade, surrounded by the halo of the rose window. Though the church is massive and imposing, it has always stood for the grace and compassion of Mary, the "mother of God."

Imagine the faith of the people who built this. They

broke ground in 1163 with the hope that someday their great-great-great-great-great-great grandchildren might attend the dedication mass two centuries later. Look up the 200-foot bell towers and imagine a tiny medieval community mustering the money and energy to build this. Master masons supervised, but the people did much of the grunt work themselves for free—hauling the huge stones from distant quarries, digging a 30-foot-deep trench to lay the foundations, and treading like rats on a wheel designed to lift the stones up, one by one. This kind of backbreaking, arduous manual labor created the real hunchbacks of Notre-Dame.

• *"Walk this way" toward the cathedral, and view it from the bronze plaque on the ground marked...*

Point Zero

You're standing at the very center of France, from which all distances are measured. The "Cité" started here in the third century B.C. In 52 B.C., the Romans booted out the Parisii tribe and built their government palace at the end of the square behind you and a Temple of Jupiter where the cathedral sits. Two thousand years of dirt and debris have raised the city's altitude. The archaeological crypt nearby offers a fascinating look at the remains of the earlier city and church below today's street level.

Still facing the church, on your right is a grand equestrian statue of Charlemagne ("Charles the Great"), whose reign marked the birth of modern Europe. Crowned in A.D. 800, he briefly united much of Europe during the Dark Ages. (Maybe even greater than Charles are nearby pay toilets—the cleanest you'll find in downtown Paris.)

Before renovation, 150 years ago, this square was much smaller, a characteristic medieval shambles facing a run-down church, surrounded by winding streets and countless buildings (look at the outlines marked in the pavement of the square, showing the medieval street plan). The huge church bell towers rose above this tangle of smaller buildings, inspiring Victor Hugo's story of a deaf, bell-ringing hunchback who could look down on all Paris.

• *Now turn your attention to the church facade. Look at the left doorway and, to the left of the door, find the statue with his head in his hands.*

Notre-Dame Facade

When Christianity began making converts in Roman Paris, the Bishop of Paris was beheaded. But these early Christians were hard to keep down. St. Denis got up, tucked his head under his arm, headed north, paused at a fountain to wash it off, and continued until he found just the right place to meet his maker. The

NOTRE DAME FACADE

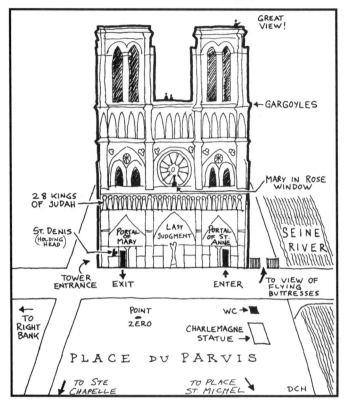

GREAT VIEW!

← GARGOYLES

MARY IN ROSE WINDOW

28 KINGS OF JUDAH →

ST. DENIS (HOLDING HEAD)

PORTAL OF MARY

LAST JUDGMENT

PORTAL OF ST. ANNE

SEINE RIVER

TOWER ENTRANCE

EXIT

ENTER

TO VIEW OF FLYING BUTTRESSES

← TO RIGHT BANK

POINT ZERO

WC

CHARLEMAGNE STATUE →

PLACE DU PARVIS

↓ TO STE CHAPELLE

TO PLACE ST. MICHEL ↘

DCH

Parisians were convinced of this miracle, Christianity gained ground, and a church soon replaced the pagan temple.

By the way, Christians think Montmartre (the one hill overlooking Paris) is named for this martyr (pagans think it was named after a Roman temple of Mars—Mount of Mars—which once stood here). Denis eventually died on the edge of town where the church of St. Denis was built (famous in history books as the first Gothic church but not much to see today).

• *Now look above the central doorway, where you'll find scenes from the Last Judgment.*

Central Portal

It's the end of the world, and Christ sits on the throne of judgment (just under the arches, holding his hands up). Below him, an angel and a demon weigh souls in the balance. The good people stand to the left, looking up to heaven. The naughty ones to the right are chained up and led off to...a six-hour tour of the Louvre on a hot day. Notice the crazy sculpted demons to the right, at the base of the arch.

• *Above the arches is a row of 28 statues, known as...*

The Kings of Judah

In the days of the French Revolution (1789–1793), these Biblical kings were mistaken for the hated French kings, and Notre-Dame represented the oppressive Catholic hierarchy. The citizens stormed the church, crying, "Off with their heads!" Plop, they lopped off the crowned heads of these kings with glee, creating a row of St. Denises that wasn't repaired for decades.

But the story doesn't end there. A schoolteacher who lived nearby collected the heads and buried them in his backyard for safekeeping. There they slept until 1977, when they were accidentally unearthed. Today, you can stare into the eyes of the original kings in the Cluny Museum, a few blocks away (see page 137).

• *Enter the church and find a spot to view the long, high central aisle.*

Notre-Dame Interior

Remove your metaphorical hat and become a simple bareheaded peasant, entering the dim medieval light of the church. Take a minute to let your pupils dilate, to take in the subtle, mysterious light show God beams through the stained glass windows. Follow the slender columns up to the praying-hands arches of the ceiling and contemplate the heavens. Let's say it's dedication day for this great stone wonder. The priest intones the words of the mass that echo through the hall: *"Terribilis est locus iste"*—"This place is *terribilis*," meaning awe inspiring or even terrifying. It's a huge, dark, earthly cavern lit with an unearthly light.

This is Gothic. Taller and filled with light, this was a major improvement over the earlier Romanesque style. Gothic architects needed only a few structural columns topped by pointed arches that crisscross the columns to support the weight of the roof. This let them build higher than ever, freeing up the walls for windows. The church is designed in the shape of a cross, with the altar where the cross beams intersect.

• *Walk up to the main altar.*

The Altar

This marks the spot where mass is said and the bread and wine of communion are prepared and distributed. In olden days, there were no chairs. The church can hold up to 10,000 faithful. Join the statue of Joan of Arc (*Jeanne d'Arc*, in the right transept) in gazing up to the rose-shaped window, the only one of the three with its original medieval glass.

This was the holy spot for Romans, Christians...and even atheists. When the Revolutionaries stormed the church, they gutted it and turned it into a "Temple for the Cult of Reason." A woman dressed up like the Statue of Liberty held court at the altar as a symbol of the divinity of Man. France today, while nominally Catholic, remains aloof from Vatican dogmatism. Instead of traditional wooden confessional booths, notice the open, glass-walled room where modern sinners seek counseling as much as forgiveness.

Just past the altar are the walls of the choir, where more intimate services can be held in this spacious building. The aisles are lined with chapels, each dedicated to a particular saint. The faithful can pause at their favorite, light a candle as an offering, and meditate in the cool light of the stained glass. (The nearby Treasury, containing lavish robes and golden relic-holders, probably isn't worth the entry fee.)

• *Amble around the ambulatory, spill back outside, and make a U-turn left. Walk to the back end of the church along the side that faces the river.*

Notre-Dame Side View

Along the side of the church, you'll notice the flying buttresses. These 50-foot stone "beams" that stick out of the church were the key to the complex architecture of Gothic. The pointed arches we saw inside caused the weight of the roof to push outward rather than downward. The "flying" buttresses support the roof by pushing back inward. Gothic architects were masters at playing architectural forces against each other to build loftier and loftier churches.

Picture Quasimodo running around along the railed balcony at the base of the roof among the gargoyles. These grotesque beasts that stick out from pillars and buttresses represent souls caught between heaven and earth. They also function as rain spouts when there are no evil spirits to do battle with.

The neo-Gothic 90-meter spire is a product of the 1860 reconstruction of the dilapidated old church. Around its base are

apostles and evangelists (the green men) as well as Viollet-le-Duc, the architect in charge of the work. Notice how the apostles look outward, blessing the city, while the architect (at top) looks up the spire, marveling at his fine work.

• *Behind Notre-Dame, squeeze through the tourist buses, cross the street, and enter the iron gate into the park at the tip of the island.*

Deportation Memorial (Mémorial de la Déportation)

This memorial to the 200,000 French victims of the Nazi concentration camps draws you into their experience. As you descend the steps, the city around you disappears. Surrounded by walls, you have become a prisoner. Your only freedom is your view of the sky and the tiny glimpse of the river below.

Enter the dark, single-file chamber up ahead. Inside, the circular plaque in the floor reads, "They descended into the mouth of the earth and they did not return."

A hallway stretches in front of you lined with 200,000 lighted crystals, one for each French citizen that died. Flickering at the far end is the eternal flame of hope. The tomb of the unknown deportee lies at your feet. Above, the inscription reads, "Dedicated to the living memory of the 200,000 French Deportees sleeping in the night and the fog, exterminated in the Nazi concentration camps." Above the exit as you leave is the message you'll find at all Nazi sights: "Forgive, but never forget."

Île St. Louis

Back on street level, look across the river to the Île St. Louis. If the Île de la Cité is a tug laden with the history of Paris, it's towing this classy little residential dinghy laden only with boutiques, characteristic restaurants, and famous sorbet shops. This island wasn't developed until much later (18th century). What was a swampy mess is now harmonious Parisian architecture.

• *From the tip of the Île de la Cité, cross the bridge to the Left Bank and turn right. Walk along the river, toward the front end of Notre-Dame. Stairs detour down to the riverbank if you need a place to picnic. This side view of the church from across the river is one of Europe's great sights.*

LEFT BANK (RIVE GAUCHE)

The Left Bank of the Seine—"left" if you were floating down-stream—still has many of the twisting lanes and narrow buildings of medieval times. The Right Bank is more modern and business oriented, with wide boulevards and stressed Parisians in suits. Here along the riverbank, the "big business" is books, displayed in the green metal stalls on the parapet. These literary entrepreneurs pride themselves on their easygoing business style. With flexible hours and literally no overhead, they run their businesses as they have since medieval times.

• *When you reach the bridge (pont au Double) that crosses over in front of Notre-Dame, veer to the left, across the street to a small park (square Viviani). Go through the park to the small rough-stone church of St. Julien-le-Pauvre. You'll pass Paris' oldest inhabitant, a false acacia tree ("Robinier") that may have once shaded the Sun King.*

Medieval Paris (1000–1400)

This church dates from the 12th century, and the area around it keeps the same feel. A half-timbered house stands to the right of the entrance. Many buildings in medieval times were built like this, with a wooden frame filled in with a plaster of mud, straw, and dung. Back then, the humble "half-timbered" structure would have been hidden by a veneer of upscale stucco.

Looking along nearby rue Galande, you'll see a few old houses built every which way. In medieval days, people were piled on top of each other, building at all angles, as they scrambled for this prime real estate near the main commercial artery of the day—the Seine. The smell of fish competed with the smell of neighbors in this knot of humanity.

These narrow streets would have been dirt (or mud). Origi-nally the streets sloped from here down into the mucky Seine, until modern quays cleaned that up. Many Latin Quarter lanes were named for their businesses or crafts. The rue de la Bucherie (or "butcher street," just around the corner, in the direction of the river) was where butchers slaughtered livestock. The blood and guts drained into the Seine and out of town.

• *At #37 rue de la Bucherie is...*

Shakespeare & Company Bookstore

Along with butchers and fishmongers, the Left Bank has been home to scholars, philosophers, and poets since medieval times. This funky bookstore—a reincarnation of the original shop from the 1920s—has picked up the literary torch. In the '20s, it was famous as a meeting place of Paris' literary expatriate elite. Ernest Hemingway, a struggling American writer, strangled and

cooked pigeons in the park and borrowed books from here to survive. Fitzgerald, Joyce, and Pound also got their English fix here.

Today it does its best to carry on that literary tradition. Struggling writers are given free accommodations upstairs in tiny, book-lined rooms with views of Notre-Dame. Downstairs, travelers enjoy the best selection of used English books in Paris. Pick up *Free Voice*, a newspaper published for today's American expatriates, and say hi to George.

• *Return to St. Julien-le-Pauvre, then turn right (west) on rue Galande, which immediately intersects with the busy rue St. Jacques (also called rue du Petit Pont). Way back in Roman times, the rue St. Jacques was the straight, wide, paved road that brought chariots racing in and out of the city. (Roman-iacs can see remains from the third-century baths, along with a fine medieval collection, at the Cluny Museum, two blocks to the left; see tour on page 137.) Cross rue St. Jacques to the small Gothic church of St. Severin.*

St. Severin

Don't ask me why, but it took a century longer to build this church than Notre-Dame. This is flamboyant, or "flame-like," Gothic, and you can see the short, prickly spires meant to make this building flicker in the eyes of the faithful. The church gives us a close-up look at gargoyles. This weird, winged species of flying mammal, now extinct, used to swoop down on unwary peasants, occasionally carrying off small children in their beaks. Today, they're most impressive in thunderstorms, when they vomit rain.

The Latin Quarter

While it may look more like the Tunisian Quarter today, this area is the Latin Quarter, named for the language you'd hear on these streets if you walked them in the Middle Ages. The university, one of the leading universities of medieval Europe, was (and still is) nearby.

A thousand years ago, the "crude" or vernacular local languages were sophisticated enough to communicate basic human needs, but if you wanted to get philosophical, the language of choice was Latin. The educated elite of Dark Ages Europe was a class that transcended nations and borders. From Sicily to Sweden, they spoke and corresponded in Latin. The most Latin thing about this area now is the beat you may hear coming from some of the subterranean jazz clubs.

Along rue St. Severin you can still see the shadow of the medieval sewer system. (The street slopes into a central channel of bricks.) In the days before plumbing and toilets, when people still went to the river or neighborhood wells for their water, flushing meant throwing it out the window. Certain times of day were flushing times. Maids on the fourth floor would holler *"Garde de l'eau!"* ("Look out for the water!") and heave it into the streets, where it would eventually wash down into the Seine.

• *At #22 rue St. Severin, you'll find the skinniest house in Paris, two windows wide. Continue along rue St. Severin to…*

Boulevard St. Michel

Busy boulevard St. Michel (or "boul' Miche") is famous as the main artery for bohemian Paris, culminating a block away (to the left), where it intersects with boulevard St. Germain. Although nowadays you're more likely to find pantyhose at 30 percent off, there are still many cafés, boutiques, and bohemian haunts nearby.

The Sorbonne—the University of Paris' humanities department—is also close, if you want to make a detour. (Turn left on boulevard St. Michel and walk two blocks. The entrance is at #47 rue des Écoles, or just gaze at the dome from the Place Sorbonne courtyard.) Founded as a theology school around the radical Peter Abelard, it became the alma mater for Thomas Aquinas, Loyola, Erasmus, and John Calvin. Children of kings and nobles were sent here to become priests, though many returned as heretics, having studied radical new secular ideas as well. Paris still is a world center for new intellectual trends.

• *Cross boulevard St. Michel. Just ahead is a tree-filled square lined with cafés and restaurants.*

Place Saint Andre des Arts

In Paris, most serious thinking goes on in cafés. (For more information, see "Les Grands Cafés de Paris" on page 187.) For centuries, these have been social watering holes, where you could buy a warm place to sit and stimulating conversation for the price of a cup of coffee. Every great French writer—from Voltaire and Rousseau to Sartre and Derrida—had a favorite haunt.

Paris honors its writers. If you visit the Panthéon (a few blocks down boulevard St. Michel and to the left), you will find great French writers and scientists buried in a setting usually reserved for warriors and politicians.

• *Adjoining this square on the river side is the triangular-shaped place St. Michel, with a Métro stop and a statue of St. Michael killing a devil.*

Place St. Michel

You're standing at the traditional core of the Left Bank's artsy, liberal, hippie, bohemian district of poets, philosophers, and winos. You'll find international eateries, far-out bookshops, street singers, pale girls in black berets, jazz clubs, and—these days—tourists. Small cinemas show avant-garde films, almost always in the *version originale* (v.o.). For colorful wandering and café-sitting, afternoons and evenings are best. In the morning, it feels sleepy. The Latin Quarter stays up late and sleeps in.

In less commercial times, place St. Michel was a gathering point for the city's malcontents and misfits. Here, in 1871, the citizens took the streets from the government troops, set up barricades "Les Miz"-style, and established the Paris Commune. In World War II, the locals rose up against their Nazi oppressors (read the plaques by the St. Michael fountain).

And in the spring of 1968, a time of social upheaval all over the world, young students battled riot batons and tear gas, took over the square, and declared it an independent state. Factory workers followed their call to arms and went on strike, toppling the de Gaulle government and forcing change. Eventually, the students were pacified, the university was reformed, and the Latin Quarter's original cobblestones were replaced with pavement, so future scholars could never again use them as weapons.

• *From place St. Michel, look across the river and find the spire of Sainte-Chapelle church, with its weathervane angel. Cross the river on pont St. Michel and continue along boulevard du Palais.*

On your left, you'll see the doorway to Sainte-Chapelle. But first, carry on another 30 meters and turn right at a wide pedestrian street, the rue de Lutece.

CITÉ "METROPOLITAIN" STOP

Of the 141 original turn-of-the-century subway entrances, this is one of 17 survivors now preserved as a national art treasure. (New York's Museum of Modern Art even exhibits one.) The curvy, plantlike iron work is a textbook example of Art Nouveau, the style that rebelled against the Erector-set squareness of the Industrial Age.

The flower market on place Louis Lepine is a pleasant detour. On Sundays this square chirps with a busy bird market. And across the way is the Prefecture de Police, where Inspector Clouseau of Pink Panther fame used to work, and where the local resistance fighters took the first building from the Nazis in August of 1944, leading to the allied liberation of Paris a week later.

• *Pause here to admire the view. Sainte-Chapelle is a pearl in an ugly architectural oyster, part of a complex of buildings that includes the Palace of Justice (to the right of Sainte-Chapelle, behind the iron and bronze gates).*

Return to the entrance of Sainte-Chapelle. You'll need to pass through a metal detector to get into Sainte-Chapelle. (It's best to leave your Uzi at the hotel.) Walk through the security scanner. Toilets are ahead on the left. The line into the church may be long. (Museum cardholders can go directly in.) Enter the humble ground floor . . .

SAINTE-CHAPELLE

Sainte-Chapelle, the triumph of Gothic church architecture, is a cathedral of glass like no other. It was built in 1248 for St. Louis IX (France's only canonized king) to house the supposed Crown of Thorns. Its architectural harmony is due to the fact that it was completed under the direction of one architect and in only five years— unheard of in Gothic times. Recall that Notre-Dame took over 200.

The exterior is ugly. But those fat buttresses are all the support needed to hold up the roof, opening up the walls for stained glass. The design clearly shows an Old Regime approach to worship. The basement was for staff and more common folks. Royal Christians worshiped upstairs. The paint job, a 19th-century restoration, helps you imagine how grand this small, painted, jew-elled chapel was. (Imagine Notre-Dame painted as this is . . . .)

• *Climb the spiral staircase to the "Haute Chapelle." Leave the rough stone of the earth and become enlightened.*

The Stained Glass

Fiat lux. "Let there be light." Christianity, like many religions, intuitively recognized the sun as the source of life on earth. Light shining through stained glass was a symbol of God's grace shining down to earth, and Gothic architects used their new technology to turn dark stone buildings into lanterns of light. For me, the glory of Gothic shines brighter here than in any other church.

SAINTE-CHAPELLE

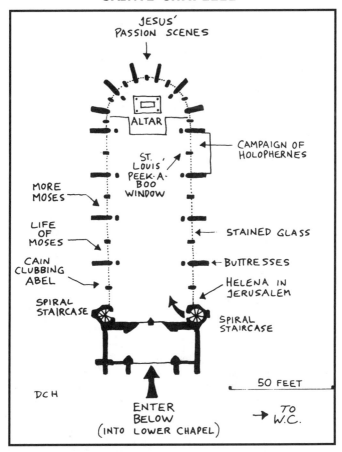

JESUS' PASSION SCENES

ALTAR

CAMPAIGN OF HOLOPHERNES

ST. LOUIS' PEEK-A-BOO WINDOW

MORE MOSES

LIFE OF MOSES

STAINED GLASS

CAIN CLUBBING ABEL

BUTTRESSES

HELENA IN JERUSALEM

SPIRAL STAIRCASE

SPIRAL STAIRCASE

DCH

50 FEET

ENTER BELOW (INTO LOWER CHAPEL)

TO W.C.

There are 15 separate panels of stained glass, with more than 1,100 different scenes, mostly from the Bible. In medieval times, scenes like these helped teach Bible stories to the illiterate. These cover the entire Christian history of the world, from the Creation in Genesis (first window on the left), to the coming of Christ (over the altar), to the end of the world (the round "rose"-shaped window at the rear of the church). Each individual scene is interesting, and the whole effect is overwhelming.

Let's look at a single scene. Head toward the altar to the fourth big window on the right. Look at the bottom circle, second

from the left. It's a battle scene (the campaign of Holophernes) showing three soldiers with swords slaughtering three men. The background is blue. The men have different colored clothes—red, blue, green, mauve, and white. Notice some of the details. You can see the folds in the robes, the hair, and facial features, and look at the victim in the center—his head is splotched with blood!

Craftsmen made glass (which is, essentially, melted sand), coloring it by mixing in metals like cobalt (blue) or copper (green). Then they'd assemble pieces of different colored glass to make, say, the soldier in blue with a green shield (upper right). The pieces were held together by lead. Details like the folds in the robes (see the victim in white, lower left) came by either scratching on the glass or by baking in imperfections. It was a painstaking process of finding just the right colors, fitting them together to make a scene...and then multiplying by 1,100. (Note: The sun lights up different windows at different times of day. Overcast days give the most even light. On bright sunny days, some sections are glorious while others look like a sheet of lead.)

Other scenes worth a look:

1) Cain clubbing Abel (first window on the left, second row of circles, far right—Cain is in red).

2) The life of Moses (second window, the bottom row of diamond panels). First panel shows baby Moses in a basket, placed by his sister in the squiggly brown river. Next, he's found by pharaoh's daughter. Then, he grows up. And finally, he's a man, a prince of Egypt on his royal throne.

3) In the next window (third on left) you'll see various scenes of Moses. He's often given "horns" because of a medieval mistranslation of the Biblical description of his "aura" of holiness.

4) Over the altar are scenes from Jesus' arrest and crucifixion. Stand at the stairs in front and look over the altar and through the canopy to find Jesus being whipped (left), Jesus in purple being crowned

It takes 13 tourists to build a Gothic church: six columns, six buttresses, and one steeple.

with thorns (right), Jesus in yellow carrying his cross (a little above), and, finally, Jesus on the cross being speared by a soldier (above, left).

5) The pagan Roman emperor Constantine sends his Christian daughter Helena to Jerusalem to find the Crown of Thorns and Crucifixion cross (first window to the right, lowest level).

If you can't read much into the individual windows, you're not alone. The medieval worshiper was a stained-glass speed reader, and we're the illiterate ones. (For some tutoring, a little book with color photos is on sale downstairs with the postcards.)

The altar was raised up high (notice the staircase for the priest to the right) to better display the relic around which this chapel was built—the Crown of Thorns. This was the crown put on Jesus when the Romans were torturing and humiliating him before his execution. King Louis was convinced he'd found the real McCoy and paid three times as much money for it as was spent on this entire chapel. Today, the supposed Crown of Thorns is kept in the Notre-Dame Treasury and shown only on Good Friday.

Notice the little private viewing window in the wall to the right of the altar. Louis was both saintly and shy. He liked to be able to go to church without dealing with the rigors of public royal life. Here he could worship still dressed in his jammies.

Lay your camera on the ground and shoot the ceiling. Those pure and simple ribs growing out of the slender columns are the essence of Gothic structure.

Palais de Justice

As you walk around the church exterior, look down and notice how much Paris has risen in the 800 years since Sainte-Chapelle was built. You're in a huge complex of buildings that has housed the local government since ancient Roman times. It was the site of the original Gothic palace of the early kings of France. The only surviving medieval parts are Sainte-Chapelle and the Conciergerie prison.

Most of the site is now covered by the giant Palais de Justice, home of France's supreme court, built in 1776. "*Liberté, Egalité, Fraternité*" over the doors is a reminder that this was also the

headquarters of the Revolutionary government. Here
they doled out justice, con-
demning many to torture in
the Conciergerie downstairs
or to have their heads
removed by "Monsieur de
Paris"—the guillotine.

Paris' City Palace in 1650, with Sainte-Chapelle, the Conciergerie, and Pont Neuf (then 30 years old) in the background.

• *Now pass through the big iron gate to the noisy boulevard du Palais and turn left (toward the Right Bank).*

On the corner is the site of the city's oldest public clock (1334). While the present clock is Baroque, it still manages to keep accurate time.

Turn left onto quai d'Horologe and walk along the river. The round medieval tower just ahead marks the entrance to the Conciergerie. Even if you don't pay to see the Conciergerie, you can visit the courtyard and lobby. Step past the serious-looking guard into the courtyard.

Conciergerie

The Conciergerie, a former prison and place of torture, is a gloomy place. Kings used it to torture and execute failed assassins. The leaders of the Revolution put it to similar good use. The tower next to the entrance, called "the babbler," was named for the painful sounds that leaked from it.

Look at the stark printing above the doorways. This was a no-nonsense revolutionary time. Everything, including lettering, was subjected to the test of reason. No frills or we chop 'em off.

Marie-Antoinette was imprisoned here. During a busy eight-month period in the Revolution, she was one of 2,600 prisoners kept here on their way to the guillotine.

The interior (requires ticket), with its huge vaulted and pillared rooms, echoes with history but is pretty barren. You can see Marie-

Antoinette's cell, with a collection of Marie-Antoinette mementos. In another room, a list of those made "a foot shorter at the top" by the guillotine includes ex-King Louis XVI, Charlotte Corday (who murdered Marat in his bathtub), and the chief Revolutionary who got a taste of his own medicine—Maximilien Robespierre.

• *Back outside, wink at the flak-vested guard (but no jokes about your Uzi), turn left, and continue your walk along the river. Across the river you can see the rooftop observatory of the Samaritaine department store, where we'll end this walk. At the first corner, veer left into a sleepy triangular square called "place Dauphine."*

Place Dauphine

It's amazing to find such coziness in the heart of Paris. This city of 2 million is still a city of neighborhoods, a collection of villages. The French Supreme Court building looms behind like a giant marble gavel. Enjoy the village-Paris feeling in the park. You may see lawyers on their lunch break playing *boules*.

• *Walk through the park to the statue of Henry IV, who in 1607 inaugurated the Pont Neuf. (If you need a romantic hideaway in the midst of this mega city, take the steps down into the park on the tip of the island and dangle your legs over the prow of this concrete island.) From the statue, turn right onto the old bridge. Walk to the little nook halfway across.*

Pont Neuf

The Pont Neuf, or "new bridge," is now Paris' oldest. Its 12 arches span the widest part of the river. The fine view includes the park on the tip of the island (note Seine boats), the Orsay, and the Louvre. These turrets were originally for vendors and street entertainers. In the days of Henry, who originated the promise of "a chicken in every pot," this would have been a lively scene.

• *The first building you'll hit on the Right Bank is the venerable old department store Samaritaine. Go through the door, veer left, and catch the elevator to the ninth floor. Climb two sets of stairs to the panorama. (Don't confuse the terrace level with the higher, better panorama. Light meals are served on the terrace. Public WCs on fifth and ninth floors.)*

THE REST OF PARIS

From the circular little crow's nest of the building, ponder the greatest skyline in Europe. Retrace the walk you just made, starting with Notre-Dame and Sainte-Chapelle. Then spin counterclockwise (or run down the stairs to hop on the Métro) and check out the rest of Paris:

The **Pompidou Center**, the wild and colorful rectangular tangle of blue and white pipes and tubes, is filled with art that makes this building's exterior look tame. See page 67.

Sacré-Coeur is a neo-Romanesque church topping Montmartre. This is an atmospheric quarter after dark, its streets filled with strolling tourists avoiding strolling artists. ★ See Montmartre Walk on page 73.

The **Louvre** is the largest building in Paris, the largest palace in Europe, and the largest museum in the Western world. ★ See Louvre Tour on page 79.

Stretching away from the Louvre, the **Tuileries Gardens**, place de la Concorde, and the Champs-Élysées lead to the Arc de Triomphe. The gardens are Paris' "Central Park," filled with families at play, cellists in the shade, carousels, pony rides, and the ghost of Maurice Chevalier.

The gardens overlook the grand **place de la Concorde**, marked by an ancient obelisk, where all of France seems to converge. It was "guillotine central" during the Revolution and continues to be a place of much festivity.

Europe's grandest boulevard, the **Champs-Élysées**, runs uphill from place de la Concorde about a mile to the Arc de Triomphe. While pretty globalized, and with rich-and-single aristocrats more rare than ever, it's still the place you're most likely to see Sylvester Stallone. ⊙ See Champs-Élysées Walk on page 57.

Napoleon began constructing the magnificent **Arc de Triomphe** in 1806 to commemorate his victory at the Battle of Austerlitz. It was finished in 1836, just in time for the emperor's funeral parade. Today it commemorates heroes of past wars. There's no triumphal arch bigger (50 meters high, 40 meters wide). And, with 12 converging boulevards, there's no traffic circle more thrilling, either on foot or behind the wheel. See page 57.

Paris, the capital of Europe, is built on an appropriately monumental plan, with an axis that stretches from the Louvre, up the Champs-Élysées, past the Arc de Triomphe, all the way to the modern Grande Arche among the skyscrapers at **La Defense**. (Find the faint shadow of this arch, just above the Arc de Triomphe.)

The **Orsay Museum**, the train-station-turned-art-museum, is just beyond the Louvre on the left bank. See page 98.

The body of Napoleon lies under the gilded dome. The giant building is **Les Invalides**, designed to house his wounded troops. Today it houses Europe's greatest military museum. See page 134. The **Rodin Museum** is nearby. See page 124.

The **Eiffel Tower** is a thousand-foot exclamation point built as a tempporary engineering stunt to celebrate the 100th anniversary of the French Revolution. Paris decided to let it be an exception to a downtown building code that allows the skyline to be broken only by a few prestigious domes and spires. See page 31.

The 52-story **Montparnasse Tower**, a city in itself (5,000 workers, 700 feet high) reminds us that, while tourists look for hints of Louis and Napoleon, work-a-day Paris looks to the future.

CHAMPS-ÉLYSÉES
WALK

Leaving Paris without strolling the Champs-Élysées is like walking out of a great restaurant before dessert. This is Paris at its most Parisian: monumental sidewalks, stylish shops, grand cafés, and glimmering showrooms. This walk covers about three miles and takes three hours if done completely. The Arc de Triomphe (open daily until 23:00 in summer) and Champs-Élysées are best at night. Métro stops are located every three blocks on the Champs-Élysées (zhahn-zay-lee-zay).

Start by taking the Métro to the Arc de Triomphe. At the Métro stop Charles de Gaulle Étoile, follow *sortie* Champs-Élysées/Avenue Friedland to "access Arc de Triomphe" signs. Exit at the top of the Champs-Élysées and face the Arc de Triomphe. Underground WCs are on the left side of Champs-Élysées, and an underground walkway leading to the arch should be in front of you on the right side of the Champs-Élysées.

Ascend the **Arc de Triomphe** via the 230 steps or the elevator—sorry, no discount for walkers (40F, daily till 23:00, Oct–May until 22:00, skip the line if you have a pass or don't want to go to the top of the arch).

A small museum near the top explains its history; the exhibits are in French, but there's a good video in English. Begun in 1806, the arch was intended to honor Napoleon's soldiers, who, in spite of being vastly outnumbered by the Austrians, scored a remarkable victory at the battle of Austerlitz. Napoleon died prior to its completion. But it was finished in time for his funeral procession to pass underneath carrying his remains from exile in St. Helena home to Paris. Today the Arc de Triomphe is dedicated to the glory of all French armies.

From the rooftop viewpoint, get your bearings with the circular orientation tables. Opposite the Champs-Élysées, the avenue Grande

CHAMPS-ÉLYSÉES WALK

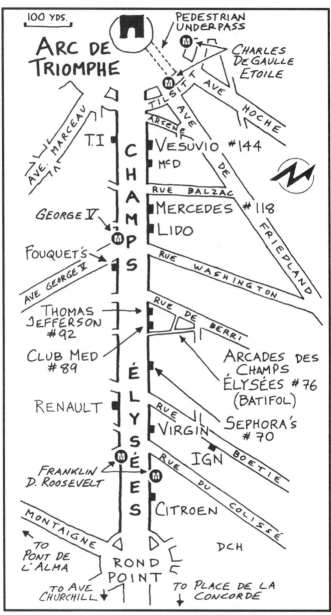

Armée leads to the skyscraper ghetto of the La Defense suburb. Notice what a contrast they make to the regular height of buildings closer to the arch. French President Mitterand had the huge white **Grande Arche de La Defense** built as a centerpiece of this mini-Manhattan (see the Sights chapter, "Northwest Paris"). It's part of the huge axis capped by the arch you're standing on and the Louvre. The wide boulevard lined with grass and trees a little to your left is avenue Foch (named after a WWI hero) and is the best address to have in Paris. (The shah of Iran and Aristotle Onassis had homes here.) The Bois de Boulogne is the big green park at the end of avenue Foch. While the arch was under construction, the land below you was a rural forest, looking much like the Bois de Boulogne.

Walk to the Champs-Élysées side and scan the cityscape of downtown Paris. Notice the uniform height and symmetry. The beauty of Paris—basically a flat basin with a river running through it—is man-made. The key to this beauty is the relationship between the width of its grand boulevards and the uniformity in the height and design of the buildings. To the right, the rude **Montparnasse Tower** looks lonely out there, standing like the box the Eiffel Tower came in. It served as a wake-up call in the early 1970s to preserve the building height restriction and strengthen urban design standards.

The 12 boulevards that radiate from the Arc de Triomphe were part of Baron Haussmann's master plan for Paris: the creation of a series of major boulevards, intersecting at diagonals with monuments (like the Arc de Triomphe) as centerpieces of those intersections. His plan did not anticipate the automobile—obvious when you watch the traffic scene below. As you gaze down at what appears a chaotic traffic mess, watch how smoothly it really functions. Cars entering the circle have the right of way, those in the circle must yield. Motorcycles are fair game. Pedestrians are used as target practice. Still, there are plenty of accidents, often caused by tourists who don't understand the rules of the game. Tired of related disputes, insurance companies split the fault and damages of any Arc de Triomphe accidents 50-50.

Look straight down the **Champs-Élysées**. The first street was built at the lower end in the early 1600s by Queen Marie de Medici, a short extension of her Tuileries Gardens. It soon became the place to cruise in your carriage. (It still is today—traffic can be jammed up even at midnight.) One hundred years later, it was extended uphill to where you are now.

Like its Roman ancestors, this arch has served as a parade gateway for triumphal armies (French or foe) and important ceremonies. From 1941 to 1944, a large swastika flew from here as Nazis goose-stepped down the Champs-Élysées. Allied troops marched triumphantly under this arch in August 1944.

Descend the arch and stand on the bronze plaque at the foot of the **Tomb of the Unknown Soldier** (from World War I). Daily at 18:30 the flame is rekindled and new flowers set in place. On the columns you'll see lists of battle victories and officers (with a line under the names of those who died in battle).

Still facing the Tomb of the Unknown Soldier, turn right and walk to the front of the arch's massive column to see its most famous sculpture. *The Departure of the Volunteers*, or *La Marseillaise*, is a rousing effort to rally the troops by what looks like an ugly reincarnation of Joan of Arc. On the right side of this column, a scene a little over halfway up the arch shows Napoleon's confident pose as he oversees his victory at Austerlitz.

Walk out to the traffic circle and look down the Champs-Élysées. Plan your walking attack from here. The Louvre is the building at the very end of the avenue through the Tuileries Gardens. You'll turn right off the Champs-Élysées about halfway there. Notice how the left sidewalk is more popular with pedestrians. While the left side is most interesting, cross over at least once for the exhilerating view from the center of the avenue's 10 lanes. The **tourist information office** is immediately on the right at #127. Le Drugstore (next door) has a small grocery store in the back.

Cross back under the tunnel to the top of the Champs-Élysées. The *nouveau* (new) Champs-Élysées is a revitalized avenue with new street benches, lamps, broader sidewalks, and an army of green-suited workers with small machines designed to keep Paris' most famous avenue spic and span.

Start your descent. The first tiny street you cross, rue de Tilsitt, is part of a shadow ring road—an option for drivers who'd like to avoid the chaos of the arch, complete with stoplights. Be careful of speedy cars on these cross streets as you descend.

On the first block down, stop by Café Vesuvio (#144, reasonable prices) to enjoy fine views of the arch with its rooftop bristling with tourists. The Big Macs for sale next door are just as popular among the French as they are at home.

At the Mercedes showroom (#118), you can pick up your new sedan and a leather jacket and purse to match.

Next to the Mercedes showroom is the famous **Lido**, Paris' largest cabaret—check out the photos, video, and prices. These sensational shows pull out every stop for floor customers. Movie-going on the Champs-Élysées is also popular. Check to see if there are films you recognize, then look for the showings (*seances*); if there is a "v.o." (*version originale*) next to the time, the film will be in its original langauge.

Now cross the boulevard where the elegant avenue George V (home to several four-star hotels and the Crazy Horse Saloon) spills into the Champs-Élysées. Fouquet's café-restaurant, under the orange awning, serves the most expensive shot of expresso I found in Paris (29F), but the setting is tops. Since the early 1900s, Fouquet's has been a favorite of French actors and actresses. The welcome mat of golden plaques honors winners of France's Oscarlike film awards, the Cesars (see "Les Grands Cafés de Paris," page 187).

Cross back to the lively side. At #92, a wall plaque marks the place Thomas Jefferson lived while minister to France (1785). A plaque just below marks the spot where Robert Birlinger died fighting the Germans during the liberation of Paris in August 1944.

Nearby are several arcades. My favorite is the Arcade des Champs-Élysées, at #76. This refuge of the belle epoque seems out of place today. Wander in. A meal at Batifol's gives you a taste of the old Champs-Élysées, (climb three steps for the most atmospheric tables; reasonable value—try the *pot-au-feu*).

Just down *les Champs*, glide down Sephora's ramp at #74 into a vast hall of cosmetics and perfumes. The young woman at the wheel of scents will explain how it works. Grab a black basket and join the frenzy. Halfway down on your left in red flashing numbers are the current prices of perfumes (*cours des parfums*) in cities throughout the world. Notice that Paris is hardly the cheapest.

The English pharmacy is open until midnight at the corner on rue Boetie, and map lovers can detour one block down this street to the Institut Geographique National, France's version of the National Geographic Society (Mon–Sat 9:30–19:00).

Virgin Megastore sells a world of music one block farther down the Champs-Élysées. The Disney and Quicksilver stores are reminders of global ecomomics—the French love these stores as much as Americans do. And near the bottom of the Champs-Élysées, Renault and Citroen showrooms glare across the avenue, each offering late-night cafés and restaurants.

At the Rondpoint the shopping ends and the park begins. This leafy circle is always colorful, lined with flowers or seasonal decorations (thousands of pumpkins at Halloween, hundreds of trees at Christmas).

Now it's decision time. You have three options: 1) You can continue straight (by Métro or foot) to reach place de la Concorde and the Tuileries Gardens; 2) A hard right turn here takes you back to the river and pont de l'Alma, down Paris' most exclusive shopping street, the avenue Montaigne, where you need an appointment to buy a dress; 3) You can finish the walk with me.

To continue, walk a block past Rondpoint, then turn right on avenue Churchill, and walk between the glass- and steel-domed

Grand and Petit Palais exhibition halls, built for the 1900 World's Fair. Today these examples of the "can do" spirit of the turn of the century host a variety of exhibits (details at tourist offices or in *Pariscope*). Impressive temporary exhibits fill the huge Grand Palais (drop in to see what's on; not covered by museum pass), while the Petit Palais (left side) houses a permanant collection of 19th-century paintings by Delacroix, Cézanne, Monet, and others (covered by museum pass).

Cross the river on pont Alexandre, eyeing the golden dome of Les Invalides. Les Invalides was built by Louis XIV as a veteran's hospital for his battle-weary troops (see Napoleon's Tomb Tour on page 132); in the Esplanade des Invalides, possibly the largest slice of accessible grass in Paris, soccer balls and Frisbees fill the air.

This exquisite bridge, spiked with golden statues and iron-work lamps, was built to celebrate a turn-of-the-century treaty between France and Russia. Like the two palaces just passed, it's a fine example of belle epoque exuberance. Notice the elegant streetlamps on the railing. The barges under the bridge are some of over 2,000 houseboats on the Seine.

At the end of the bridge, turn left and follow the Seine past the Air France bus terminal and Ministry of Foreign Affairs (#37) to the Greek temple–like Assemblée Nationale (at the next bridge). France's 600 members of parliament convene here. If the gates are open, climb to the top of the steps for a fantastic view over the place de la Concorde.

From here, pont de la Concorde leads to place de la Concorde. The bridge, built of stones from the Bastille prison (which was demolished by the Revolution in 1789), symbolizes that, with good government, *concorde* (harmony) can come from chaos. Walk to the far (right) side of the bridge and begin crossing it. Stand near the center of the bridge and gaze upriver. Using a clock as a compass, the L'Orangerie (closed for renovation) is at 10:00 and the tall building with the skinny chimneys (at 11:00) is the architectural caboose of the sprawling Louvre Palace. The park between is the Tuileries Gardens. The thin spire of Sainte-Chapelle is dead center at 12:00, with the twin towers of Notre-Dame to its right. The Orsay Museum is closer on the right (just this side of the next bridge), opposite the Tuileries.

Leaving the bridge, you'll cross a freeway underpass similar to the one at pont de L'Alma, three bridges downstream, where Princess Diana lost her life in the tragic 1997 car accident.

Continue to the **place de la Concorde**, the 21-acre square with the obelisk. Walk to the island in the center from the cross-walk on the far side of the square. During the Revolution, this was the place de la Revolution. Over 1,300 heads lost their bodies here during the Reign of Terror. The guillotine sat here. A bronze plaque on the Arc de Triomphe side of the obelisk memorializes the place where Louis XVI and Marie-Antoinette, among many others, were made a foot shorter at the top. Three worked the guillotine: one managed the

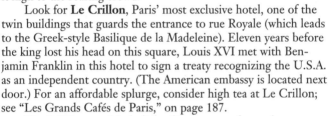

blade, one held the blood bucket, and one caught the head, raising it high to the roaring crowd.

Look for **Le Crillon**, Paris' most exclusive hotel, one of the twin buildings that guards the entrance to rue Royale (which leads to the Greek-style Basilique de la Madeleine). Eleven years before the king lost his head on this square, Louis XVI met with Benjamin Franklin in this hotel to sign a treaty recognizing the U.S.A. as an independent country. (The American embassy is located next door.) For an affordable splurge, consider high tea at Le Crillon; see "Les Grands Cafés de Paris," on page 187.

The 2,300-year-old **obelisk of Luxor** now forms the centerpiece of place de la Concorde. It was carted here from Egypt in 1829, a gift to the French king. The gold pictures on the obelisk tell the story of its incredible journey.

The obelisk also forms a center point along a line locals call the "royal perspective." From this straight line (Louvre—Obelisk—Arc de Triomphe—Grand Arche de la Defense) you can hang a lot of history. The Louvre symbolized the old regime (divine right rule by kings and queens). The obelisk and place de la Concorde symbolize the peoples' revolution (cutting off the king's head). The Arc de Triomphe calls to mind the triumph of nationalism (victorious armies carrying national flags under the arch). And the huge modern arch in the distance, surrounded by the headquarters of multinational corporations, heralds a future where business entities are more powerful than nations.

The beautiful **Tuileries Gardens** lead through the iron gates to the Louvre (with a public WC just inside on the right). If high tea at Le Crillon isn't your cup of tea, pull up a chair next to the pond or find one of the cafés in the gardens.

MARAIS
WALK

This walk takes you through one of Paris' most characteristic quarters, the Marais, and finishes in Beaubourg. When in Paris, you naturally want to see the big sights, but to experience Paris you need to visit a vital neighborhood.

The **Marais** neighborhood contains more pre-Revolutionary lanes and buildings than anywhere else in town and is more atmospheric than touristy. It's medieval Paris. This is how much of the city looked until, in the mid-1800s, Napoleon III had Baron Haussmann blasted out the narrow streets to construct broad boulevards (wide enough for the guns and ranks of the army, too wide for revolutionary barricades), creating modern Paris.

This walk is about three miles long. Allow two hours, and add another hour if you visit the Carnavalet Museum. Paris Walks offers in-depth guided tours of this area (see "Organized Tours," page 25).

Start by riding the Métro to Bastille. At **place de la Bastille**, there are more revolutionary images in the Métro station murals than on the square. Exit the Métro following signs to rue Saint Antoine (not the signs to rue Saint Antoine du Faubourg). Ascend onto a noisy square dominated by the bronze **Colonne de Juillet** (July Column). Victims of the revolutions of 1830 and 1848 are buried in a vault 55 meters below this gilded statue of liberty. The actual Bastille, a royal fortress-then-prison that once symbolized old-regime tyranny and now symbolizes the Parisian emancipation, is long gone. While only a brick outline of the fortress' round turrets survives (under the traffic where rue Saint Antoine hits the square), the story of the Bastille is indelibly etched on the city's psyche.

For centuries the Bastille was used to defend the city (mostly from its own people). On July 14, 1789, the people of Paris stormed the prison, releasing its seven prisoners and hoping to find arms. Instead, they found heads. They demolished the brick

————— MARAIS WALK —————

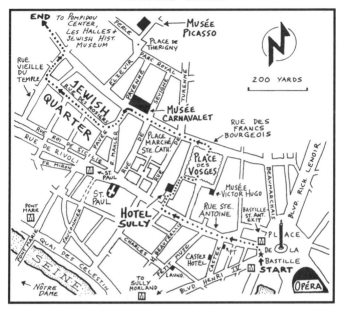

fortress and decorated their pikes with the heads of a few big wigs. By shedding blood, the leaders of the gang made sure it would be tough to turn back the tides of revolution. Ever since, the French have celebrated July 14 as their independence day—Bastille Day.

The flashy, glassy-grey, and controversial **Opéra-Bastille** dominates (some say overwhelms) the square. Designed by the Canadian architect Carlos Ott, this latest Parisian grand project was opened with great fanfare by François Mitterrand on the 200th Bastille Day, July 14, 1989. (For ticket information, see page 198.)

Turn your back to the statue and, passing the Banque de France on your right (good rates, long lines, opposite a fine map of the area), head down rue Saint Antoine about four blocks into the Marais.

Leave rue Saint Antoine at #62 and turn right through two elegant courtyards of **Hôtel de Sully** (62 rue Saint Antoine, open until 19:00, fine bookstore inside). Originally a swamp (*marais*), during the reign of Henry IV, it became the hometown of the French aristocracy. In the 17th century, big shots built their private mansions (*hôtels*), like this one, close to Henry's place des Vosges. *Hôtels* that survived the revolution now house museums, libraries, and national institutions. The aristocrats may be gone, but the Marais—which, until recently, was a dumpy bohemian quarter—is today a thriving, trendy, but real community and a joy to explore.

To get to the **place des Vosges** park, continue through Hôtel de Sully (if it's closed, backtrack to rue de Biraque to reach place des Vosges). The small door on the far right corner of the second courtyard pops you out into one of Paris' finest squares (closes at dusk). Walk to the center, where Louis XIII sits on a horse surrounded by locals enjoying their community park. Children frolic in the sandbox, lovers warm benches, and pigeons guard their fountains, while

trees shade this retreat from the glare of the big city. Henry IV built this centerpiece of the Marais in 1605. As hoped, this turned the Marais into Paris' most exclusive neighborhood. **Victor Hugo** lived at #6, and you can visit his house (22F, Tue–Sun 10:00–17:40, closed Mon, corner closest to the Bastille, see page 37).

Walk behind Louis' horse to the arcade. Follow it left past art galleries and antique shops onto the boutique-filled rue des Francs Bourgeois. Browse Francs Bourgeois for two blocks to the corner of rue de Sévigné, where you'll see the Musée Carnavalet (on right).

The **Carnavalet Museum** focuses on the history of Paris and is housed inside a Marais mansion (35F, Tue–Sun 10:00–17:00, closed Mon, 23 rue de Sévigné, see page 37).

Go another block along rue des Francs Bourgeois (peeking through the gate on the right) and turn left at the post office. (The **Picasso Museum**, described on page 37, is up 1 block to the right: 30F, Wed–Mon 9:30–18:00, closed Tue, 5 rue Thorigny.)

Go right onto rue Rosiers, which runs straight for three blocks through Paris' Jewish Quarter, lively every day except Saturday.

The **Jewish Quarter** is lined with colorful shops and kosher eateries. Check out Jo Goldenberg's delicatessen/

restaurant (1st corner on left, #7, scene of a terrorist bombing in darker times). You'll be tempted by kosher pizza and plenty of 20F falafel to go (*emporter* = to go) joints. Rue Rosiers dead-ends into rue du Vieille du Temple. Turn right.

Frank Bourgeois is waiting at the corner postcard/print shop. Turn left on rue des Francs Bourgeois, which leads past the national archives (peek inside the courtyard) and turns into rue Rambuteau; continue for several blocks on rue Rambuteau. As you approach the Pompidou Center, you'll pass within a few doors of the new **Jewish history museum**—to the right on rue du Temple (40F, not covered by museum pass, Mon–Fri 11:00–18:00, Sun 10:00–18:00, closed Sat, 71 rue du Temple, see page 36).

The pipes and glass of the newly renovated **Pompidou Center** mark your exit from the Marais and reintroduce you to our century. Pass that huge building on your left to join the fray in front of the center (also called the Centre Beaubourg). Survey this popular spot from the top of the sloping square. Tubular escalators lead up to a great view (free) and the modern art museum (see page 36).

The Pompidou Center follows with gusto the 20th-century architectural axiom "form follows function." To get a more spacious and functional interior, the guts of this exoskeletal building are draped on the outside and color coded: vibrant red for people lifts, cool blue for air-conditioning, eco-green for plumbing, don't-touch-it yellow for electrical stuff, and white for bones (compare the Pompidou Center to another exoskeletal building, Notre-Dame). Enjoy the adjacent *Homage to Stravinsky* **fountain.** Jean Tingley designed this as a tribute to the composer: every fountain represents one of his hard-to-hum scores. For low-stress meals try **Le Mélodine**, a self-service cafeteria at the Rambuteau Métro stop, or the fun **Dame Tartine**, which overlooks the *Homage to Stravinsky* fountain and serves a young clientele and good, cheap meals.

With your back to the Pompidou Center's escalators, walk the cobbled pedestrian mall, crossing the busy boulevard Sebastopol to the ivy-covered pavilions of **Les Halles**. Paris' down-and-dirty central produce market of 800 years was replaced by a glitzy but soulless shopping center in the late 1970s. The mall's most endearing layer is its grassy rooftop park. The Gothic Saint Eustache church overlooking this contemporary scene has a famous 8,000-pipe organ. The Louvre and Notre-Dame are not far away. The mall is served by Paris' busiest Métro hub (Chatelet–Les Halles).

RUE CLER
WALK

The Art of Parisian Living

Paris is changing fast, but a stroll down this street puts you into a thriving traditional Parisian neighborhood.

Shopping for groceries is an integral part of daily life here. Parisians shop almost daily for three good reasons: Refrigerators are small (expensive electricity, tiny kitchens), produce must be fresh, and it's an important social event. Shopping is a chance to hear about the butcher's vacation plans, see photos of the florist's new grandchild, relax over *un café*, and kiss the cheeks of friends (twice for regular acquaintances, three times for friends you haven't seen in a while).

Rue Cler—traffic free since 1984—offers plenty of space for tiny stores and their shoppers to spill into the street. It's an ideal environment for this ritual to survive and for you to explore. The street is lined with all the necessary shops—wine, cheese, chocolate, bread—as well as a bank, and a post office. And the shops of this community are run by people who've found their niche ... boys who grew up on quiche, girls who know a good wine.

If you wish to learn the fine art of living Parisian-style, rue Cler provides an excellent classroom. And if you wish to assemble the ultimate French picnic, there's no better place. This is the only walking tour in this guidebook you should start hungry.

(Do this walk when the market is open and lively: Tue–Sat 8:30–13:00 or 17:00–19:00, Sun 8:30–12:00, dead on Mon).

1. Bakery: Start your walk where the pedestrian section of rue Cler does, at rue de Grenelle (Mo. École Militaire). The corner bakery is typical of a newer breed of bakeries with space in the corner for coffee drinkers and fast-fooders. The almond croissants here are famous among locals. Like locals, we'll buy our baguette later to avoid damaging the slender loaves.

RUE CLER WALK

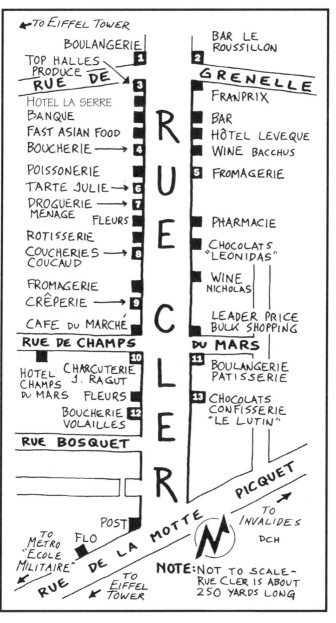

2. Café Roussillon: This café across the street is typical.
Drinks at the always-active bar (*comptoir*) are about half the price of drinks at the tables. The *"tickets restaurant"* and *"cheque déjeuner"* decals on the door advertise that this café accepts lunch checks. In France, an employee lunch subsidy program is an expected perk. Employers issue checks (worth about 30F or $5) for the number of days an employee works in a month. Few workers bring sack lunches. A good lunch is sacred.

3. Top Halles Produce: Fresh produce is trucked in each
morning from the huge Rungis market near Orly airport. Rungis' location, outside of town, is handy for small farmers bringing in their goods. Notice the lack of bags (paper or plastic?). Most locals bring their own.

Parisians shop with their nose. Try it. Insist on quality. Smell the cheap Spanish strawberries. Then smell the French Gariguette. Find the herbs. Is today's delivery in? *Ooh la la*, look at the price of those melons. What's the country of origin? It must be posted. If they're out of season, they come from Guadeloupe. Many people buy only French products.

The Franprix across the street is a small Safeway-type store. Opposite Hôtel Leveque is Asie Traiteur. Fast Asian food to go is popular in Paris. These shops—about as common as bakeries now—are making an impact on Parisian eating habits.

4. Butcher: Next to Asie Traiteur is the Triperie/Boucherie.
Look for things you may want to avoid in restaurants: *rognons* (kidneys), *foie* (liver), *coeur de boeuf* (heart of beef). Next door is fish, brought in daily from ports on the English Channel, just 100 miles away. Across the street is a wine shop. Next to that, smell the...

5. Fromagerie: A long, narrow, canopied cheese table brings the
fromagerie into the street. Wedges, cylinders, balls, and mini–hockey pucks all powdered white, grey, and burnt marshmallow—it's a festival of mold. Most of the street cart is devoted only to the goat cheeses. *Ooh la la* means you're impressed. If you like cheese, show greater excitement with more *la*s. *Ooh la la la la*. My local friend held the stinkiest glob close to her nose, took an orgasmic breath, and exhaled, "Yes, it smells like zee feet of angels." Try it.

Step inside and browse through some of the 400 different types of French cheese. Behind the heavy plastic curtains in the back room are *les meules,* the big, 170-pound wheels of cheese (250 gallons of milk go into each wheel). The "hard" cheeses are cut from these. Don't eat the skin of these big ones...they roll them on the floor. But the skin on the smaller cheeses—the Brie,

the Camembert—is part of the taste. "It completes the package."

At dinner tonight you can take the cheese course just before or as the dessert. On a good cheese plate you have a hard cheese (like Emmentaler), a flowery cheese (maybe Brie or Camembert), a blue, and a goat.

6. Tarte Julie: Perhaps the most tempting storefront on rue Cler is Tarte Julie's. The front windows are filled with various pies. The shop's classy old storefront is a work of art that survives from the previous occupant. The inset stones and glass advertise horse meat: *Boucherie Chevaline*. The decorated front, from the '30s and signed by the artist, would fit in a museum. But it belongs right here. And everyone knows this is a place for a fine tart, not horse meat.

7. Droguerie Ménage and More: This French drugstore sells everything but drugs. It's the classic kitchen/hardware store where you buy corkscrews, brooms, knives, and so on.

Wander on past the flower shop, pharmacy (in France the first diagnosis and prescription is made by the pharmacist—if it's out of his league, he'll recommend a doctor), rotisserie (quarter of a roasted chicken with a salad and a drink to go?), and another wine shop. In France, when invited to dinner, it's bad style to bring a bottle of wine. The host cooks with a particular wine in mind. Bring flowers or chocolates instead.

8. Butcher: At Coucheries Coucaud, sort through pigeons, quail, and rabbit. Hoist a duck and check the feet; they should be rough and calloused—an indication that they weren't stuck in an industrial kennel but ran wild on a farm. While Americans prefer beef, pork, and chicken, the French eat more rabbit, lamb, duck, and horse.

9. Crêperie and More: Almost next door you'll find the smallest, friendliest business on rue Cler, the Crêperie. Savory crêpes come with ingredients we'd put in an omelet (cheese, ham, mushrooms, and so on). They're called *galettes*, and the pancake is made from buckwheat flour. Dessert crêpes are made of wheat flour and come with everything you might enjoy on your ice-cream sundae. The Café du Marché, on the corner, is the best place to sit and enjoy the rue Cler action. For a reasonable meal, grab a chair and the waiter will prop the chalky menu listing the *plat du jour* (blue plate special) on an empty chair. The shiny, sterile Leader Price grocery store (across the street) is a French Costco selling bulk items. Because storage space is so limited in most Parisian apartments, bulk purchases are unlikely to become a big deal here.

10. Charcuterie J. Ragut: Across the street, a *charcuterie* sells mouthwatering deli food to go (try their homemade potato chips). Because kitchens are so small, these gourmet delis are handy, allowing hosts to concentrate on the main course and buy beautifully prepared side dishes to complete a fine dinner. Notice the system: Pay the cashier and return with the receipt to pick up your food.

11. Boulangerie: Locals debate the merits of rue Cler's rival *boulangeries*. It's said that a baker cannot be both a good bread man and a good pastry man: When you do good bread, you have no time to do good pastry. The baker at the rue Grenelle bakery (stop #1) specializes in pastry. The bread suffers. Here, the baker does good bread. He has a man who does the tasty little pastries for him.

12. Butcher Shop: Locals know that here Mom and Pop buy the veal only "on the foot." Each of the red-and-gold medals, which now hang like a necklace across the ceiling, once hung around the neck of a prize-winning little cow . . . proof of top quality.

The well-dressed butcher is following his father's act. The dad is 87 now. He used to change his apron three times a day . . . so customers expect his son to do the same. The dad lives upstairs but still comes down to see that things are done right.

Over 35 years ago, the butcher married the daughter of the couple who ran the fish shop down the street. Their kids have no interest in taking over the butcher shop. Mom and Pop fear it's the end of an era.

13. Le Lutin Gourmand Chocolats Confiseries: Corinne recently took over the shop from a woman who kept this neighborhood in fine chocolates for 30 years. The wholesalers want you to take the new products, but she keeps the old traditional candies too. "The old ladies, they want the same sweets they had 80 years ago."

Corinne dips and decorates her chocolates in the back, where the merchants used to live. Traditionally in rue Cler shops, the merchants lived and produced in the back and sold in the front.

Rue Cler ends at the post office. The École Militaire Métro stop is just around the corner. If you bought a rue Cler picnic, you'll find benches and gardens nearby; from the post office, avenue la Motte Picquet leads to two fine parks: left to Les Invalides or right to the Eiffel Tower. *Bon appétit!*

MONTMARTRE WALK

While most tourists make the almost obligatory trek to the top of Paris' touristy Montmartre, eat an overpriced crêpe, and marvel at the view, the neighborhood has a fascinating charm and history missed by most and uncovered with this short walk.

You'll walk about two miles, up and down, on this 90-minute, 12-stop tour. To avoid the tourist crowds, arrive in the morning by 9:30. To avoid the climb, either take the funicular or catch a taxi (about 70F from the Eiffel Tower or Bastille to Sacré-Coeur) and begin the tour at the church on top. And wear your money belt!

To reach Sacré-Coeur by Métro, get off at Anvers. When you exit the Métro, look up the only real hill in Paris. The peeling and neglected Elysées Montmartre theater at 74 boulevard de Roche-chouart is the oldest cancan dance hall in Paris and sets the stage for this area in transition (it's a rowdy rock-and-roll dance hall today). From artists to Arabs, people have always moved to this area for cheap rent. The area still feels neglected, though some urban gentrification is underway as young professionals restore neglected apartments and hotels renovate for a more upscale clientele.

Walk two blocks up rue de Steinkerque (the street to the right of Elysées Montmartre) through waves of tourists and past cheap clothing and souvenir shops to the grassy parkway below the white Sacré-Coeur church. Hike to the church or ride the funicular (costs one Métro ticket). At the top is a fountain and a grand view, but one level below the top you'll find benches and a quieter panoramic perch.

1. Sacré-Coeur Church and View: From Paris' highest point (427 feet), the City of Light fans out at your feet. The big triangular roof on your left is the Gare du Nord train station; the golden dome out there on the right is Les Invalides. The colorful

Pompidou Center is straight ahead, and the domed Panthéon lies just beyond to the right, on Paris' only other butte. The Montparnasse ("Awful") Tower is farther off, and the skyscrapers beyond define the southern limit of central Paris. Now walk up to the church.

The Sacré-Coeur ("Sacred Heart") church, with its onion domes and bleached-bone pallor, looks ancient but was built only a century ago by Parisians chastened by German invaders. Otto von Bismark's Prussian army laid siege to Paris for over four months in 1870. Things got so bad for residents that urban hunting for dinner (to cook up cats and dogs) became accepted behavior. The church was erected as a "praise the Lord anyway" gesture after France's humiliation by Germany.

The five-dome Romano-Byzantine basilica took 40 years to build. The church is dedicated to the "sacred heart" of Jesus, which enables Him to understand human needs and feelings. The contrast between the brilliant white exterior and the sooty interior is jarring. Explore the impressive mosaics, especially of Christ with his sacred heart above the altar. Walk clockwise around the ambulatory behind the altar. Notice the colorful mosaic stations of the cross as you walk behind the altar on your right. Between VII and VIII, rub St. Peter's bronze foot and look up to the ceiling.

For an unobstructed panoramic view of Paris, climb 262 feet up the tight and claustrophobic spiral stairs to the top of the dome (15F, daily 10:00–18:00, Jun–Sept access is outside church and downstairs to the right, especially worthwhile if you have kids with excess energy). Skip the crypt (15F); it's just a big empty basement.
• *Leaving the church, turn right and follow the tree-lined street. At rue St. Eleuthere turn right and walk uphill to the Church of St. Pierre (at top on right).*

2. Church of St. Pierre: Originally a headquarters for nuns,
the church is one of Paris' oldest—some say Dante prayed here. Older still are the four grey columns inside that may have stood in a temple of Mercury and Mars in Roman times. (Two flank the entrance, and two are behind the altar.) The name "Montmartre" comes from the Roman "Mount of Mars," though later generations, thinking of their beheaded patron St. Denis, preferred a less pagan version, "Mount of Martyrs."

In front of the church, the Café and Caberet La Boheme remind visitors that the community was a haunt of the bohemian crowd in the 19th and early 20th centuries. The artist-filled place du Tertre awaits.

3. Bohemian Montmartre—Place du Tertre: In 1800 a
wall separated Paris from this village on the hill. You had to pay a toll

MONTMARTRE WALK

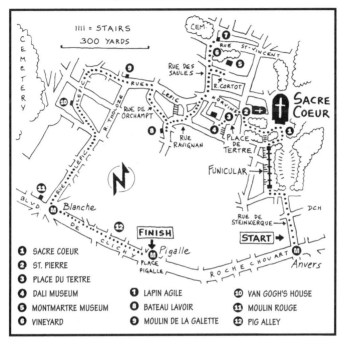

❶ SACRE COEUR		
❷ ST. PIERRE		
❸ PLACE DU TERTRE		
❹ DALI MUSEUM	❼ LAPIN AGILE	❿ VAN GOGH'S HOUSE
❺ MONTMARTRE MUSEUM	❽ BATEAU LAVOIR	⓫ MOULIN ROUGE
❻ VINEYARD	❾ MOULIN DE LA GALETTE	⓬ PIG ALLEY

to get in. Montmartre was a mining community (the local gypsum was the original plaster of Paris) where the wine flowed cheap and easy. Life here was a working-class festival of cafés, bistros, and dance halls. Painters came here for the ruddy charm, the light, and the low rents. In 1860 Montmartre was annexed into the growing city of Paris. The "bohemian" ambience survived and attracted sophisticated Parisians ready to get down and dirty in the belle epoque of cancan.

Lined with cafés and filled with artists, hucksters, and tourists, the scene mixes charm and kitsch in ever-changing proportions. The place du Tertre artists, who at times outnumber the tourists, are the great-great-grandkids of the Renoirs, van Goghs, and Picassos who once roamed here—poor, carefree, seeking inspiration, and occasionally cursing a world too selfish to bankroll their dreams.

The Syndicat d'Initiative on the corner is a tourist office (daily 10:00–19:00).

4. Dalí Museum: Is place du Tertre too surreal? Escape down-hill, to the opposite corner of the square from which you entered, into the tiny place du Calvaire for a great view (and a peaceful café with a fine panorama to your left).

Not surreal enough? Turn right, walking past the café Chez Plumeau, and visit the Salvador Dalí Museum. The museum— a beautifully lit black gallery with the right music—offers a walk through statues, etchings, and paintings by Dalí. Don't miss the printed interview on the exit stairs (35F, not covered by museum pass, daily 10:00–18:00, well described in English, 11 rue Poulbot).

Exit the museum to the right, where rue Poulbot leads to rue Norvins, the spine and main tourist drag of the comunity. Turn left down rue Norvins to the crossroads with rue des Saules. The venerable *boulangerie* on the left (dating from 1900) is one of the last surviving bits of the old-time community. From here we'll side-trip three blocks down the backside of the *mont*, then return to carry on past the *boulangerie*.

From rue Norvins turn right on rue des Saules and notice the dome of Sacré-Coeur rising above the rooftops just after the café Consulat. Painters such as Maurice Utrillo (1883–1955), captured views like this, making the neighborhood famous. Utrillo the son of a free-spirited single mom, grew up in Montmartre's streets. He fought, broke street lamps, and haunted the cafés and bars, buying drinks with masterpieces.

5. Montmartre Museum: Follow rue des Saules downhill into the less-touristed backside of Montmartre. A right up rue Cortet (at Maison Rose restaurant) leads up an exclusive street with vine-covered homes to the Montmartre Museum, at #12. Utrillo once lived here with his mom. (Composer Erik Satie lived at #16.) The museum fills eight rooms in this creaky 17th-century manor house with paintings, posters, old photos, music, and memorabilia recreating the traditional cancan and caberet Montmartre scene (25F, not covered by museum pass, Tue–Sun 11:00–18:00, closed Mon, reasonably well described in English).

• *Return to the rue des Saules and walk downhill past the Maison Rose restaurant one block to Paris' last remaining vineyard.*

6. Clos Montmartre Vineyard: What originally drew artists to Montmartre was its country charm. With vineyards, wheat fields, windmills, animals, and a village tempo of life, it was the perfect escape from grimy Paris. Today's vineyard is off-limits to tourists except for the annual grape-harvest fest (first Saturday in October), when a thousand costumed locals bring back the boisterous old days and the vineyard's annual production of 300 liters is auctioned off to support local charities.

• *Continue downhill to the foot of the vineyard.*

7. Lapin Agile Caberet: The faded poster above the door gives the place its name. A rabbit (*lapin*) makes an agile leap into a pot while balancing a bottle of wine. This was the village's hot spot. Picasso and other artists and writers would gather for "performances" that ranged from serious poetry, dirty limericks, sing-alongs, and parodies of the famous to anarchist manifestos. Once they tied a paintbrush to the tail of the owner's donkey and entered the "abstract painting" that resulted in the Salon—it won critical acclaim and sold for a nice price.

You now have two options. Most will want to walk back up the rue des Saules to the bakery at the top of the hill, where we'll continue our walk. But if you want to return to the bakery via Renoir's home, walk one block up the rue des Saules, turn right at la Maison Rose, and follow rue de l'Abbreuvoir to the small walkway at the end, which leads to Renoir's home, at #6. Meet the others at the bakery on rue des Saules by angling up through the small park on your left after Renoir's home and turning left up the rue Norvins.
• *Once reunited at the bakery, we all go downhill, hugging the buildings on our left—don't curve right on rue Lepic. Turn right on rue Ravignan and follow it to the "TIM Hotel." Next door, at 13 place Emile-Goudeau, is Bateau-Lavoir.*

8. Bateau-Lavoir, Picasso's Studio: Modern art was born here in this humble artists' abode, where as many as 10 artists lived and worked. The fading photos in the window show Picasso and the studio where he and his friends Georges Braque and Juan Gris revolutionized art. Sharing paints, ideas, and girlfriends, they created art, such as Picasso's *Demoiselles d'Avignon*, that shocked the world. Modigliani and the poet Apollinaire also lived here. The original studio burned down in 1970. Picasso wrote, "I know one day we'll return to Bateau-Lavoir. It was there that we were really happy—where they thought of us as painters, not strange animals."
• *Walk back uphill one short block, turn left on rue d'Orchampt, squirt out the end, and (at rue Lepic and rue d'Orchampt) come face-to-face with a wooden windmill.*

9. Moulin de la Galette: Only two windmills (*moulins*) remain on a hill that was once dotted with them. Originally they pressed grapes and crushed stones. When the gypsum mines closed and vineyards became apartments, this one turned into a popular outdoor dance hall. Renoir's *Bal du Moulin de La Galette* (at the Orsay) shows it in its heyday—a sunny Sunday afternoon in the leafy gardens, with ordinary folk dancing, eating, and laughing. Some call it the quintessential Impressionist painting.
• *Rue Lepic winds down the hill. The green-latticed building to your*

*right was all part of the Moulin de la Galette. Continue past the main
entry of Moulin de la Galette down rue Lepic to #54 to find...*

10. Van Gogh's House: In the two short years (1886–1888) he
stayed here with his brother, Vincent van Gogh transformed from a
gloomy Dutch painter of brown and grey peasant scenes into an inspired visionary with wild ideas and Impressionist colors.

• *Follow the rue Lepic downhill as it makes a right to place Blanche;
check out the horse butcher at number 30 as you descend. Notice the
happy horses on the price stickers. This leg of the rue Lepic is little
changed from when Vincent lived here. Enjoy that notion for the delightful last stretch of rue Lepic before it hits the big street and a big change.
On busy place Blanche is the...*

11. Moulin Rouge: *Ooh
la la!* The new Eiffel Tower
at the 1889 World's Fair was
nothing compared to the
sight of pretty cancan girls
spreading their legs at the
newly opened "Red Wind-
mill." The nightclub seemed
to sum up the belle epoque,
the age of elegance, opulence,

sophistication, and worldliness. On most nights, you'd see a small
man in a sleek black coat, checked pants, a green scarf, and a bowler
hat peering through his pince-nez glasses at the dancers and making
sketches of them—Henri de Toulouse-Lautrec. Perhaps he'd order
an absinthe, the dense green liqueur that was the toxic muse for so
many great and forgotten artists. Toulouse-Lautrec's sketches of
dancer Jane Avril and comic La Goulue hang in the Orsay. Walk in
and mull over the photos, show options, and prices.

12. Pig Alley: The stretch of boulevard de Clichy from place
Blanche eastward (toward Sacré-Coeur) to place Pigalle is the den
mother of all iniquities. Plaster of Paris from the gypsum found on
this mount was loaded sloppily at place Blanche...the white place.
Today, sex shops, peep shows, live sex shows, and hotdog stands
line the busy boulevard de Clichy. Dildos abound.

　　Although raunchy now, the area has always been the place
where bistros had tax-free status, wine was cheap, and prostitutes
roamed free. WWII GIs nicknamed Pigalle "Pig Alley."

　　End your tour at the place Blanche Métro stop (if you want to
skip the raunchiness) or hike through Pigalle, escaping home from
the fine Art Nouveau Métro stop, Pigalle.

LOUVRE TOUR

⑨

paris

Paris walks you through history in two world-class museums—
the Louvre (ancient world to 1850) and the Orsay (1850–1914,
including Impressionism). Start your art-yssey at the Louvre.
The Louvre's collection—more than 30,000 works of art—is
a full inventory of Western civilization. To cover the entire
collection in one visit is in-Seine. We'll enjoy just three of the
Louvre's specialties—Greek sculpture, Italian painting, and
French painting.

Orientation

Cost: 45F, 26F after 15:00 and on Sun, free on first Sun of month
and for those under 18; covered by museum pass. Tickets good all
day; re-entry allowed.

Hours: Wed–Mon 9:00–18:00, closed Tue. Open Wed eve
until 21:45. On Mon eve Richelieu Wing (only) open until
21:45. Galleries start closing 30 minutes early. Closed Jan 1,
Easter, May 1, Nov 1, and Dec 25. Crowds are worst on Sun,
Mon, Wed, and mornings. Save money by visiting in the
afternoon.

Getting There: The Métro stop Palais Royale/Musée du Louvre
is closer to the new entrance than the stop called Louvre Rivoli.

There is no grander entry than through the pyramid, but
metal detectors create a long line at times. There are several
ways to avoid the line. Museum pass holders can use the group
entrance in the pedestrian passageway between the pyramid and
rue de Rivoli. Otherwise, you can enter the Louvre underground
from the Carrousel shopping mall. Enter the mall at 99 rue de
Rivoli (the door with the red awning), or directly from the Métro
stop Palais Royale/Musée du Louvre (exit following signs to
"Musée du Louvre").

THE LOUVRE–A BIRD'S EYE VIEW

Checkrooms: The coat check does not take bags. The bag check is separate from the coat check and may have a much shorter line.

Photography: Photography without a flash is allowed.

Cuisine Art: The underground shopping mall has a dizzying assortment of good-value eateries (up the escalator near the inverted pyramid). There's also a post office, handy tourist office, SNCF train office, glittering boutiques, and the Palais-Royal Métro entrance. Stairs at the far end take you right into the Tuileries Gardens, a perfect antidote to the stuffy, crowded rooms of the Louvre.

Length of Our Tour: Two hours

Louvre Tours: The 90-minute English-language tours leave six times daily except Sun (33F, tour tel. 01 40 20 52 09, info tel. 01 40 20 51 51, www.louvre.fr). Clever 30F audioguides (after ticket booths, at top of escalators) give you a directory of about 130 masterpieces, allowing you to dial a rather dull commentary on included works as you stumble upon them; we recommend the free, self-guided tour described below.

Starring: *Vénus de Milo, Winged Victory, Mona Lisa,* Raphael, Michelangelo, and the French painters.

Surviving the Louvre

Pick up the map at the information desk under the pyramid as you enter. The Louvre, the world's largest museum, fills three wings in this immense U-shaped palace. The north wing (Richelieu) houses French, Dutch, and Northern art. The east wing (Sully) houses the extensive French painting collection.

For this tour, we'll concentrate on the Louvre's south wing (Denon), which houses the superstars: ancient Greek sculpture, Italian Renaissance painting, and French neoclassical and Romantic painting.

Expect changes. The Louvre is in flux for several years as they shuffle the deck. If you can't find a particular painting, ask a guard where it is. Point to the photo in your book and ask, *"Où est?"* (oo ay).

THE TOUR BEGINS — GREEK STATUES (600 B.C.–A.D. 1)

Every generation defines beauty differently. For Golden Age Greeks, beauty was balance, combining opposites in just the right proportions. They thought that the human body—especially the female form—embodied the order they saw in the universe. In the Louvre, we'll see a series of "Venuses" throughout history. Their different poses and gestures tell us about the people that made them. We'll see how the idea of beauty (as balance) began in ancient Greece, how it evolved into Hellenism (tipping the balance from stability to movement), and then how it resurfaced in the Renaissance, 2,000 years later.

• *From inside the big glass pyramid, you'll see signs to the three wings. Head for the Denon wing.*

Escalate up one floor. After showing your ticket, take the first left you can, climbing a set of stairs to the brick-ceilinged Salle (Room) 1: "Antiquités grecques, etrusques, et romaines." Enter prehistory.

Pre-Classical Greece

These statues are noble but crude. The Greek Barbie dolls (3000 B.C.) are older than the pyramids, as old as writing itself. These pre-rational voodoo dolls whittle women down to their life-giving traits. Farther along, a woman (*Core*) is

PRE-CLASSICAL GREECE

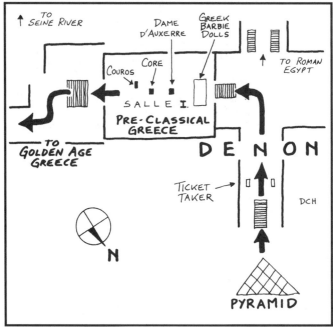

essentially a column with breasts. Another (*Dame d'Auxerre*) pledges allegiance to stability. A young naked man (*Couros*) seems to have a gun to his back—his hands at his sides, facing front, with sketchy muscles and a masklike face. "Don't move."

The early Greeks who admired such statues found stability

more attractive than movement. Like their legendary hero, Odysseus, the Greek people had spent generations wandering, war-weary, and longing for the comforts of a secure home. The noble strength and sturdiness of these works looked beautiful.

• *Exit Salle 1 and climb the stairs one flight. At the top, veer 10-o'clock left, where you'll soon see* Vénus de Milo *rising above a sea of heads. As you approach her, turn right into Salle 7, where you'll find two carved panels from the Parthenon on the wall.*

Golden Age Greece

The great Greek cultural explosion that changed the course of history happened in a 50-year stretch (around 450 B.C.) in Athens, a Greek town smaller than Muncie, Indiana. They dominated the ancient world through brain, not brawn, and the art shows their love of rationality and order.

In a sense, we're all Greek. Democracy, mathematics, theater, philosophy, literature, and science were practically invented in ancient Greece. Most of the art that we'll see in the Louvre either came from Greece or was inspired by it.

Parthenon Frieze (Fragment de la Frise des Panathenees), c. 440 B.C.

These stone fragments once decorated the exterior of the greatest Athenian temple, the Parthenon. The right panel shows a half-man/half-horse creature sexually harassing a woman. It tells the story of how these rude Centaurs crashed a party of humans. But the Greeks fought back and threw the brutes out, just as Athens (metaphorically) conquered its barbarian neighbors and became civilized.

The other relief shows the sacred procession of young girls who marched up the hill every four years with an embroidered veil for the 40-foot statue of Athena, the goddess of wisdom. The maidens, carved in only a few inches of stone, are amazingly realistic—more so than anything we saw in the pre-Classical period. They glide along horizontally (their belts and shoulders all in a line), while the folds of their dresses drape down vertically. The man in the center is relaxed and realistic. Notice the veins in his arm.

Greeks of the Golden Age valued the Golden Mean, that is, balance. The ideal person was well rounded—an athlete and a bookworm, a lover and a philosopher, a realtor who plays the piano, a warrior and a poet. In art, the balance between timeless stability and fleeting movement made beauty. The maidens' pleated dresses make them look as stable as fluted columns, but their arms and legs step out naturally—the human form is emerging from the stone.

• *Now seek the Goddess of Love. You'll find her floating above a sea of worshiping tourists. It's been said that, among the warlike Greeks, this was the first statue to unilaterally disarm.*

Vénus de Milo (Aphrodite), c. 100 B.C.

The *Vénus de Milo* (or Goddess of Love from the Greek island of Milos) created a sensation when it was discovered in 1820. Europe

GREEK STATUES

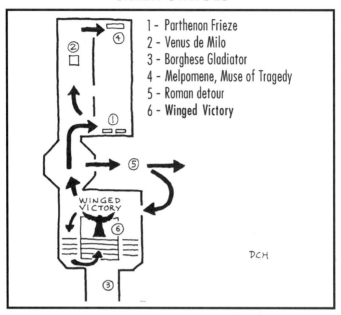

1 - Parthenon Frieze
2 - Venus de Milo
3 - Borghese Gladiator
4 - Melpomene, Muse of Tragedy
5 - Roman detour
6 - Winged Victory

was already in the grip of a classical fad, and this statue seemed to sum up all that ancient Greece stood for. The Greeks pictured their gods in human form, telling us they had an optimistic view of the human race.

Most "Greek" statues are actually later Roman copies. This is a rare Greek original. This "epitome of the Golden Age" was

actually sculpted three centuries later, though in the style of the earlier.

Vénus de Milo is a harmonious balance of opposites. Venus is stable, resting her weight on one leg (called *contrapposto*, or "counterpose"), yet her other leg is slightly raised, ready to take a step. This slight movement sets her whole body in motion, though she remains perfectly still.

Split *Vénus* down the middle (left and right) and see how the movement of the two halves balance each other. As she lifts her left leg, her right shoulder droops down. And as her knee points one way, her head turns the other. The twisting pose gives an S-curve to her body (especially noticeable from the back view) that the Greeks and succeeding generations found beautiful.

Other opposites balance as well, like the rough-cut texture of her dress (size 14) that sets off the smooth skin of her upper half. She's actually made from two different pieces of stone plugged together at the hips (the seam is visible). The face is realistic and anatomically accurate, but it's also idealized, a goddess, too generic and too perfect. This isn't any particular woman but Every-woman—all the idealized features that the Greeks found beautiful.

What were her missing arms doing? Several archeologists' theories are on a plaque nearby. Some say her right arm held her dress while her left arm was raised. Others say she was hugging a man statue or leaning on a column. I say she was picking her navel.

• *This statue is interesting and different from every angle. Remember the view from the back—we'll see it again later. Orbit* Vénus. *Make your re-entry to Earth as you wander among Greek statues. Try to find even one that's not* contrapposto. *Oh yes, there is one.*

Borghese Gladiator (*Guerrier Combattant, Dit Gladiateur Borghese*)

We see a fighting gladiator at the peak of action. He blocks a blow with the shield that used to be attached to his left arm while his right hand, weighted with an early version of brass knuckles, prepares to deliver the counterpunch. His striding motion makes a diagonal line from his left foot up his leg, along the body and out the extended arm. It's a dramatic, precariously balanced pose.

This is the motion and emotion of Greece's Hellenistic Age, the time after the culture of Athens was spread around the Mediterranean by Alexander the Great (c. 325 B.C.).

The earlier Golden Age Greeks might have considered this statue ugly. His rippling, knotted muscles are a far cry from the more restrained Parthenon sculptures and the soft-focus beauty of *Vénus*. And the statue's off-balance pose leaves you hanging, like an unfinished melody. But Hellenistic Greeks loved these cliff-hanging scenes of real-life humans struggling to make their mark. The artist himself made his mark, signing the work proudly on the tree trunk: "Agasias of Ephesus, son of Dositheos, did this."

• *Before heading upstairs to the* Winged Victory, *find the "Antiquités romaines" and take a . . .*

Roman Detour

The Romans were great conquerors but bad artists. Fortunately for us, they had a huge appetite for Greek statues and made countless copies. They took the Greek style and wrote it in capital letters—like the huge statue of Melpomene, holding the frowning mask of tragic plays.

One area the Romans excelled in was realistic portrait busts, especially of their emperors, who were worshiped as gods on earth. Stroll among the Caesars and try to see the man behind the public persona—Augustus, the first emperor, and his wily wife, Livia; Nero ("Neron"), who burned part of his own city; Hadrian, who popularized the beard; crazy Caligula; the stoic Marcus Aurelius; Claudius of "I" fame; and the many faces of the ubiquitous Emperor Inconnu.

The Roman rooms also contain sarcophagi and an impressive mosaic floor. Weary? Relax with the statues in the Etruscan Lounge.

• *Now ascend the staircase, making a U-turn up to the…*

Winged Victory of Samothrace (*Victoire de Samothrace*)

This woman with wings, poised on the prow of a ship, once stood on a hilltop to commemorate a great naval victory. Her clothes are windblown and sea sprayed, clinging to her body like the winner of a wet T-shirt contest. (Notice the detail in the folds of her dress around the navel, curving down to her hips.) Originally her right arm was stretched high celebrating the victory like a Super Bowl champion, waving a "we're-number-one" finger.

This is the *Vénus de Milo* gone Hellenistic—a balance of opposites that produces excitement, not grace. As *Victory* strides forward, the wind blows her and her wings back. Her feet are firmly on the ground, but her wings (and missing arms) stretch upward. She is a pillar of vertical strength while the clothes curve and whip around her. These opposing forces create a feeling of great energy, making her the lightest two-ton piece of rock in captivity.

In the glass case nearby is *Victory*'s open right hand, discovered in 1950, a century after the statue itself was unearthed. Also in the case is *Victory*'s finger. When the French discovered this was in Turkey, they negotiated with the Turkish government for rights to it. Considering all the other ancient treasures the French had looted from Turkey in the past, the Turks thought it only appropriate to give France the finger.

• *Enter the octagonal room to the left of the* Winged Victory, *with Icarus bungee-jumping from the ceiling. Bench yourself under a window and look out towards the pyramid.*

FRENCH HISTORY

The Louvre as a Palace

The Louvre, a former palace, was built in stages over several centuries. On your right (the east wing) was the original medieval fortress. Next, another palace, the Tuileries, was built 500 yards to the west—in the open area past the pyramid and past the triumphal arch. Succeeding kings tried to connect these two palaces, each one adding another section onto the long, skinny north and south wings. Finally, in 1852, after three centuries of building, the two palaces were connected, creating a rectangular Louvre. Soon after that, the Tuileries Palace burned down during a riot, leaving the U-shaped Louvre we see today.

The glass pyramid was designed by the American architect I. M. Pei. Many Parisians hated the pyramid, like they used to hate another new and controversial structure 100 years ago—the Eiffel Tower.

The plaque above the doorway to the Apollo Gallery (Galerie d'Apollon) explains that France's Revolutionary National Assembly (the same people who brought you the guillotine) founded this museum in 1793. What could be more logical? You behead the king, inherit his palace and art collection, open the doors to the masses, and, Voilà! You've got Europe's first public museum. Major supporters of the museum are listed on the walls—notice all the Rothschilds.

• *Enter the Apollo Gallery ("Galerie d'Apollon").*

Apollo Gallery

The Gallery gives us a feel for the Louvre as the glorious home of the French kings (before Versailles). Imagine a chandelier-lit party in this room, drenched in stucco and gold leaf, with tapestries of leading Frenchmen and paintings with mythological and symbolic themes.

In the glass case at the far end, you'll find the crown jewels. There's the jewel-studded crown of Louis XV; the

140-carat Regent Diamond, worn by Louis XV, Louis XVI, and Napoleon; and the dragon-shaped 107-carat Côte de Bretagne Ruby. You'll also see the pearl-and-diamond earrings worn by Napoleon's wife, Josephine, and the golden crown of the pin-headed Empress Eugenie.

In another glass case is the cameo crown of that great champion of democracy, Napoleon—we'll see this crown in a painting later.

The inlaid tables made from marble and semiprecious stones and many other art objects show the wealth of France, Europe's number one power for two centuries.

• *The Italian collection ("Peintures Italiennes") is on the other side of the Winged Victory. Cross to the other side and pause at the two fresco paintings on the wall to the left.*

ITALIAN RENAISSANCE

A thousand years after Rome fell, plunging Europe into the Dark Ages, the Greek ideal of beauty was "reborn" in 15th-century Italy. This was the Renaissance, the cultural revival of ancient art.

In these two frescoes by the Italian Renaissance artist Botticelli, we see echoes of ancient Greece. The maidens, with

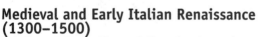

their poses, clear sculptural lines, and idealized beauty, are virtual *Vénus de Milo*s with clothes. The Renaissance was a time of great optimism, exploration, and liberation, and here we see it in its fresh-faced springtime.

The key to Renaissance painting was realism, and for the Italians "realism" was spelled "3-D." Painters were inspired by the realism and balanced beauty of Greek sculpture.

• *The Italian collection—including* Mona Lisa—*is scattered throughout the next few rooms, in the long Grand Gallery, and in adjoining rooms. To see the paintings in chronological order may require a little extra shoe leather. When in doubt, show the photo to a guard and ask,* "Où est?"

Medieval and Early Italian Renaissance (1300–1500)

Painting a 3-D world on a 2-D surface is tough, and after a millennium of Dark Ages, artists were rusty. Living in a religious age, they painted mostly altarpieces full of saints, angels, Madonnas, and crucifixes floating in an ethereal gold-leaf

heaven. Gradually, though, they brought these otherworldly scenes down to earth.

Painters like Giotto, Fra Angelico, and Uccello broke Renaissance ground by learning to paint realistic, 3-D humans. They placed them in a painted scene with a definite foreground, background, and middle ground to create the illusion of depth. Composition was simple but symmetrically balanced in the Greek style—two angels to the left, two to the right, and so on. Art was a visual sermon, appreciated for its moral message, not its beauty.

• *The long Grand Gallery displays Italian Renaissance painting, some masterpieces, some not.* Mona Lisa *is in a room about halfway down on the right.*

The Grand Gallery

The Grand Gallery was built in the late 1500s to connect the old palace with the Tuileries Palace. From the doorway look to the far end and consider this challenge: I hold the world's record for the Grand Gallery Heel-Toe-Fun-Walk-Tourist-Slalom—end to end in one minute 58 seconds, two injured. Time yourself—it's a good break, if a bit of a detour.

Along the way, notice some of these features of Italian Renaissance painting:

1) Religious: Lots of Madonnas, children, martyrs, and saints.

2) Symmetrical: The Madonnas are flanked by saints, two to the left, two to the right, and so on.

3) Realistic: Real-life human features are especially obvious in the occasional portrait.

4) Three-Dimensional: Every scene gets a spacious setting with a distant horizon.

5) Classical: You'll see some Greek gods and classical nudes, but even Christian saints pose like Greek statues, and Mary is a "Venus" whose face and gestures embody all that was good in the Christian world.

THE GRAND GALLERY

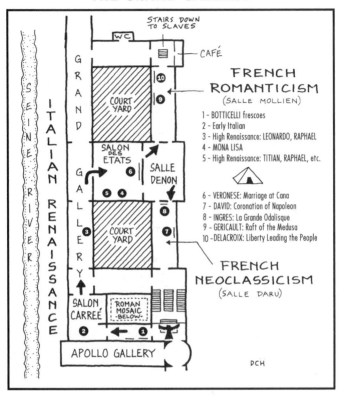

STAIRS DOWN
TO SLAVES

WC

CAFÉ

GRAND

SEINE RIVER

ITALIAN RENAISSANCE

COURT YARD

SALON DES ETATS

GALLERY

SALLE DENON

COURT YARD

SALON CARREÉ

ROMAN MOSAIC BELOW

APOLLO GALLERY

FRENCH ROMANTICISM
(SALLE MOLLIEN)

1 - BOTTICELLI frescoes
2 - Early Italian
3 - High Renaissance: LEONARDO, RAPHAEL
4 - MONA LISA
5 - High Renaissance: TITIAN, RAPHAEL, etc.

6 - VERONESE: Marriage at Cana
7 - DAVID: Coronation of Napoleon
8 - INGRES: La Grande Odalisque
9 - GERICAULT: Raft of the Medusa
10 - DELACROIX: Liberty Leading the People

FRENCH NEOCLASSICISM
(SALLE DARU)

DCH

Mantegna—*St. Sebastian*

This isn't the patron saint of porcupines. St. Sebastian was a Christian martyr, although here he looks more like a classical Greek statue. Notice the *contrapposto* stance (all of his weight resting on one leg) and the Greek ruins scattered around him. His executioners look like ignorant medieval brutes who are bewildered by this enlightened Renaissance Man. Italian artists were begining to learn how to create human realism and earthly beauty on the canvas. Let the Renaissance begin.

Italian High Renaissance (1500–1600)

The two masters of Renaissance grace and balance were Raphael and Leonardo da Vinci.

Leonardo was the consummate Renaissance Man. Musician, sculptor, engineer, scientist, and sometimes painter, he combined knowledge from all areas to create beauty. If he were alive today, he'd create a Unified Field theory in physics—and set it to music.

• *Look for the following masterpieces by Leonardo and Raphael in the Grand Gallery.*

Leonardo da Vinci—*Virgin, Child, and St. Anne (La Vierge, l'Enfant Jesus, et Sainte Anne)*

Three generations—grandmother, mother, and child—are arranged in a pyramid form with Anne's face as the peak and the lamb as the lower right corner. Within this balanced structure, Leonardo sets the figures in motion. Anne's legs are pointed to our left. (Is Anne *Mona*? Hmm.) Her daughter Mary, sitting on her lap, reaches to the right. Jesus looks at her playfully while turning away. The lamb pulls away from him. But even with all the twisting and turning, this is still a placid scene. It's as orderly as the geometrically perfect universe created by the Renaissance God.

There's a psychological kidney punch in this happy painting. Jesus, the picture of childish joy, is innocently playing with a lamb—the symbol of his inevitable sacrificial death.

The Louvre has the greatest collection of Leonardos in the world—all five of them. Don't miss the neighboring *Madonna of the Rocks* and his androgynous *John the Baptist.*

Raphael—*La Belle Jardinière*

Raphael (roff-eye-ELL) perfected the style Leonardo pioneered. This Madonna, Child, and John the Baptist is also a balanced pyramid with hazy grace and beauty. Mary is a mountain of maternal tenderness (the title translates as "The Beautiful Kindergarten Teacher"), eyeing her son with a knowing look. Jesus looks up innocently, standing *contrapposto* like a chubby Greek statue.

With Raphael, the Greek ideal of beauty reborn in the Renaissance reached its peak. His work spawned so many imitators who cranked out sickly sweet generic Madonnas that we often take him for granted. Don't. This is the real thing.

While the *Jardinière* has an idealized beauty, Raphael could deliver photo-realism, too. See his portrait of black-hatted, clear-eyed Balthazar Castiglione.

• *Have a seat and prepare for the* Mona Lisa *mob scene. Best to read ahead here. Then follow the crowds and signs to* Mona Lisa *in the Salle des Etats.*

Leonardo da Vinci—*Mona Lisa*

Leonardo was already an old man when François I invited him to France. Determined to pack light, he took only a few paintings with

him. One was a portrait of a Lisa del Giocondo, the wife of a wealthy Florentine merchant. When he arrived, François immediately fell in love with the painting, making it the centerpiece of the small collection of Italian masterpieces that would, in three centuries, become the Louvre museum. He called it *La Gioconda*. We know it as a contraction of the Italian for "my lady Lisa"—*Mona Lisa*.

Advance warning: *Mona* may disappoint you. She's smaller than you'd expect, darker, engulfed in a huge room, and hidden behind a glaring pane of glass. So, you ask, "Why all the hubbub?" Let's take a closer look. Like any lover, you've got to take her for what she is, not what you'd like her to be.

The famous smile attracts you first. Leonardo used a hazy technique called *sfumato*, blurring the edges of *Mona*'s mysterious smile. Try as you might, you can never quite see the corners of her mouth. Is she happy? Sad? Tender? Or is it a cynical supermodel's smirk? Every viewer reads it differently, projecting his own mood onto *Lisa*'s enigmatic face. *Mona* is a Rorschach ink blot... so how are you feeling?

Now look past the smile and the eyes that really do follow you (most eyes in portraits do) to some of the subtle Renaissance elements that make this work work. The body is surprisingly massive and statuelike, a perfectly balanced pyramid turned at an angle so that we can see its mass. Her arm is resting lightly on the chair's armrest almost on the level of the frame itself, like she's sitting in a window looking out at us. The folds of her sleeves and her gently folded hands are remarkably realistic and relaxed. The typical Leonardo landscape shows distance by getting hazier and hazier.

The overall mood is one of balance and serenity, but there's also an element of mystery. Her smile and long-distance beauty are subtle and elusive, tempting but always just out of reach, like strands of a street singer's melody drifting through the Métro tunnel. *Mona* doesn't knock your socks off, but she winks at the patient viewer.

• *Near* Mona *look for...*

Titian—*Pastoral Symphony* (*Le Concert Champêtre*)

Venus enters the Renaissance in this colorful work by Titian the Venetian (they rhyme). The nymph turning toward the well at left is like a Titian reconstruction of the *Vénus de Milo*, but what a difference! The Greek Venus was cold and virginal, but these babes are hot, voluptuous, sensual. The two couples are "making music," if you catch my drift.

The three figures on the grass form a pyramid, giving the scene a balanced, classical beauty, but this appeals more to the senses than to the mind. The golden glow of the skin, the ample flesh, and the hazy outlines became the standard of female nudes for centuries. French painters, especially, learned from Titian's rich colors and sensual beauty.

• *The huge canvas at the far end of the Salle des États is...*

Veronese—*Marriage at Cana*

Stand 10 steps away from this enormous canvas to where it just fills your field of vision, and suddenly...you're in a party! Pull up a glass of wine. This is the Renaissance love of beautiful things gone hog-wild. Venetian artists like Veronese painted the good life of rich, happy-go-lucky Venetian merchants.

In a spacious setting of Renaissance architecture we see colorful lords and ladies decked out in their fanciest duds, feasting on a great spread of food and drink while the musicians fuel the fires of good fun. Servants prepare and serve the food, jesters play, and animals roam.

In the upper left, a dog and his master look on. A sturdy linebacker in yellow pours wine out of a jug, while nearby a ferocious cat battles a lion. The man in white samples some wine and thinks, "Hmm, not bad." The wedding couple at the far left is almost forgotten.

Believe it or not, this is a religious work showing the wedding celebration where Jesus turned water into wine. And there's Jesus in the dead center of 130 frolicking figures, wondering if maybe wine coolers might not have been a better choice. With true Renaissance optimism, Venetians pictured Christ as a party animal, someone who loved the created world as much as they did.

Now, let's hear it for the band! On bass—the bad cat with the funny hat—Titian the Venetian! And joining him on viola—Crazy Veronese!

• *Exit behind the* Marriage at Cana *into the Salle Denon. The dramatic Romantic room is to your left, and the grand neoclassical room is to your right. They feature the most exciting French canvases in the Louvre. In the neoclassical room, kneel before the largest canvas in the Louvre.*

FRENCH PAINTING—NEOCLASSICAL (1780–1850)

J. L. David—*The Coronation of Napoleon*

France's last kings lived in a fantasy world, far out of touch with the hard lives of their subjects. The people revolted, and this decadent world was decapitated—along with the head of state, Louis XVI. Then, after a decade of floundering under an inefficient revolutionary government, France was united by a charismatic, brilliant, temperamental upstart general who kept his feet on the ground, his eyes on the horizon, and his hand in his coat—Napoleon Bonaparte.

Napoleon quickly conquered most of Europe and insisted on being made emperor (not merely king) of this "New Rome." He staged an elaborate coronation ceremony in Paris. The painter David (dah-veed) recorded it for posterity.

We see Napoleon holding aloft the crown—the one we saw in the Apollo Gallery. He has just made his wife, Josephine, the

empress, and she kneels at his feet. Seated behind Napoleon is the Pope who journeyed from Rome to place the imperial crown on his head. But Napoleon felt that no one was worthy of the task. At the last moment, he shrugged the Pope aside, grabbed the crown, held it up for all to see...and crowned himself. The Pope looks p.o.'d.

The radiant woman in the gallery in the background center wasn't actually there. Napoleon's mother couldn't make it to see her boy become the most powerful man in Europe, so he had her painted in anyway. (There's a key on the frame telling who's who in the picture.)

The traditional place of French coronations was the ultra-Gothic Notre-Dame cathedral. But Napoleon wanted a setting that would reflect the glories of Greece and the grandeur of Rome. So interior decorators erected stage sets of Greek columns and Roman arches to give the cathedral the architectural political correctness you see in this painting. (The *Pietà* statue on the right edge of the painting is still in Notre-Dame today.)

David was the new republic's official painter and propagandist, in charge of costumes, flags, and so on for all public ceremonies and spectacles. (Find his self-portrait in the *Coronation*, way up in the second balcony, far right, with the curly grey hair.) His "neoclassical" style influenced French fashion. Take a look at his portrait of *Madame Juliet Récamier* nearby, showing a modern Parisian woman in ancient garb and Pompeii hairstyle reclining on a Roman couch. Nearby paintings such as *The Death of Socrates* and the *Oath of the Horatii (Le Serment des Horaces)* are fine examples of neoclassicism, with Greek subjects, patriotic sentiment, and a clean, simple style.

Ingres—*La Grande Odalisque*

Take *Vénus de Milo*, turn her around, lay her down, and stick a hash pipe next to her and you have the *Grande Odalisque*. Okay, maybe you'd have to add a vertabra or two.

Using clean, polished, sculptural lines, Ingres (ang-gruh, with a soft "gruh") exaggerates the S-curve of a standing Greek nude. As in the *Vénus de Milo*, rough folds of cloth set off her smooth skin. The face too

has a touch of *Vénus'* idealized features (or like Raphael's kindergarten teacher), taking nature and improving on it. Also, contrast the cool colors of this statuelike nude with Titian's golden girls. Ingres preserves *Vénus'* backside for posterior—I mean, posterity.

• *Cross back through the Salle Denon and into the opposite room gushing with . . .*

ROMANTICISM (1800–1850)

Géricault—*The Raft of the Medusa* (*Le Radeau de la Méduse*)

Not every artist was content to copy the simple, unemotional style of the Golden Age Greeks. Like the ancient Hellenists, they wanted to express motion and emotion. In the artistic war between hearts and minds, the heart style was known as Romanticism. It was the complete flip side of neoclassicism, though they both flourished in the early 1800s.

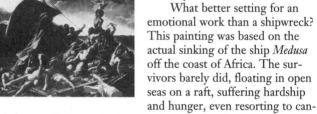

What better setting for an emotional work than a shipwreck? This painting was based on the actual sinking of the ship *Medusa* off the coast of Africa. The survivors barely did, floating in open seas on a raft, suffering hardship and hunger, even resorting to cannibalism—all the exotic elements for a painter determined to shock the public and arouse their emotions.

That painter was young Géricault (zher-ee-ko). He'd honed his craft sketching dead bodies in the morgue and the twisted faces of lunatics in asylums. Here he paints a tangle of bodies and lunatics sprawled over each other. The scene writhes with agitated, ominous motion—the ripple of muscles, churning clouds, and choppy seas. On the right is a deathly green corpse sprawled overboard. In the face of the man at left cradling a dead body, we see the despair of spending weeks stranded in the middle of nowhere.

But wait. There's a stir in the crowd. Someone has spotted something. The bodies rise up in a pyramid of hope culminating in a waving flag. They wave frantically trying to catch the attention of the tiny, tiny ship on the horizon, their last desperate hope...which did finally save them. Géricault uses rippling movement and powerful colors to catch us up in the excitement. If Art controls your heartbeat, this is a masterpiece.

Delacroix—*Liberty Leading the People* (*La Liberté Guidant le Peuple*)

France is the symbol of modern democracy. They weren't the first (America was), nor are they the best working example of it, but they've had to work harder to achieve it than any other country. No sooner would they throw one king or dictator out than they'd get another. They're now working on their Fifth Republic.

In this painting, the year is 1830. The Parisians have taken to the streets once again to fight royalist oppressors. There's a hard-bitten proletarian with a sword (far left), an intellectual with a top hat and a sawed-off shotgun, and even a little boy brandishing pistols.

Leading them on through the smoke and over the dead and dying is the figure of Liberty, a strong woman waving the French flag. Does this symbol of victory look familiar? It's the *Winged Victory*, wingless and topless.

To stir our emotions, Delacroix uses only three major colors—the red, white, and blue of the French flag.

This symbol of freedom is a fitting tribute to the Louvre, the first museum ever opened to the common rabble of humanity. The good things in life don't belong only to a small wealthy part of society, but to everyone. The motto of France is "Liberté, Egalité, Fraternité"—liberty, equality, and the brotherhood of all.

• *Exit the room at the far end (past the café) and go downstairs, where you'll bump into the bum of a large, twisting male nude looking like he's just waking up after a thousand-year nap.*

Michelangelo Buonarotti—*Slaves* (*L'Esclave Mourant* and *L'Esclave Rebelle*), c. 1513

These two statues by earth's greatest sculptor are a fitting end to this museum—works that bridge the ancient and modern worlds. Michelangelo, like his fellow Renaissance artists, learned from the Greeks. The perfect anatomy, twisting poses, and idealized faces look like they could have been done 2,000 years earlier.

The so-called *Dying Slave* (also called the Sleeping Slave, who looks like he should be stretched out on a sofa) twists listlessly against his T-shirt-like bonds, revealing his smooth skin. Compare the polished detail of the rippling, bulging left arm with the sketchy details of the face and neck. With Michelangelo, the body does the talking.

This is probably the most sensual nude ever done by the master of the male body.

The *Rebellious Slave* fights against his bondage. His shoulders turn one way while his head and leg turn the other, straining to get free. He even seems to be trying to free himself from the rock he's made of. Michelangelo said that his purpose was to carve away the marble to reveal the figures God put inside. This *Slave* shows the agony of that process and the ecstasy of the result.

• *Finished? I am.* Où est la sortie?

ORSAY TOUR

⑩

The Musée d'Orsay (mew-zay dor-say) houses French art of the 1800s (specifically, art from 1848–1914), picking up where the Louvre leaves off. For us, that means Impressionism, the art of sun-dappled fields, bright colors, and crowded Parisian cafés. The Orsay houses the best general collection of Manet, Monet, Renoir, Degas, van Gogh, Cézanne, and Gauguin anywhere. If you like Impressionism, visit this museum. If you don't like Impressionism, visit this museum. I personally find it a more enjoyable and rewarding place than the Louvre. Sure, ya gotta see *Mona* and *Vénus de Milo*, but after you get your gottas out of the way, enjoy the Orsay.

Orientation

Cost: 40F, 27F for ages 18 to 25 and over 60, under 18 free; covered by museum pass. Tickets are good all day. Museum pass holders can enter to the left of the main entrance.

Hours: Tue–Sat 10:00–18:00, Thu until 21:45, Sun 9:00–18:00, closed Mon. From Jun 20–Sept 20, the museum opens at 9:00. Last entrance 30 minutes before closing. Galleries start closing 30 minutes early. Note: The Orsay is crowded on Tue, when the Louvre is closed.

Getting There: Directly at the RER-C stop called Musée d'Orsay. The nearest Métro stop is Solferino, three blocks south of the Orsay. From the Louvre, it's a 15-minute walk across the river and downstream (west) to the Orsay.

Information: The booth near the entrance gives free floor plans in English (tel. 01 40 49 48 48).

Photography: Photography without a flash is allowed.

Cuisine Art: The elegant second-floor restaurant has a buffet salad bar. A simple fourth-floor café is sandwiched between the Impressionists.

Length of Our Tour: Two hours
Orsay Tours: English-language tours usually run daily except Sun at 11:30. The 90-minute tours cost 38F and are available on audio-tape; we recommend the free, self-guided tour described below.
Starring: Manet, Monet, Renoir, Degas, van Gogh, Cézanne, and Gauguin

Gare d'Orsay: The Old Train Station

• *Pick up the free English map at the info desk, buy your ticket, and check bags to the right. Belly up to the stone balustrade overlooking the main floor and orient yourself.*

Trains used to run right under our feet down the center of the gallery. This former train station, or *gare*, barely escaped the wrecking ball in the 1970s when the French realized it'd be a great place to house their enormous collections of 19th-century art scattered throughout the city.

The main floor has early 19th-century art (as usual, Conservative on the right, Realism on the left). Upstairs (not visible from here) is the core of the collection—the Impressionist rooms. Finally, we'll end the tour with "the other Orsay" on the mezzanine level you see to the left. Clear as Seine water? *Bon.*

THE ORSAY'S 19TH "CENTURY" (1848–1914)

Einstein and Geronimo. Abraham Lincoln and Karl Marx. The train, the bicycle, the horse and buggy, the automobile, and the balloon. Freud and Dickens. Darwin's *Origin of Species* and the Church's Immaculate Conception. Louis Pasteur and Billy the Kid. V. I. Lenin and Ty Cobb.

The 19th century was a mix of old and new side by side. Europe was entering the modern Industrial Age, with cities, factories, rapid transit, instant communication, and global networks. At the same time it clung to the past with traditional, rural—almost medieval—attitudes and morals.

According to the Orsay, the "19th century" began in 1848 with the socialist and democratic revolutions (Marx's *Communist Manifesto*). It ended in 1914 with the pull of an assassin's trigger, igniting World War I and ushering in the modern world.

The museum shows art that is also both old and new, conservative and revolutionary. We'll start with the Conservatives and early rebels on the ground floor, then head upstairs to see how a

—— ORSAY GROUND FLOOR—OVERVIEW ——

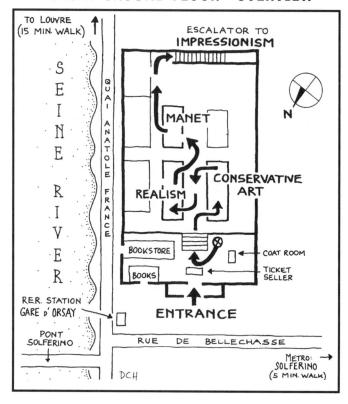

few visionary young artists bucked the system and revolutionized the art world, paving the way for the 20th century.

• *Walk down the steps to the main floor, a gallery filled with statues.*

Conservative Art

No, this isn't ancient Greece. These statues are from the same century as the Theory of Relativity. It's the Conservative art of the French schools that was so popular throughout the 19th century. It was popular because it's beautiful. The balanced poses, the perfect anatomy and sweet faces, the curving lines, the gleaming white stone—all this is very beautiful. (I'll be bad-mouthing it later, but for now appreciate the exquisite craftsmanship of this "perfect" art.)

• *Take your first right into the small Room 1, marked "Ingres." Look for a nude woman with a pitcher of water.*

Ingres—*The Source* (*La Source*)

Let's start where the Louvre left off. Ingres (ang-gruh, with a soft "gruh"), whose works help cap the Louvre collection, championed a neoclassical style. *The Source* is virtually a Greek statue on canvas. Like *Vénus de Milo*, she's a balance of opposite motions—her hips tilt one way, her breasts the other; one arm goes up, the other down; the fluid curve of her body is matched by the water falling from the pitcher.

Ingres worked on this over the course of 35 years and considered it his "image of perfection." Famous in its day, *The Source* influenced many artists whose classical statues and paintings are in the Orsay gallery.

In this and the next few rooms you'll see more of these visions of idealized beauty—nude women in languid poses, Greek myths, and so on. The "Romantics," like Delacroix, added bright colors, movement, and emotion to the classical coolness of Ingres.

• *Walk uphill (quickly, this is background stuff) to the last room, with a pastel blue-green painting.*

Cabanel—*Birth of Venus* (*Naissance de Vénus*)

This goddess is a perfect fantasy, an orgasm of beauty. The Love Queen stretches back seductively, recently birthed from the ephemeral foam of the wave. This is art of a pre-Freudian society,

when sex was dirty and mysterious and had to be exalted into a more pure and divine form. The sex drive was channeled into an acute sense of beauty. French folk would literally swoon in ecstasy before these works of art.

Get a feel for the ideal beauty and refined emotion of these Greek-style works. You'll find a statue with a pose similar to Venus' back out in the gallery. Go ahead, swoon. If it feels good, enjoy it.

• *Now, take a mental cold shower, grab a bench in the main gallery of statues, and read on.*

Academy and Salon

Who liked this stuff? The art world was dominated by two conservative institutions: the Academy (the state art school) and the Salon, where works were exhibited to the buying public.

Now let's literally cross over to the "wrong side of the tracks" to the art of the early rebels.
• *Head back toward the entrance and turn right into Room 4, marked "Daumier" (opposite the Ingres room).*

Realism—Early Rebels

Daumier—36 Caricature Busts (Ventre Legislatif)
This is a liberal's look at the stuffy bourgeois establishment that controlled the Academy and the Salon. In these 36 bust-lets, Daumier, trained as a political cartoonist, exaggerates their most distinct characteristic to capture
with vicious precision the pomposity and self-righteousness of these self-appointed arbiters of taste. The labels next to the busts give the name of the person being caricatured, his title or job (most were members of the French parliament), and an insulting nickname (like "gross, fat, and satisfied" and Monsieur "Platehead"). Give a few nicknames yourself. Can you find
Reagan, Clinton, Yeltsin, Thatcher, and Gingrich?

These people hated what you're about to see. Their prudish faces tightened as their fantasy world was shattered by the Realists.
• *Go uphill four steps and through a few romantic and pastoral rooms to the final room, #6.*

Millet—*The Gleaners (Les Glaneuses)*
Millet (mee-yay) shows us three gleaners, the poor women who pick up the meager leavings after a field has already been harvested by the wealthy. Millet grew up on a humble farm. He didn't attend the Academy and hated the uppity Paris art scene. Instead of idealized gods, goddesses, nymphs, and winged babies, he painted simple rural scenes. He was strongly affected by the Revolution of 1848, with its affirmation of the working class. Here he

captures the innate dignity of these stocky, tanned women who work quietly in a large field for their small reward.

This is "Realism" in two senses. It's painted "real"-istically, unlike the prettified pastels of Cabanel's *Birth of Venus*. And it's

REALISM—THE REBELS

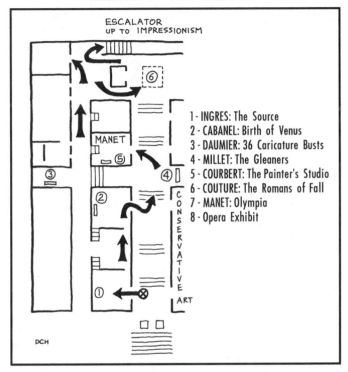

ESCALATOR
UP TO IMPRESSIONISM

MANET

1 - INGRES: The Source
2 - CABANEL: Birth of Venus
3 - DAUMIER: 36 Caricature Busts
4 - MILLET: The Gleaners
5 - COURBERT: The Painter's Studio
6 - COUTURE: The Romans of Fall
7 - MANET: Olympia
8 - Opera Exhibit

CONSERVATIVE ART

DCH

the "real" world—not the fantasy world of Greek myth, but the harsh life of the working poor.

• *Swoon briefly back out into the main gallery and hang a U-turn left, climbing the steps to a large alcove with two huge canvases. On the left...*

Courbet—*The Painter's Studio* (*L'Atelier du Peintre*)

In an age when "Realist painter" was equated with "bomb-throwing Socialist," it took great courage to buck the system. Rejected by the so-called experts, Courbet (coor-bay) held his own one-man exhibit. He built a shed in the middle of Paris, defiantly hung his art out, and basically "mooned" the shocked public.

Here we see Courbet himself in his studio, working diligently on a Realistic landscape, oblivious to the confusion around him. Looking on are ordinary citizens (not Greek heroes), a nude

model (not a goddess but a
woman), and a little boy with an
adoring look on his face. Perhaps
it's Courbet's inner child admiring
the artist who sticks to his guns,
whether it's popular or not.
• *Return to the main gallery. Back
across the tracks, the huge canvas you
see is . . .*

Couture—*The Romans of the Fall* (*Les Romains de la Décadence*)

We see a *fin de siècle* (end-of-
century) society that's stuffed with
too much luxury, too much classical beauty, too much pleasure,
wasted, burned-out, and in decay.
The old, backward-looking order
was about to be slapped in the face.
• *Continue up the gallery, then left
into Room 14 ("Manet, avant 1870").
Find the reclining nude.*

Manet—*Olympia*

"This brunette is thoroughly ugly. Her face is stupid, her skin
cadaverous. All this clash of colors is stupefying." So wrote a critic

when Edouard Manet's nude
hung in the Salon. The public
hated it, attacking Manet (man-
nay) in print and literally
attacking the canvas.

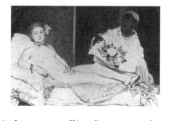

　　Think back on Cabanel's
painting, *The Birth of Venus*—an
idealized, pastel, Vaseline-on-
the-lens beauty. Cabenel's nude
was soft-core pornography, the kind you see selling lingerie and
perfume. The public lapped it up (and Napoleon III purchased it).

　　Manet's nude doesn't gloss over anything. The pose is classic, used by Titian, Goya, and countless others. But the sharp
outlines and harsh contrasting colors are new and shocking.
Her hand is a clamp, and her stare is shockingly defiant, with
not a hint of the seductive, hey-sailor look of most nudes. This
prostitute, ignoring the flowers sent by her last customer, looks
out to us as if to say "next." Manet replaced soft-core porn with
hard-core art.

Manet had an upper-class upbringing and some formal art training, and he had been accepted by the Salon. He could have cranked out pretty nudes and been a successful painter. Instead he surrounded himself with a group of young artists experimenting with new techniques. With his reputation and strong personality, he was their master, though he learned equally from them. Let the Impressionist revolution begin.

• *Continue to the end of the gallery. Before taking the covered escalator up to the often-crowded Impressionist rooms, take a break and read ahead. Or you could visit the exhibit near the escalator.*

Opera Exhibit

Expand to 100 times your size and hover over a scale model section of the city. There's the 19th-century Garnier Opera House with its green roof in a diamond-shaped block in the center.

You'll also see a cross-section model of the Opera House. You'd enter from the right end, buy your ticket in the foyer, then move into the entrance hall with its grand staircase, where you could see and be seen by *tout* Paris. At curtain time, you'd find your seat in the golden auditorium, topped by a glorious painted ceiling. (The current ceiling is even more wonderful than the model, done by Marc Chagall.) Notice that the stage is as big as the seating area, with elaborate riggings to raise and lower scenery. Nearby, there are models of set designs from some famous productions. These days, Parisians enjoy their Verdi and Gounod at the new opera house at place Bastille.

IMPRESSIONISM

The camera threatened to make artists obsolete. A painter's original function was to record reality faithfully like a journalist. Now a machine could capture a better likeness faster than you could say Etch-a-Sketch.

But true art is more than just painting reality. It gives us reality from the artist's point of view, putting a personal stamp on the work. It records not only the scene—a camera can do that—but the artist's impressions of the scene. Impressions are often fleeting, so you have to work quickly.

The Impressionist painters rejected camera-like detail for a quick style more suited to capturing the passing moment. Feeling stifled by the rigid rules and stuffy atmosphere of the Academy, the Impressionists' motto was "out of the studio, into the open air." They grabbed their berets and scarves and took excursions to the country, setting up their easels on riverbanks and hillsides or sketching in cafés and dance halls. Gods, goddesses, nymphs, and fantasy scenes were out; common people and rural landscapes were in.

EARLY IMPRESSIONISM

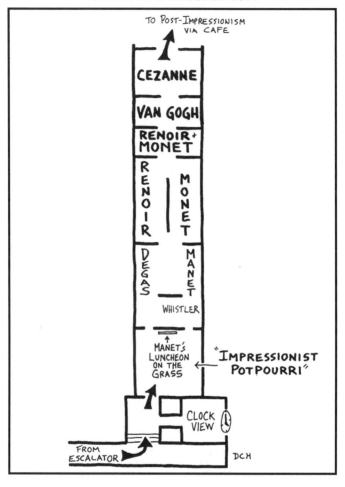

The quick style and simple subjects were ridiculed and called childish by the "experts." Rejected by the Salon, the Impressionists staged their own exhibition in 1874. They brashly took their name from an insult thrown at them by a critic who laughed at one of Monet's "Impressions" of a sunrise. During the next decade, they exhibited their own work independently. The public, opposed at first, was slowly drawn in by the simplicity, the color, and the vibrancy of Impressionist art.

• *Ride the escalator to the top floor. Take your first left for a commanding view of the Orsay. Second left takes you between a bookshop and a giant "backwards" clock to the art.*

The Impressionist collection is scattered somewhat randomly through the next 10 or so rooms. Shadows dance and the displays mingle. You'll find nearly all of these paintings, but exactly where they're hung is a lot like their brushwork...delightfully sloppy. (If you don't see a described painting, move on. It's either hung farther down or on holiday.) Now, let there be...

Impressionism—Manet, Degas, Monet, Renoir

Light! Color! Vibrations! You don't hang an Impressionist canvas— you tether it. Impressionism features light colors, easygoing open-air scenes, spontaneity, broad brush strokes, and the play of light.

The Impressionists made their canvases shimmer by a simple but revolutionary technique. If you mix, say, red, yellow, and blue together you'll get brown, right? But Impressionists didn't bother to mix them. They'd slap a thick brushstroke of yellow down, then a stroke of green next to it, then red next to that. Up close all you see are the three messy strokes, but as you back up...*voilà!* Brown! The colors blend in the eye at a distance. But while your eye is saying "bland brown," your subconscious is shouting, "Red! Yellow! Blue! Yes!"

There are no lines in nature. Yet someone in the classical tradition (Ingres, for example) would draw an outline of his subject, then fill it in with color. But the Impressionists built a figure with dabs of paint...a snowman of color.

Manet—*Luncheon on the Grass* (*Le Déjeuner sur l'Herbe*)

Manet really got a rise out of people with this one. Once again the public judged the painting on moral terms rather than artistic ones.

What are these scantily clad women doing with these fully clothed men, they wondered? Or rather, what will they be doing after the last baguette is eaten?

A new revolutionary movement is budding: Impressionism. Notice the messy brushwork of the trees and leaves in the background, and the play of light on the pond in back and filtering through the trees onto the hazy woman stooping behind. And the strong contrasting colors (white skin, black clothes, green grass). And the fact that this is a true out-of-doors painting, not a studio production. The first shot had been fired.

Whistler—*Whistler's Mother* (*Portrait de la Mére de l'Auteur*)

Why so famous? I don't know either. It shouldn't be, of course, but it is. Perhaps because it's by an American, and we see in his mother some of the monumental solidity of our own ancestral moms made tough by pioneering the American wilderness.

Or perhaps because it was so starkly different in its day. In a roomful of golden goddesses, it'd stand out like a fish in a tree. The experts hated it and didn't understand it. (If music is the fear of silence, is art the fear of reality?) The subtitle is "Arrangement in Grey and Black," and the whole point is the subtle variations on dark shades softened by the rosy tint of her cheeks, but the critics kept waiting for it to come out in Colorization.

Degas—*The Dance Class* (*La Classe de Danse*)

Clearly, Degas loved dance and the theater. (Also catch his statue, *Tiny Dancer, 14 Years Old*, in the glass case.) The play of stage lights off his dancers, especially the halos of ballet skirts, is made

to order for an Impressionist.

Edgar Degas (day-gah) was a rich kid from a family of bankers who got the best classical-style art training. Adoring Ingres' pure lines and cool colors, he painted in the Conservative style. His work was exhibited in the Salon. He gained success and a good reputation and then...he met the Impressionists.

Degas blends classical lines with Impressionist color and spontaneity. His dancers have outlines, and he's got them in a classic 3-D setting—with the floor lines slanting to the upper right.

So why is Degas an Impressionist? First off, he's captured a candid, fleeting moment, a momentary "impression"—the dancers are tired and bored, at the tail end of a long rehearsal. Look at the girl on the left scratching her back restlessly and the cuddly little bundle of dog in the foreground. Degas loved the unposed "snapshot" effect, catching his models off guard.

Finally, he's got that Impressionistic "fury" of the brush. In *The Dance Class*, look at the bright green bow on the girl with her back to us. Not only are the outlines sketchy, but see how he slopped green paint onto her dress and didn't even say, *"Excusez-moi."*

Degas—*The Glass of Absinthe* (*Au Café, dit L'Absinthe*)

Degas hung out with low-life Impressionists discussing art, love, and life in the cheap cafés and bars in Montmartre (the original Bohemia-ville). He painted Impressionistic snapshots of everyday people. Here a weary lady of the evening meets morning with a last lonely coffin-nail drink in the glaring light of a four-in-the-morning café. The pale green drink forming the center of the composition is that toxic substance absinthe that fueled many artists and burned out many more.

Look across the room at some later works by Manet. The old dog was learning new tricks from his former disciples.

• *The next rooms feature works by two Impressionist masters at their peak, Monet and Renoir. You're looking at the quintessence of Impressionism.*

Monet—*La Gare St. Lazare*

Claude Monet (mo-nay) is the father of Impressionism. He learned from Manet (*a* before *o*) but quickly went beyond even Manet's shocking slabs of colors. Monet fully explored the possi-

bilities of open-air painting and lighter, brighter colors.

He could even make this drab train station glow with reflected light. The sun diffuses through the skylight and mingles with the steam from the engine. The yellow buildings in the background merge with the blue smoke in the foreground to illuminate an otherwise colorless scene.

Stand a good six feet from the canvas and look at the tall building with the slanted Mansard roof behind the station. Looks fine? Now get close up. At six inches it's a confusing pile of color blobs. And the smoke is truly "thick." Light on!

Monet—*The Cathedral of Rouen* (*La Cathédrale de Rouen*), a series of five paintings

Monet went to Rouen, rented a room across from the cathedral, set up his easel...and waited. He wanted to catch "a series of

differing impressions" of the
cathedral facade at different times
of day and year. He often had
several canvases going at once. In
all he did 30 canvases, and each is
unique. The time-lapse series
shows the sun passing slowly
across the sky, creating different
colored light and shadows. These
five are labeled: in the morning,

in grey weather, morning sun, full view, full sunlight.

As Monet zeroes in on the play of colors and light, the
physical subject—the cathedral—is dissolving. It has become
only a rack upon which to hang the light and color. Later artists
would boldly throw away the rack, leaving purely abstract modern
art in its place.

Monet—Paintings from Monet's Garden at Giverny
One of Monet's favorite places to paint was the garden of his home

in Giverny, west of Paris (and worth a
visit if you like Monet more than you
hate crowds). You'll find several different views of it along with the painter's
self-portrait. The *Blue Water Lilies* is
similar to the large and famous water lily
paintings in the nearby L'Orangerie
Museum (closed for restoration—
another reason to return to Paris) across
the river in the Tuileries Gardens.

Renoir—*Dance at the Moulin de la Galette*
(*Bal du Moulin de la Galette*)
On Sunday afternoons, working-class folk would dress up and head

for the fields on Butte Montmartre
(near Sacré-Coeur church) to
dance, drink, and eat little cakes
(*galettes*) till dark. Renoir (ren-wah)
liked to go there to paint the common Parisians living and loving in
the afternoon sun. The sunlight filtering through the trees creates a
kaleidoscope of colors, like a 19th-

century mirrored ball throwing darts of light on the dancers.

This dappled light is the "impression" that Renoir came
away with. He captures it with quick blobs of yellow. Look at the

sun-dappled straw hat (right of center) and the glasses (lower right). Smell the powder on the ladies' faces. The painting glows with bright colors. Even the shadows on the ground, which should be grey or black, are colored a warm blue. As if having a good time was required, even the shadows are caught up in the mood, dancing. Like a photographer who uses a slow shutter speed to show motion, Renoir paints a waltzing blur.

Renoir—*The City Dance/The Country Dance* (*La Danse à la Ville/La Danse à la Campagne*)

In contrast to Monet's haze of colors, Renoir clung to the more traditional technique of drawing a clear outline, then filling it in.

This two-panel "series" by Renoir shows us his exquisite draftsmanship, sense of beauty, and smoother brushwork. Like

Degas, Renoir had classical training and exhibited at the Salon.

Renoir's work is lighthearted with light colors, almost pastels. He seems to be searching for an ideal, the pure beauty we saw on the ground floor. In later years he used more and more red tones as if trying for even more warmth.

• *On the divider in the center of the room, you'll find...*

Pissarro and Others

We've neglected many of the founders of the Impressionist style. Browse around and discover your own favorites. Pissarro is one of mine. His grainy landscapes are more subtle and subdued than the flashy Monet and Renoir, but, as someone said, "He did for the earth what Monet did for the water."

You may find the painting *Young Girl in the Garden* (*Jeune Fille en Jardin*) with a pastel style as pretty as Renoir's. It's by Mary Cassatt, an American who was attracted to the strong art magnet that was and still is Paris.

• *Take a break. Look at the Impressionist effect of the weather on the Paris skyline. Notice the skylight above you—these Impressionist rooms are appropriately lit by ever-changing natural light. Then carry on...*

POSTIMPRESSIONISM

Take a word, put "-ism" on the end, and you've become an intellectual. Commune-ism, sex-ism, cube-ism, computer-ism... Postimpression-ism.

"Postimpressionism" is an artificial and clumsy concept to

POSTIMPRESSIONISM

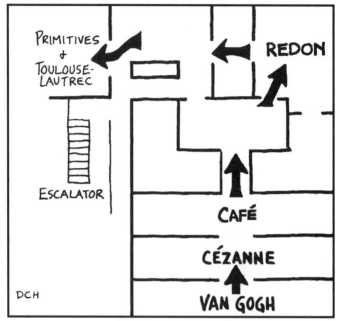

describe those painters who used Impressionist techniques after Monet and Renoir. It might just as well be called something like "Premodernism," because it bridged Impressionism with the 20th century... or you could call it bridge-ism.

• *The Orsay's Postimpressionist collection (we'll see van Gogh, Cézanne, Gauguin, Rousseau, Seurat, and Toulouse-Lautrec) flip-flops back and forth between here and the end of this gallery. Be prepared to skip around.*

Van Gogh

Impressionists have been accused of being lightweights. The colorful style lends itself to bright country scenes, gardens, sunlight on the water, and happy crowds of simple people. It took a remarkable genius to add profound emotion to the Impressionist style.

Vincent van Gogh (van-go, or van-HOCK to the Dutch and the snooty) was the son of a Dutch minister. He too felt a religious calling, and he spread the gospel among the poorest of the poor—peasants and miners. When he turned to painting, he channeled this same spiritual intensity into his work. Like Michelangelo,

Beethoven, Rembrandt, Wayne Newton, and a select handful of others, he put so much of himself into his work that art and life became one. In this room you'll see both van Gogh's painting style and his life unfold.

Van Gogh—*Peasant* (*Paysanne près de l'Atre*)

As a young man, van Gogh left his steady clerking job to work with poor working people in overcast Belgium and Holland. He painted these hardworking, dignified folks in a crude, dark style reflecting the oppressiveness of their lives...and the loneliness of his own as he roamed northern Europe in search of a calling.

Van Gogh—*Self-Portrait, Paris* (*Portraite de l'Artiste*), 1887

Encouraged by his art-dealer brother, van Gogh moves to Paris, and *voilà!* The color! He meets Monet and hobnobs with Gauguin and

Toulouse-Lautrec. He rents a room in Montmartre, learning the Impressionist style. (See how he builds a bristling brown beard using thick strokes of reds and greens side by side.)

At first he paints like the others but soon develops his own style. By using thick swirling brush strokes, he infuses life into even inanimate objects. Van Gogh's brush strokes curve and thrash around like a garden hose pumped with wine.

Van Gogh—*Midday* (*La Méridienne*), 1890, based on a painting by Millet

The social life of Paris becomes too much for the solitary van Gogh. He moves to the south of France. At first, in the glow of the bright spring sunshine, he has a period of incredible creativity and happiness, overwhelmed by the bright colors—an Impressionist's dream. Here again we see his love of the common people taking a glowing siesta in the noon sun.

Van Gogh—*Van Gogh's Room at Arles* (*La Chambre de Van Gogh à Arles*), 1889

But being alone in a strange country begins to wear on him. An ugly man, he finds it hard to get a date. The distorted perspective of this painting makes his tiny rented room look even more

cramped. He invites his friend
Gauguin to join him, but after two
months together arguing passion-
ately about art, nerves get raw. Van
Gogh threatens Gauguin with a
knife, driving him back to Paris. In
crazed despair, van Gogh mutilates
his own ear.

The people of Arles realize they have a madman on their
hands and convince van Gogh to seek help. He enters a mental
hospital.

Van Gogh—*The Church at Auvers-sur-Oise* (*L'Église d'Auvers-sur-Oise*), 1890

Van Gogh's paintings done in the peace of the mental hospital are

more meditative—fewer bright landscapes,
more closed-in scenes with deeper and almost
surreal colors.

There's also a strong sense of mystery.
What's behind this church? The sky is
cobalt blue and the church's windows are
also blue, like we're looking right through
the church to an infinite sky. There's something mysterious lurking on the other side.
You can't see it, but you feel its presence
like the cold air from an approaching Métro
train still hidden in the tunnel. There's a road that leads from us
to the church, then splits to go behind. A choice must be made.
Which way?

Van Gogh—*Self-Portrait, St. Remy* (*Portrait de l'Artiste*), 1889

Van Gogh wavered between happiness and
madness. He despaired of ever being sane
enough to continue painting.

This self-portrait shows a man engulfed
in a confused but beautiful world. The background brush strokes swirl and rave, setting in
motion the waves of the jacket. He's caught in
the current, out of control. But in the midst
of this rippling sea of mystery floats a still,
detached island of a face with probing,
questioning, wise eyes.

Do his troubled eyes know that only a few months later he
would take a pistol and put a bullet through his chest?

Cézanne

Cézanne's art brought Impressionism into the 20th century. There's less color here, less swirling brushwork, less passion. It's cleaner, chunkier, more intellectual. Cézanne (say-zahn) can be difficult to appreciate after the warmth of Renoir, and he won't give you the fireworks of van Gogh. But he's worth the effort.

Cézanne—*Self-Portrait* (*Portrait de l'Artiste*)

Cézanne was virtually unknown and unappreciated in his lifetime. He worked alone, lived alone, and died alone, ignored by all but a few revolutionary young artists who understood his efforts.

And Cézanne couldn't draw. His brush was a blunt instru-

ment. With it, he'd bludgeon reality into submission, drag it across a canvas, and leave it there to dry. But Cézanne the mediocre painter was a great innovator. His works are not perfected, finished products but revolutionary works-in-progress—gutter balls with wonderful spin. His work spoke for itself—which is good

because, as you can see here, he had no mouth.

Cézanne—*Landscape* (*Rochers près des Grottes au dessus de Château-Noir*)

Cézanne used chunks of color as blocks to build three-dimensional forms. The rocky brown cliffs here consist of cubes of green, tan, and blue that blend at a distance to create a solid 3-D structure. It only makes sense from a distance. Try this: Start at six inches and fade back. At some point the messy slabs become reality on the rocks.

Why is this revolutionary? Past artists created the illusion of 3-D with lines (like when we draw receding lines to turn a square into a cube). The Impressionists pioneered the technique of using blobs of color, not lines, to capture a subject. But most Impressionist art is flat and two dimensional, a wall of color like Monet's *Rouen Cathedral* series. Cézanne went 3-D with chunks.

These chunks are like little "cubes." No coincidence that his experiments in reducing forms to their geometric basics influenced the...cubists.

Cézanne—*The Card Players* (*Les Joueurs de Cartes*)

These aren't people. They're studies in color and pattern. The subject matter—two guys playing cards—is less important than the pleasingly balanced pattern they make on the canvas, two sloping

forms framing a cylinder (a bottle) in the center. Later, abstract artists would focus solely on the shapes and colors.

Again, notice how the figures are built with chunks of color. The jacket of the player at right consists of tans, greens, and browns. As one art scholar put it: "Cézanne confused intermingled forms and colors, achieving an extraordinarily luminous density in which lyricism is controlled by a rigorously constructed rhythm." Just what I said—chunks of color.

Cézanne—*A Modern Olympia* (*Une Moderne Olympia*)

Is this Cézanne himself paying homage to Manet? And dreaming up a new, more radical style of painting? We've come a long way since Manet's *Olympia*, which seems tame to us now.

• *Exit to the café and consider a well-deserved break. From the café, continue ahead, walking under the large green beam, following signs saying, "suite de la visite."*

A hallway leads past WCs to . . .

Redon

Now flip out the lights and step into his mysterious world. If the Orsay's a zoo, this is the nocturnal house. Prowl around. This is wild, wild stuff, intense—imagine Richard Nixon on mushrooms playing sax.

• *At cockcrow pass into the gallery lined with metal columns containing the primitive art of Rousseau and Gauguin. Start in the first alcove to the left.*

PRIMITIVISM

Henri Rousseau—*War* (*La Guerre ou La Chevauchée de la Discorde*)

Some artists, rejecting the harried, scientific, and rational world, remembered a time before "-isms," when works of art weren't scholarly "studies in form and color" but voodoo dolls full of mystery and magic power. They learned from the art of primitive tribes in Africa and the South Seas, trying to recreate a primal Garden of Eden of peace and wholeness. In doing so, they created another "ism": primitivism.

One such artist was Rousseau, a man who painted like a child. He was an amateur artist who palled around with all the great painters, but they never took his naive style of art seriously.

This looks like a child's drawing of a nightmare. The images are primitive—flat and simple, with unreal colors—but the effect is both beautiful and terrifying. War in the form of a woman with a sword flies on horseback across the battlefield, leaving destruction in her wake—broken bare trees, burning clouds in the background, and heaps of corpses picked at by the birds.

Gauguin—*The Beautiful Angel* (*La Belle Angele*)

A woman in peasant dress sits in a bubble like the halos in a medieval religious painting. Next to it is a pagan idol. This isn't a scene but an ordered collage of images with symbolic overtones. It's left to us to make the connection.

Paul Gauguin (go-gan) learned the bright clashing colors from the Impressionists but diverged from this path about the time van Gogh waved a knife in his face.

Gauguin simplifies. His figures are two dimensional with thick dark outlines filled in with basic blocks of color. He turned his back on the entire Western tradition of realism begun in the Renaissance, which tried to recreate the 3-D world on a 2-D canvas. Instead he returns to an age where figures become symbols.

Gauguin—*Arearea* (*Pleasantries*) (*Joyeusetes*)

Gauguin got the travel bug early in childhood and grew up wanting to be a sailor. Instead he became a stockbroker. In his spare time he painted and was introduced to the Impressionist circle. At the age of 35, he got fed up with it all, quit his job, abandoned his wife (see her stern portrait bust), and took refuge in his art. He traveled to the South Seas in search of the exotic, finally settling on Tahiti.

In Tahiti, Gauguin found his Garden of Eden. He simplified his life to the routine of eating, sleeping, and painting. He simplified his painting still more to flat images with heavy black outlines filled in with bright, pure colors. He painted the native girls in their naked innocence (so different from Cabanel's seductive *Venus!*).

But this simple style had a deep under-current of symbolic meaning.

Arearea shows native women and a dog. In the "distance" (there's no attempt at traditional 3-D here), a pro-cession goes by with a large pagan idol. What's the connection between the idol and the foreground figures who are apparently unaware of it? Gauguin makes us dig deep down into our medulla oblongata to make a mystical connection between the beau-tiful women, the dog, and religion. In primitive societies, religion permeates life. Idols, dogs, and women are holy.

Seurat—*The Circus* (*Le Cirque*)

With "pointillism," Impressionism is brought to its logical conclusion—lit-tle dabs of different colors placed side by side to blend in the viewer's eye. Using only red, yellow, blue, and green points of paint, Seurat (sur-rah) creates a mosaic of colors that shim-mers at a distance, capturing the wonder of the dawn of electric lights.

Toulouse-Lautrec—*The Clownesse Cha-U-Kao*

Henri de Toulouse-Lautrec was the black sheep of a noble family. At age 15 he broke both legs, which left him a cripple. Shunned by his family, a freak to society, he felt more at home in the underworld of other outcasts—prostitutes, drunks, thieves, dancers, and actors. He painted the nightlife lowlife in the bars, cafés, dance halls, and brothels he frequented. Toulose-Lautrec died young of alcoholism.

This is one of his fellow freaks, a fat lady clown who made her living being laughed at. She slumps wearily after a performance, indifferent to the applause, and adjusts her dress to prepare for the curtain call.

Toulouse-Lautrec was a true "impression"-ist, catching his models in candid poses. He worked spontaneously, never correct-ing his mistakes, as you can see from the blotches on her dark skirt and the unintentional yellow sash hanging down. Can you see a bit of Degas here, in the subject matter, snapshot pose, and colors?

Toulouse-Lautrec—*Jane Avril Dancing*

Toulouse-Lautrec hung out at the Moulin Rouge dance hall in Montmartre. One of the most popular dancers was this slim, graceful, elegant, and melancholy woman who stood out above the

rabble of the Moulin Rouge. Her legs keep dancing while her mind is far away. Toulouse-Lautrec the artistocrat might have identified with her noble face—sad and weary of the nightlife, but stuck in it.

• *You've seen the essential Orsay and are permitted to cut out (the exit is straight below you). But there's an "Other Orsay" I think you'll find entertaining.*

To reach the mezzanine ("niveau median"), cross to the other side of the gallery and go down three flights. At the foot of the escalator, the mezzanine (which overlooks the main floor) is to your right. But first, go left to the palatial room of mirrors and chandeliers, marked "Salle des Fetes" or "Arts et Decors de la IIIème République" (Room 52).

THE "OTHER" ORSAY—MEZZANINE

The beauty of the Orsay is that it combines all the art of the 1800s (1848–1914), both modern and classical, in one building. The classical art, so popular in its own day, has been maligned and forgotten in the 20th century. It's time for a reassessment. Is it as gaudy and gawdawful as we've been led to believe? From our end-of-century perspective, let's take a look at the opulent, *fin de siècle* ("end of the century") French high society and its luxurious art.

The Grand Ballroom (Arts et Decors de la IIIème République)

This was one of France's most luxurious nightspots when the Orsay hotel was here. You can easily imagine gowned debutantes and white-gloved dandies waltzing the night away to the music of a chamber orchestra.

Notice:

1) The interior decorating: raspberry marble-ripple ice-cream columns, pastel ceiling painting, gold work, mirrors, and leafy strands of chandeliers.

2) The statue *Bacchante Couchée* sprawled in the middle of the room. Familiar pose? If not, you flunk this tour.

3) The statue *Aurore*, with her canopy of hair, hide-and-seek face, and silver-dollar nipples.

4) The large painting *The Birth of Venus (La Naissance de Venus)* by William

THE OTHER ORSAY

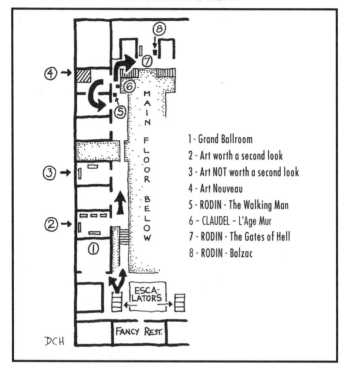

1 - Grand Ballroom
2 - Art worth a second look
3 - Art NOT worth a second look
4 - Art Nouveau
5 - RODIN - The Walking Man
6 - CLAUDEL - L'Age Mur
7 - RODIN - The Gates of Hell
8 - RODIN - Balzac

DCH

Bouguereau. Van Gogh once said: "If I painted like Bouguereau, I could hope to make money. The public will never change—they love only sweet things."

5) *La Nature*, with the only see-through veil of marble I've ever seen through.

So here's the question—is this stuff beautiful or merely gaudy? Divine or decadent?

• *Return to the mezzanine overlooking the main gallery. Head toward the far end. Enter the first room on the left (#55).*

Art Worth a Second Look

We've seen some great art; now let's see some not-so-great art—at least, that's what modern critics tell us. This is realistic art with a subconscious kick, art from a neurotic society before Freud articulated its demons.

• *Working clockwise, you'll see . . .*

Cain

The world's first murderer, with the murder weapon still in his belt, is exiled with his family. Archeologists had recently discovered a Neanderthal skull, so the artist shows them as a prehistoric hunter/gatherer tribe.

The Dream (*Le Rêve*)

Soldiers sleep, while visions of Gatling guns dance in their heads.

Payday (*La Paye des Moissonneurs*)

Peasants getting paid, painted by the man called "the grandson of Courbet and Millet." The subtitle of the work should be "Is this all there is to life?"

The Excommunication of Robert Le Pieux

The bishops exit after performing the rite. The king and queen are stunned, the sceptre dropped. The ritual candle has been snuffed out; it falls, fuming, echoing through the huge hall.... Again, is this art or only cheap theatrics?

• *Return to the mezzanine. Skip the next room, then go left into Room 59, labeled "Symbolisme."*

Art Not Worth a Second Look

The Orsay's director said: "Certainly we have bad paintings. But we have only the greatest bad paintings." And here they are.

Serenity

An idyll in the woods. Three nymphs with harps waft off to the right. These people are stoned on something.

The School of Plato (*L'École de Platon*)

Subtitled "The Athens YMCA." A Christlike Plato surrounded by adoring, half-naked nubile youths gives new meaning to the term "Platonic relationship."

Will the pendulum shift so that one day art like *The School of Plato* becomes the new, radical avant-garde style?

• *Return to the mezzanine and continue to the far end. Enter the last room on the left (#65) and head for the far corner.*

ART NOUVEAU

The Industrial Age brought factories, row houses, machines, train stations, geometrical precision—and ugliness. At the turn of the century, some artists reacted against the unrelieved geometry of harsh, pragmatic, iron-and-steel Eiffel Tower art with a "new art"—Art Nouveau (art new-vo). Hmm. I think I had a driver's ed teacher by that name.

Charpentier—*Dining Room of Adrien Benard* (*Boiserie de la Salle à Mangé de la Propriété Benard*)

Like nature, which also abhors a straight line, Art Nouveau artists used the curves of flowers and vines as their pattern. They were convinced that "practical" didn't have to mean "ugly" as well. They turned everyday household objects into art.

This wood-paneled dining room, with its organic shapes, is one of the finest examples of the Art Nouveau style (called Jugendstil in Germanic countries). Another is the curvy wrought-iron work of some of Paris' early Métro entrances (some survive), built by the same man who commissioned this dining room for his home.

• *Browse through the Art Nouveau rooms to the left. You'll spill out back onto the mezzanine. Grab a seat in front of the Rodin statue of a man missing everything but his legs.*

Auguste Rodin

Rodin completes the tour—from classical sculpture to Impressionist painting to an artist who brought them both together. Rodin combined classical solidity with Impressionist surfaces to become the greatest sculptor since Michelangelo.

Rodin—*The Walking Man* (*L'Homme Qui Marche*)

This muscular, forcefully striding man could be a symbol of the Renaissance Man with his classical power. With no mouth or hands, he speaks with his body. But Rodin also learned a thing or two from the comparatively lightweight Impressionist painters. Get close and look at the statue's surface. This rough "unfinished" look reflects light like the rough Impressionist brushwork, making the statue come alive, never quite at rest in the viewer's eye.

• *Near the far end of the mezzanine you'll see a small bronze couple (L'Âge Mur) by Camille Claudel, a student of Rodin's.*

Claudel—*The Ages of Life* (*L'Âge Mur*)

Camille Claudel, Rodin's student and mistress, may have portrayed their doomed love affair here. A young girl desperately reaches out to an older man, who is led away reluctantly by an older woman. The center of the composition is the empty space left when their hands separate. In real life, Rodin refused to leave his wife, and Camille (see her head sticking up from a block of marble) ended up in an insane asylum.

Rodin—*The Gates of Hell* (*Porte de l'Enfer*)

Rodin worked for decades on these doors depicting Dante's Hell, and they contain some of his greatest hits, small statues that he later executed in full size. Find *The Thinker* squatting above the doorway, contemplating Man's fate. And in the lower left is the same kneeling man eating his children (*Ugolin*) you'll see in full size nearby. Rodin paid models to run, squat, leap, and spin around his studio however they wanted. When he saw an interesting pose he'd yell "freeze" (or "statue maker") and get out his sketch pad.

Rodin—*Balzac*

The great French novelist is given a heroic, monumental ugliness. Wrapped in a long cloak, he thrusts his head out at a defiant angle, showing the strong individualism and egoism of the 19th-century

Romantic movement. Balzac is proud and snooty—but his body forms a question mark, and underneath the twisted features we can see a touch of personal pain and self doubt. This is hardly camera-eye realism—Balzac wasn't that grotesque—but it captures a personality that strikes us even if we don't know the man.

From this perch, look over the main floor at all the classical statues between you and the big clock and realize how far we've come—not in years but in style changes. Many of the statues below—beautiful, smooth, balanced, and idealized—were done at the same time as Rodin's powerful, haunting works. Rodin is a good place to end the tour. With a stable base of 19th-century stone, he launched art into the 20th century.

RODIN
MUSEUM
TOUR

Auguste Rodin (1840–1917) is a modern Michelangelo, sculpting human figures on an epic scale, revealing through the body their deepest thoughts and feelings. Like many of Michelangelo's unfinished works, Rodin's statues rise from the raw stone around them, driven by the life force. With missing limbs and scarred skin, these are prefab classics, making ugliness noble. Rodin's people are always moving restlessly. Even the famous *Thinker* is moving. While he's plopped down solidly...his mind is a million miles away. The museum presents a full range of Rodin's work, housed in a historic mansion where he once lived and worked. The gardens are picnic perfect (BYO) or consider the pleasant, if pricey, café.

Orientation

Cost: 28F, 18F on Sun and for seniors, students, and those under 18; 5F for garden only; all covered by museum pass.
Hours: Tue–Sun 9:30–17:45 Apr–Sept, garden closes at 18:45. Tue–Sun 9:30–16:45 Oct–Mar, garden closes at 17:00. Closed Mon.
Getting There: It's near Napoleon's Tomb (77 rue de Varennes, Mo: Varenne).
Tour Length: One hour.
Information: Tel. 01-44-18-61-10, www.musee-rodin.fr

Entrance Hall

Two bronze men stride forward, as bold as the often-controversial Rodin. *The Walking Man* (*L'Homme Qui Marche*) plants his back foot forcefully as though he's about to step, while his front foot already has stepped. Rodin, who himself had one foot in the past, one in the future, captures two poses at once. Just ahead, a white-marble couple locks lips in *The Kiss*, one of many statues of lovers entwined. We don't need to see their faces to tell us what they feel.

——— RODIN MUSEUM AND GARDENS ———

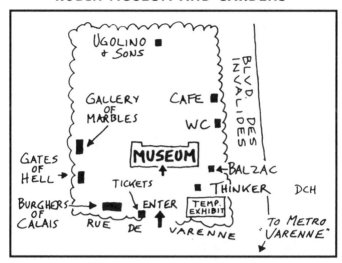

• *Pick up a museum plan with room numbers and walk left, through the shop, and to the far corner to start a circular tour of the ground floor.*

Room 1: Rodin's early works match the style of the time—pretty portrait busts and classical themes. Born of working-class roots, Rodin taught himself art by sketching statues at the Louvre and then sculpting copies.

The Man with the Broken Nose (*L'homme au nez casse*)—a deliberately ugly work—was 23-year-old Rodin's first break from the norm. He meticulously sculpted this deformed man (one of the few models the struggling sculptor could afford), but then the clay statue froze in his unheated studio, and the back of the head fell off. Rodin loved it! The Salon hated it. Rodin persevered.

See the painting of Rodin's future wife, Rose Beuret (*Portrait de Madame Rodin*), who suffered with him through obscurity and celebrity.

Room 2: To feed his new family, Rodin cranked out small works with his boss's name on them—portraits, ornamental vases, nymphs, and knickknacks to decorate buildings. Still, the series of mother-and-childs (Rose and baby Auguste?) allowed him to experiment on a small scale with the intertwined twosomes he'd do later.

His job gave him enough money to visit Italy, where he was inspired by Michelangelo's boldness, monumental scale, restless figures, and "unfinished" look. Rapidly approaching middle age, Rodin was ready to rock.

Room 3: He moved to Brussels, where his first major work, *The Bronze Age* (*L'âge d'arain*), brought controversy and the fame that surrounds it. This nude youth, perhaps inspired by Michelangelo's *Dying Slave* in the Louvre, awakens to a new world. It was so lifelike that Rodin was accused of not sculpting it himself but simply casting it directly from a live body. The boy's left hand looks like he should be leaning on a spear, but it's just that missing element that makes the pose more tenuous and interesting.

The art establishment still snubbed Rodin the outsider, and no wonder. Look at his ultraintense take on the symbol of France (*La Defense*)—this Marseillaise screams "Off with their heads" at the top of her lungs. Rodin was a slave to his muses, and some inspired monsters.

Room 4: Like the hand of a sculptor, *The Hand of God* (*La main de Dieu*) shapes Adam and Eve from the mud of the earth to which they will return. Rodin himself worked in "mud," using his hands to model clay figures, which were then reproduced in marble or bronze, usually by his assistants. Spin this masterpiece on its turntable. Rodin wants you to see it from every angle. He first worked from the front view, then checked the back and side pro- files, then filled in the in-between.

Other works in this room show embracing couples who seem to emerge from the stone just long enough to love. Rodin left many works "unfinished," reminding us that all creating is a hard process of dragging a form out of chaos.

Room 5: The two hands that form the arch of *The Cathedral* (*La Cathedrale*) are actually two right hands (a man's and a woman's?).

In *The Kiss*, a passionate woman twines around a solid man for their first, spontaneous kiss. In their bodies, we can almost read the thoughts, words, and movements that led up to this meeting of lips. *The Kiss* was the first Rodin work the public loved. Rodin despised it, thinking it simple and sentimental.

Rodin worked with many materials— he chiseled marble (*The Kiss*), used clay (the smaller, red-brown *Kiss*—opposite the big kiss), cast bronze, worked plaster, painted, and sketched. He often did different versions of the same subject in a different medium.

Room 6: This room displays works by Camille Claudel, mostly in the style of her master. The 44-year-old Rodin took 18-year-old Camille as his pupil, muse, colleague, and lover. We can follow the arc of their relationship:

Rodin was inspired by young Camille's beauty and spirit, and he often used her as a model. You'll see her head emerging from a block of marble.

As his student, "Mademoiselle C" learned from Rodin, doing portrait busts in his lumpy style. Her bronze bust of Rodin (by the door) shows the steely-eyed sculptor with strong front and side profiles, barely emerging from the materials he worked with.

Soon they were lovers. *The Waltz* (*La Valse*) captures the spinning exuberance the two must have felt as they embarked together on a new life. The couple twirls in a delicate balance.

But Rodin was devoted as well to his lifelong companion, Rose. *Maturity* (*L'Âge Mur*) shows the breakup. A young girl on her knees begs the man not to leave her, as he's led away reluctantly by an older woman. The center of the composition is the hole left when their hands drift apart.

Rodin did leave Camille. Overwhelmed by grief and jealousy, she went crazy and had to be institutionalized until she died. *The Wave* (*La Vague*), carved in onyx in a very un-Rodin style, shows fragile women huddled under a wave about to engulf them.

Rooms 7–8: What did Rodin think of women? Here are many different images from which you can draw conclusions.

Eve buries her head in shame, hiding her nakedness. But she can't hide the consequences of that first sin—she's pregnant.

Rodin became famous, wealthy, and respected, and society ladies all wanted him to do their portraits. In Room 8, you'll also see his last mistress (*La Duchesse de Choiseul*), who lived with him here in this mansion.

Room 9: This dimly lit room is filled with Rodin's sketches. The first flash of inspiration for a huge statue might be a single line sketched on notepaper. Rodin wanted nude models in his studio at all times—walking, dancing, and squatting—in case they struck some new and interesting pose. Rodin thought of sculpture as simply "drawing in all dimensions."

• *Upstairs you'll find a glass display case that tries hard to explain how…* Rodin made his bronze statues by pouring molten bronze into the narrow space between an original clay model and the mold around it. Once you had a mold, you could produce other copies, which is why there are famous Rodin bronzes all over the world.

As the display case clearly fails to make clear, the classic "lost wax" technique works like this:

1) The artist sculpts a clay model.

2) It is covered with materials that harden to make a shell that's hard on the outside, flexible inside. The shell is removed by cutting it into two halves that can be pieced back together—this is your mold that can be used over and over.

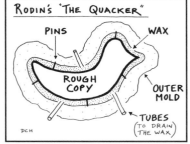

3) Cement is poured into the mold to make a durable, rough copy. The mold is removed.

4) The surface of the copy is sanded down slightly.

5) The mold is put back over it, using pins to keep quarter-inch space between the mold and the rough copy. Hot wax is poured into the space, it cools, and the mold is removed. The artist touches up the wax "skin" of the rough copy into its final form.

6) It is covered again with the mold and ventilation tubes.

7) The whole contraption is coated with heat-resistant materials.

8) The wax is heated—it melts and drains away (gets "lost"), leaving a quarter-inch of open space between the rough copy and the mold. Molten bronze is poured in to fill the space. As the bronze cools, it takes the shape of the mold.

9) The mold and the tubing are removed, the bronze is lifted off the rough copy, and you're left with a hollow bronze statue ready to be polished and varnished.

Rooms 10–11: For decades, Rodin wrestled with a massive project—a doorway encrusted with characters from Dante's *Inferno*. These *Gates of Hell* were never completed (see unfinished piece in the garden), but his studies created some of Rodin's masterpieces—including *The Thinker*, who was to be the centerpiece.

Rodin's figures struggle to come into existence. Rodin was fascinated with the theory of evolution—not Darwin's version of the survival of the fittest but the Frenchman Lamarck's. His figures survive not by the good fortune of random mutation (Darwin), but by their own striving (Lamarck). They are driven by the life force, a restless energy that animates and shapes dead matter (Lamarck and Bergson). Rodin must have felt that force even as a child when he first squeezed soft clay and saw a worm emerge.

In Room 11 you'll see studies of the female body in all its aspects—open, closed, wrinkled.

Room 12: A virtual unknown until his mid-30s, Rodin slowly began receiving major commissions for public monuments. *The Burghers of Calais* depicts the actual event in 1347, when, in order to save their people, the city fathers surrender the keys of the city—and their own lives—to the enemy. Rodin portrays them, not in some glorious pose drenched in pomp and allegory but as a simple example of men sacrificing their lives together. As they head to the gallows, with ropes already around their necks, each shows a distinct emotion: from courage to despair. Compare the small plaster model in the glass case with the final, life-size bronze group out the window in the garden (near the street behind the ticket booth).

Room 15: Rodin's feverish attempts to capture a portrait of the novelist Balzac ranged from a pot-bellied Bacchus to a headless nude cradling an erection. In a moment of inspiration, Rodin threw a plaster-soaked robe over the nude and watched it dry into what would become the final, definitive version.

Room 17: Legendary lovers kiss, embrace, and intertwine in yin-yang bliss.

Room 14: Rodin's portrait busts of celebrities and some paintings by (yawn, are we through yet?) van Gogh, Monet, and Renoir. Rodin enjoyed discussions with Monet and other artists, incorporating their ideas in his work. Rodin is often considered an Impressionist because he captured spontaneous "impressions" of figures and created rough surfaces that catch reflected light.

Room 13: By the end of his life Rodin was more famous than his works. The P.R. film clip shows Rodin making the marble chips fly. In fact, he rarely picked up a chisel, leaving that to assistants. Compare Rodin's small plaster "sketches" (in the glass case) with the final, large-scale marble versions executed by others.

The Gardens

Rodin lived and worked in this mansion, renting rooms alongside Matisse, the poet Rilke (Rodin's secretary), and the dancer Isadora Duncan. He loved placing his creations in the overgrown gardens. These are his greatest works, Rodin at his most expansive. The epic human figures are enhanced, not dwarfed, by nature.

• *Leaving the house, there are five more stops: two on the left and three on the right. Beyond these stops is a big breezy garden ornamented with statues, a cafeteria, and WC.*

The Thinker: Leaning slightly forward, tense and compact, every muscle working toward produc-

ing that one great thought, Man contemplates his fate. No constipation jokes, please.

This is not an intellectual but a linebacker who's realizing there's more to life than frat parties. It's the first man evolving beyond his animal nature to think the first thought. It's any-one who's ever worked hard to reinvent themselves or to make something new or better. Said Rodin: "It is a statue of myself."

There are 29 other authorized copies of this statue, arguably the most famous in the world.

• *To the left of* The Thinker *you'll find...*

Balzac: The iconoclastic novelist turns his nose up at the notion he should be honored with a statue. This final version also stands in the Musée d'Orsay and on a street median in Montparnasse. When the statue was unveiled, the crowd booed, a fitting tribute to both the defiant novelist and the bold man who sculpted him.

• *Along the street near the ticket booth are...*

The Burghers of Calais: The six city fathers trudge to their execution, and we can read in their faces and poses what their last thoughts are. They mill about, dazed, as each one deals with the decision he's made to sacrifice himself for his city.

• *Circling counterclockwise...*

The man carrying the key to the city tightens his lips in determination. The bearded man is weighed down with grief. Another buries his head in his hands. One turns, seeking reassurance from his friend, who turns away and gestures helplessly. The final key bearer (in back) has been stoic, but now he's raising his hand to his head.

Each is alone in his thoughts, but they're united by their mutual sacrifice, by the base they stand on, by their height, and by their weighty robes—gravity is already dragging them down to their graves.

Pity the poor bastards, then salute King Edward III, who, at the last second, pardoned them.

• *Follow* The Thinker*'s gaze to the opposite side of the house. Standing before a tall white backdrop is a big dark door—the* Gates of Hell.

The Gates of Hell: These doors (never meant to actually open) were never finished for a museum that was never built. But the vision of Dante's trip into hell gave Rodin a chance to explore the full range of human experience, including the dark side. "Abandon hope all ye who enter in," was hell's motto. The Three Shades at the top of the door point down—that's where we're going. Beneath The Shades, pondering the whole scene from above, is Dante as The Thinker. Below him, the figures emerge from the darkness just long enough to tell their sad tale of depravity. There's Paolo and Francesca (in the center of the right door), who were driven by the life force into an illicit love affair that brought them here. Ugolino (left door, just below center) crouches in prison over his kids. This poor soul was so driven by hunger that he ate the corpses of his own children. On all fours like an animal, he is the dark side of natural selection. Finally, find what some say is Rodin himself (at the very bottom, inside the right door jamb, where it just starts to jut out), crouching humbly.

You'll find some of these figures writ large in the garden. *The Thinker* is behind you, *The Shades* are 30 yards to the right, and *Ugolino* dines in the fountain at the far end.

It's appropriate that *The Gates*—Rodin's "cathedral"—remained unfinished. He was always a restless artist for whom the process of discovery was as important as the finished product.

• *To the right of the* Gates of Hell *is a glassed-in building, the*...

Gallery of Marbles: Unfinished, they show human features emerging from the rough stone. Imagine Rodin in his studio working to give them life.

Victor Hugo (at the far end of the Gallery), the great champion of Les Miz progress, leans back like Michelangelo's nude *Adam*, waiting for the spark of creation. He tenses his face and cups his ear, straining to hear the vague call from the blurry Muse above him. Once inspired, he can bring the idea to life with the strength of his powerful arms. Rodin must have often felt this as he awaited the energizing life force. It's been said that all of Rodin's work shows the struggle of mind over matter, of brute creatures emerging from the mud and evolving into a species of thinkers.

If you've ever considered being absolute dictator of a united Europe, come here first. Hitler did, before going out and making the same mistakes as his mentor. (Hint: Don't invade Russia.)

Napoleon's tomb rests beneath the golden dome of Les Invalides church. In addition, you can visit various military museums housed in this former veterans' hospital built by Louis XIV.

Orientation

Cost and Hours: 38F, covered by museum pass, daily 10:00–17:45, closes off-season at 16:45 (Napoleon's Tomb open in summer until 19:00). Closed Jan 1, May 1, Nov 1, Dec 25. Tel. 01 44 42 37 72.

Getting There: The tomb is at Hôtel Les Invalides (near Rodin Museum, Mo: La Tour Maubourg, Varennes, or Invalides).

Tour Length: Women–one hour, men–two hours, Republican men–all day.

• *Start at Napoleon's tomb, underneath the golden dome. It's at the back end (farthest from the Seine) of this vast complex of churches and museums.*

NAPOLEON'S TOMB

Enter the church, gaze up the dome, then lean over the railing and bow to the emperor lying inside the red porphyry, scrolled tomb. If the lid were opened, you'd find an oak coffin inside, which holds another ebony coffin, housing two lead ones, then mahogany, then tinplate... until finally you'd find Napoleon himself staring up, with his head closest to the door. When his body was exhumed from the original grave site and transported here, even after 19 years in the ground, it was found to be perfectly preserved.

Born of humble Italian heritage on the French-owned isle of Corsica, Napoleon Bonaparte (1769–1821) went to school at Paris'

École Militaire (Military School), then rose quickly through the ranks amid the chaos of the Revolution. The charismatic "Little Corporal" won fans by fighting for democracy at home and abroad. In 1799, he assumed power and, within five short years, conquered most of Europe. The great champion of the Revolution had become a dictator, declaring himself emperor of a new Rome.

Napoleon's red tomb on its green base stands 15 feet high in the center of a marble floor. It's exalted by the dome above (where dead Frenchmen cavort with saints and angels), forming a golden halo over Napoleon.

Napoleon is surrounded by family. After conquering Europe, he installed his big brother Joseph as king of Spain (turn around to see Joseph's tomb in the alcove to the left of the door); his little brother Jerome became king of Westphalia (to right of door); and his baby boy, Napoleon Junior (downstairs), sat in diapers on the throne of Rome.

In other alcoves, you'll find more dead war heroes (including World War I's Marshall Foch) and many painted saints, making this the French Valhalla in the Versailles of churches.

The Crypt

• *The stairs behind the altar (with the corkscrew columns) take you down to crypt level for a closer look at the tomb.*

Wandering clockwise, read the names of Napoleon's battles inlaid on the floor. Rivoli marks the battle where the rookie 26-year-old general took a ragtag band of "citizens" and thrashed the professional Austrian troops in Italy. He returned to Paris a celebrity. In Egypt (Pyramides), he fought Turks and tribesmen to a standstill, but the exotic expedition caught the public eye, and he returned home a legend.

Austerlitz made him Europe's top dog. At the head of the million-man Grand Army, he made a three-month blitz attack through Germany and Austria. As a general he was daring, relying on a mobile force of independent armies. His personal charisma on the battlefield was said to be worth 10,000 additional men.

Pause in the battles to gaze at the grand statue of Napoleon the emperor in the alcove at the head of the tomb—royal sceptre and orb of Earth in his hands. By 1805, all of Europe was at his feet. He held an elaborate ceremony in Notre-Dame, where he proclaimed his wife, Josephine, as Empress, and himself—the 36-year-old son of humble immigrants—as Emperor. The laurel wreath, the robes, and the Roman eagles proclaim him the equal of the Caesars. The floor at the statue's feet marks the grave of his son, Napoleon II (Roi de Rome).

Around the crypt are relief panels showing Napoleon's constructive side. Dressed in toga and laurel leaves, he dispenses justice, charity, and pork-barrel projects to an awed populace.
• *In the first panel to the right of the statue...*

He establishes an Imperial University to educate naked boys throughout *"tout l'empire."* The roll of great scholars links modern France with those of the past: Plutarch, Homer, Plato, and Aristotle.

Hail Napoleon. Then, at his peak, came his fatal mistake.
• *Continue around the tomb to the Battle of Moscow (Moscowa)...*

Napoleon invaded Russia with 600,000 men and returned to Paris with 100,000 frostbitten survivors. Two years later, the Russians marched into Paris, and Napoleon's days were numbered. After a brief exile on the isle of Elba, he skipped parole, sailed to France, bared his breast and said, "Strike me down or follow me!" For 100 days they followed him, finally into Belgium, where the British finished him off at the Battle of Waterloo (conspicuously absent on the floor decor). Exiled again by a war tribunal, he spent his last days in a crude shack on the small South Atlantic island of St. Helena.

LES INVALIDES AND THE ARMY MUSEUM (MUSÉE DE L'ARMEE)

Your tomb ticket also admits you to several military museums scattered around the complex (listed in free English map/ guide in ticket hall). If you like dummies in uniforms and endless glass cases full of muskets, without historical context, you'll love the Army Museum.

Exiting the church with Napoleon's tomb, make a U-turn right, marching past the ticket hall and café. Halfway down the long hallway, on the right, you'll see the three bare stone slabs beside weeping willows that originally marked Napoleon's grave on St. Helena island. There was no epitaph, since the French and British wrangled over what to call the hero/tyrant. The stones read simply, "Here Lies...."

Continuing on, you spill out into the large Courtyard of Honor, where Napoleon honored his troops and de Gaulle once kissed Churchill. An Army Museum is on either side of the Courtyard.

LES INVALIDES

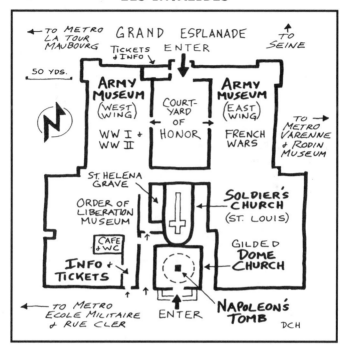

To Metro La Tour Maubourg ← / GRAND ESPLANADE / To Seine ↑ / Tickets & Info / ENTER / 50 YDS. / ARMY MUSEUM (WEST WING) / WW I + WW II / COURTYARD OF HONOR / ARMY MUSEUM (EAST WING) / FRENCH WARS / To Metro Varenne & Rodin Museum → / St. Helena Grave / ORDER OF LIBERATION MUSEUM / CAFE & WC / INFO & TICKETS / SOLDIER'S CHURCH (ST. LOUIS) / GILDED DOME CHURCH / To Metro Ecole Militaire & Rue Cler ← / ENTER / NAPOLEON'S TOMB / DCH

Army Museum: East Wing

This traces uniforms and weapons through French history, from Louis XIV to World War I. This is interesting for Napoleo-philes.

• *Enter under golden letters and go up to the second floor.*

As you circle this floor, you follow the history and art of French warfare from about 1700 to 1850: Pre-Revolution, Revolution, Napoleon, Restoration.

The "First Republic: 1793–1804" section has early Napoleonic exhibits. In the Salle Boulogne are the emperor's hat and sword. The tent (behind screen) shows his bivouac equipment—a bed with mosquito netting, a director's chair, and a table that you can imagine his generals hunched over, making battle plans.

In the rooms covering "Napoleon and The Empire 1804–1814" (first room: Salle Austerlitz), you'll find the famous portrait by Ingres of Napoleon at his peak of power, stretching his right arm to supernatural lengths. Then comes Napoleon's beloved horse, Le Vizir, who weathered many a campaign and grew old with him in exile (stuffed in a glass case, third room: Salle Eylau).

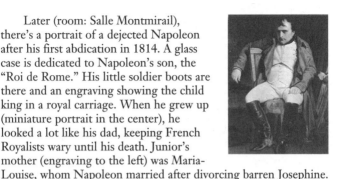

Later (room: Salle Montmirail), there's a portrait of a dejected Napoleon after his first abdication in 1814. A glass case is dedicated to Napoleon's son, the "Roi de Rome." His little soldier boots are there and an engraving showing the child king in a royal carriage. When he grew up (miniature portrait in the center), he looked a lot like his dad, keeping French Royalists wary until his death. Junior's mother (engraving to the left) was Maria-Louise, whom Napoleon married after divorcing barren Josephine.

Napoleon's big white dog suffered the same fate as his horse (in a glass case after you turn the corner into the long blue Corridor de Tarascon). On the wall to the left of the dog hang proclamations of thanks and good-byes Napoleon sent to his soldiers and the French people, announcing the surrender at Waterloo. Directly behind the dog, a shining breastplate shows the effectiveness of British artillery in the Battle of Waterloo. In about the middle of the long blue room, you'll find Napoleon's death mask and a reconstruction of his final home on St. Helena. Picture a lonely man suffering from ulcers sitting here in his nightcap and slippers, playing chess not war.

After the Salle Restauration (the mid-1800s, when France brought back the royalty), the last display before the exit is an American flag in a glass case, honoring General La Fayette of France, who helped George Washington take Yorktown. It has the only English-language description in the entire place.

Army Museum: West Wing

Across the courtyard is a twin museum in the West Wing. The ground floor covers military implements from stone axes to Axis powers. Near the entry, two huge, interesting rooms of armor and medieval weaponry have some good English descriptions.

Hitler-phobes should climb to the second floor, where de Gaulle greets you as if to say, "World War I on your left, World War II on your right." Photos and films spice up the uniforms and guns.

Musée des Plans Reliefs (top floor of West Wing) has 18th-century models of fortified cities (see flier at the door).

The Musée de l'Ordre de la Liberation (free, no English, located in another building back near Napoleon's gravestones) tells the story of the Resistance in World War II. The French refer to World War II as the War of '39–40, but this proud collection makes it clear that the French were busy during the Nazi occupation.

CLUNY MUSEUM TOUR

Musée National du Moyen Age

The name of this museum means the National Museum of the Middle Ages. The Middle Ages don't seem quite so boring as I myself approach middle age. Aside from the solemn religious art, there is some lively stuff here.

Paris emerged on the world stage in the "Middle" Ages, the time between ancient Rome and the Renaissance. Europe was awakening from a thousand-year slumber. Trade was booming, people actually owned chairs, and the Renaissance was moving in like a warm front from Italy.

Orientation

Cost and Hours: 38F, 28F on Sun, covered by museum pass, Wed–Mon 9:15–17:45, closed Tue, tel. 01 53 73 78 00

Getting There: It's at 6 place Paul-Painlevé, near the corner of boulevards St. Michel and St. Germain (Mo: Cluny/La Sorbonne, St. Michel, or Odéon).

Baggage Check: Required and free

Tour Length: One hour

Room 2: The first art you see is not some grim grey crucifixion but a colorful tapestry depicting grape-stomping peasants during the *Vendange* (the annual autumn harvest/celebration). A peasant man treads grapes in a vat, while his wife collects the juice. A wealthy man gives orders. Above that, a peasant with a pimple turns a new-fangled mechanical press. On the right, you'll see the joy of picking—pawns, knights, and queens all working side by side.

Having survived their Y1K crisis, these people realize the world won't end, and they turn their attention to the beauty of the world around them.

Room 3: Colorful woven fabrics were brought back to France by Crusaders, who went off to conquer barbarian infidels but returned with tales of enlightened peoples on the fringes of Europe.

Room 4: Six tapestries in wool and silk show the rich enjoying the simple, secular pleasures of their estate. The humans mingle harmoniously with the trees, flowers, and animals of the glorious physical world.

Reading clockwise: 1) A lady with a puppy spins wool while her husband relaxes with the morning paper; 2) Out in the garden, the sexes mingle unchaperoned by the Church. A lady takes a breath mint while a troubadour puts the moves on her servant; 3) A lady embroiders a pillow; 4) The family picks fruit from their plentiful orchards; 5) A lord goes hunting with his falcon, dog, and servant; 6) A naked woman takes an (obviously chilly) bath, enjoying fruits, jewels, and music—the good things of a world becoming increasingly less sinful.

Room 6: Enter the Dark Ages, when life was harsh and violent, angels and demons made regular appearances, and the Church was your only refuge. Stained glass gave the poor a glimpse of the glories of heaven and served as a visual aid for teaching the illiterate masses. These panels (many from the cathedral of light, Sainte-Chapelle) give us a window into the magical, supernatural, miraculous—and often violent—medieval mind. What were these people thinking?

Reading clockwise around the room, lowest level: 1) The angel Gabriel blasts his horn on Resurrection morning, rousting the grateful dead from their coffins. Notice that Gabriel's royal purple robe is made up of several different pieces of glass—purples, whites, blues—held together with lead; 2) King Herod seems—shocked? pleased?—to see the head of John the Baptist presented to him on a plate by Salome, his dancing stepdaughter; 3) A red-faced, horned, horny demon (with his equally lascivious wolf and henchman) carries off a frightened girl in red to do unspeakable acts; 4) Blond, pious Joseph is sold into slavery to camel merchants by his plotting brothers.

Next wall: 5) Samson is about to pull down the temple... 6) having had his eyes gouged out by Philistines; 7) Slaughter on the battlefield. Men with blood-stained hands and faces hack at each other with golden swords; 8) Aaron, disobeying God and Moses, worships a golden calf; 9) A king on a throne closes his eyes to all this wickedness.

Next wall (with some panels from the first Gothic church, St. Denis): 10) Two monks with prayer books gaze up as one of their brothers disappears into heaven. The Latin inscription (*"hec est via"*) means "This is the way"; 11) Seated Jesus, in a royal purple robe, is consoled by two angels; 12) Theophilus ("Lover of God") has struck a Faustian deal with the Devil and is now feeling buyer's remorse; 13) Sleeping St. Martin is visited by a heavenly vision; 14) Angels in Rock and Roll Heaven.

Last wall: Four apostles—John ("Ioanneus"), James, Peter ("Petrus," with key), and Paul.

Again, what were these people thinking? Bizarre stuff.

Room 8: These 21 stone heads (sculpted 1220–1230) of the kings of Judah from the Bible once decorated the front of Notre-Dame. Then in 1793 an angry and misinformed mob of revolutionaries mistook the kings of Judah for the kings of France and abused and decapitated the statues. (Today's heads on the Notre-Dame statues are reconstructions.) Someone gathered up the heads and buried them in his backyard near the present-day Opéra. There they slept for two centuries, unknown and noseless, until 1977, when some diggers accidentally unearthed them and brought them to an astounded world. Their stoic expressions accept what fate, time, and liberals have done to them.

The statue of Adam that's here is also from Notre-Dame. He's is scrawny and flaccid by Renaissance standards. And it will be another two hundred years before naked Adam can step out from behind that bush.

Room 9: This echoing cavern was a Roman frigidarium. Pretty cool. The museum is located on the site of a Roman bathhouse, a reminder of the Romans' centuries of occupation. After hot baths and exercise in adjoining rooms, ordinary Romans would take a cold dip in the sunken pool (in the alcove), then relax cheek to cheek with notables such as Emperor Julian the Apostate (see his statue), who lived right next door. The 40-foot ceiling is the largest Roman vault in France, and it took the French another thousand years to improve on that crisscross-arch technology. The sheer size of this room, built in A.D. 200 when Rome was at its peak, gives an idea of the epic scale the Romans built on, inspiring Europeans to greatness all during the less-civilized Middle Ages.

The four old square columns (*Pilier des Nautes*) are the oldest man-made objects you'll see from Paris. These pillars once supported a 20-foot-high altar to the king of the gods in the Temple of Jupiter, where Notre-Dame now stands. The carving on one says it was built in the time of the Emperor Tiberius, A.D. 14–37 ("TIB. CAESARE"), paid for by the Parisian boatmen's union (see them holding their canoe-shaped boats).

Room 10: Rome lived on after the Fall. The carved Byzantine ivories (first glass case) show how pagan gods, emperors, and griffins became Christian saints, gargoyles, and icons. Constantinople—the eastern half of the Empire that survived the Fall—preserved Roman tastes and imagery, like the willowy, bare-breasted, dreamy-eyed *Ariadne* (*"Ariane"*) with the sneaky satyr peeking out. In painting, Byzantine gold-background icons inspired medieval altar pieces like others in the room.

Rome also lived on in the Romanesque grandeur of Christian churches like St. Germain-des-Près (the 12-column capitals). The central capital shows Christ in robes on a throne ruling the world as a Roman emperor. These capitals were originally painted, much like the painted wooden statues across the room. Don't leave this room before eyeing the tusk of a narwhal (on the wall), which must have convinced superstitious folk to believe in unicorns.

• *Go upstairs to...*

"The Lady and the Unicorn" Tapestries

As Europeans emerged from the Dark Ages, they rediscovered the beauty of the world around them.

These six mysterious tapestries, designed by an unknown (but probably French) artist before 1500 and woven in Belgium out of wool and silk, are loaded with symbols, some serious, some playful. They have been interpreted many ways, but the series deals with each of the five senses.

• *Moving clockwise around the room...*

Taste: A blond lady takes candy from a servant's dish to feed it to her parakeet. A unicorn and a lion look on. At her feet, a monkey also tastes something, while the little white dog behind her wishes he had some. This was the Age of Discovery, when Columbus and Vasco da Gama spiced up Europe's bland gruel with new fruits, herbs, and spices.

The lion (symbol of knighthood?) and unicorn (symbol of "bourgeois nobility"? purity? fertility?) wave flags with the coat of arms of the family that bought the tapestries—three silver crescent moons in a band of blue.

Hearing: Wearing a stunning dress, the lady plays sweet music on an organ, soothing the savage beasts around her. The pattern and folds of the tablecloth are lovely. Humans and their fellow creatures live in harmony in a blue, enchanted garden filled with flowers, set in a red background.

Sight: The unicorn cuddles up and looks at himself in the lady's mirror, pleased with what he sees. The lion turns away and snickers. As the Renaissance dawns, vanity is a less-than-deadly sin.

Admire the great artistic skill in some of the detail work, such as the necklace and the patterns in her dress. This tapestry had quality control in all its stages—drawing the scene, enlarging and transferring it to a cartoon, and weaving it. Still, the design itself is crude by Renaissance 3-D standards. The fox and rabbits, supposedly in the distance, simply float overhead, as big as the animals at the lady's feet.

Smell: The lady picks flowers and weaves them into a sweet-smelling wreath. On a bench behind, the monkey apes her. The flowers, trees, and animals are exotic and varied. Each detail is exquisite alone, but stepping back, they blend together into pleasing patterns.

Touch: This is the most basic and dangerous of the senses. The lady "strokes the unicorn's horn," if you know what I mean, and the lion gets the double-entendre. Unicorns, a species extinct since the Age of Reason, were so wild that only the purest virgins could entice and tame them. Medieval Europeans were exploring the wonders of love and the pleasures of sex. The Renaissance is coming.

Tapestry #6: The most talked-about tapestry gets its name from the words on our lady's tent: *A Mon Seul Desir* ("To My Sole Desire"). What *is* her only desire?

Is it jewelry, as she grabs a necklace from the jewel box? Or is she putting the necklace away, renouncing material things in order to follow her only desire?

Our lady has tried all things sensual and is now prepared to follow the one true impulse. Is it God? Or love? Her friends the unicorn and lion open the tent doors. Flickering flames cover the tent. Perhaps she's going in to meet the object of her desire. An old, dark age is ending and a new Renaissance world dawns.

VERSAILLES
TOUR

14

paris

If you've ever wondered why your American passport has French writing in it, you'll find the answer at Versailles (vehr-sigh). The powerful court of Louis XIV at Versailles set the standard of culture for all of Europe right up to modern times. Versailles was every king's dream palace, and today if you're planning to visit just one palace in all of Europe, make it Versailles.

Orientation

Cost: 45F; 35F after 15:30, on Sun, and for those over 60 or ages 18–25; under 18 free. To supplement this with a guided tour through the other sections, you'll need to pay the 45F base price (covered by museum pass), then add 25F for a one-hour guided tour, 37F for a 90-minute guided tour (door D for both guided tours), or 30F for a self-guided Walkman-cassette tour (door C)—tours are not covered by the museum pass. Individuals join the longest line (door A1). Those with the Paris Museum Pass (or who took the private guided tour) are allowed in through B without a wait.

The grounds are free, except for fountain-filled Sundays (25F, Sun 11:15–11:35, 15:30–17:00 May–Oct).

The Grand Trianon costs 25F, and the Petit Trianon is 15F; one ticket for both is 30F.

Hours: Tue–Sun 9:00–18:30, closed Mon, 9:00–17:30 Oct–Apr, last entry 30 minutes before closing. (Grand and Petit Trianon open at 10:00 year-round.) In summer, Versailles is especially crowded around 10:00 and 13:00, Tue, and Sun. Remember, the crowds gave Marie-Antoinette a pain in the neck too, so relax and let them eat cake. It's less crowded early and late. To minimize crowds and get a reduced entry ticket, arrive after 15:30, but beware: last guided tours of the day generally depart at 15:00. To beat the crowds and get a tour, arrive by 9:00, when the palace opens. The gardens and palace are great late. On my last visit, at 18:00 I was the only tourist in the Hall of Mirrors... even on a Tuesday.

Getting There: Take the RER-C train (28F round-trip, 30 min) to Versailles R.G. (not Versailles C.H., which is farther from the palace). Trains, usually named "Vick," leave about five times an hour for the palace. Get off at Versailles Rive Gauche (the end of the line). RER-C trains leave from these RER/Métro stops: Invalides (Napoleon's Tomb, Rodin museum), Champ de Mars (Eiffel Tower), Musée d'Orsay, St. Michel (Notre-Dame, Latin Quarter), and Gare d'Austerlitz. Then walk 10 minutes to the palace.

Your Eurailpass covers this inexpensive trip, but it uses up a valuable "flexi" day; consider seeing Versailles on your way in or out of Paris. To get free passage, show your railpass at an SCNF ticket window, for example at the Les Invalides or Musée d'Orsay RER stops, and get a *contremarque de passage*; keep this ticket to exit the system.

When returning from Versailles, look through the windows past the turnstiles for the departure board. Any train leaving Versailles goes as far as downtown Paris (they're marked "all stations until d'Austerlitz").

Information: A helpful tourist information office is across the street from Versailles' R.G. station (tel. 01 39 50 36 22), two information desks are on the approach to the palace, and a very helpful tourist office is at entrance C. The useful brochure, "Versailles Orientation Guide," explains your sight-seeing options. Versailles info: tel. 01 30 84 76 18 or 01 30 84 74 00. WC and phones are near the main entrance.

Cuisine Art: The cafeteria is near the general entrance. Restaurants line the street to the right of equestrian statue. A handy McDonald's is immediately across from the train station (WC without crowds).

Tour Length: Allow two hours for the palace and two for the gardens. Including two hours to cover your round-trip transit time, it's a six-hour day trip from Paris.

Starring: Louis XIV and the Old Regime.

KINGS AND QUEENS AND GUILLOTINES

• *Read this on the train ride out there. Relax, the palace is the last stop.*

Come the Revolution, when they line us up and make us stick out our hands, will you have enough calluses to keep them from shooting you? A grim thought, but Versailles raises questions like that. It's the symbol of the Old Regime, a time when society was divided into rulers and rulees, when you were born to be rich or to be poor. To some it's the pinnacle of civilization, to others

VERSAILLES

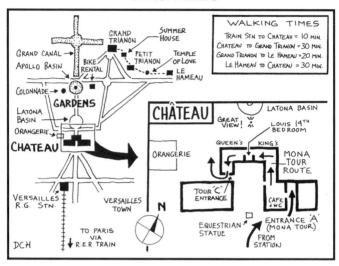

the sign of a civilization in decay. Either way it remains one of Europe's most impressive sights.

Versailles was the residence of the king and seat of France's government for a hundred years. Louis XIV (reigned 1643–1715) moved out of the Louvre in Paris, the previous royal residence, and built an elaborate palace in the forests and swamps of Versailles, 12 miles west. The reasons for the move were partly personal—Louis loved the out-of-doors and disliked the sniping environs of stuffy Paris—and partly political.

Louis was creating the first modern, centralized state. At Versailles he consolidated Paris' scattered ministries so he could personally control policy. More important, he invited to Versailles all of France's nobles so he could control them. Living a life of almost enforced idleness, the "domesticated" aristocracy couldn't interfere with the way Louis ran things. With 18 million people united under one king (England had only 5.5 million), a booming economy, and a powerful military, France was Europe's number one power.

Versailles was also the cultural heartbeat of Europe. Every king wanted a palace like Versailles. Everyone learned French. French taste in clothes, hairstyles, table manners, theater, music, art, and kissing spread across the Continent. That cultural dominance continued to some extent right up to our century.

Louis XIV

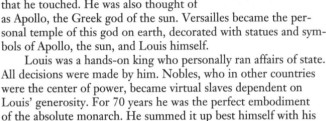

At the center of all this was Europe's greatest king. He was a true Renaissance Man, a century after the Renaissance— athletic, good-looking, a musician, dancer, horseman, statesman, art lover, lover. For all his grandeur, he was one of history's most polite and approachable kings, a good listener who could put even commoners at ease in his presence.

Louis called himself the Sun King, because he gave life and warmth to all that he touched. He was also thought of as Apollo, the Greek god of the sun. Versailles became the personal temple of this god on earth, decorated with statues and symbols of Apollo, the sun, and Louis himself.

Louis was a hands-on king who personally ran affairs of state. All decisions were made by him. Nobles, who in other countries were the center of power, became virtual slaves dependent on Louis' generosity. For 70 years he was the perfect embodiment of the absolute monarch. He summed it up best himself with his famous rhyme—*"L'etat, c'est moi!"* ("The state, that's me!").

Only Two More Louis To Remember

Three kings lived in Versailles during its century of glory. Louis XIV built it and established French dominance. Louis XV, his great-grandson (Louis XIV reigned for 72 years), carried on the tradition and policies but without the Sun King's flair. During Louis XV's reign, France's power abroad was weakening and there were rumblings of rebellion from within.

France's monarchy was crumbling, and the time was ripe for a strong leader to re-establish the old feudal order. They didn't get one. Instead, they got Louis XVI, a shy, meek bookworm, the kind of guy who lost sleep over Revolutionary graffiti... because it was misspelled. Louis XVI married a sweet girl from the Austrian royal family, Marie-Antoinette, and together they retreated into the idyllic gardens of Versailles while revolutionary fires smoldered.

Arriving at Versailles

• *Leave the Versailles R.G. train station and turn right, following signs to "château." Walk about a hundred yards, turn left, and make the grand approach over Europe's biggest cobblestones up to the palace. Enter the iron-work gates and stop at the equestrian statue in the middle of the large court.*

This tour covers the ceremonial center of the palace (The State Apartments) and the extensive grounds.

The only way to see the "King's Apartments"—the actual bedroom and private rooms—is to pay for a guided tour (Tour C). The advantages of Tour C are 1) these rooms are more lavishly  furnished than the ones we'll see; 2) you visit the Opera House, the single most stunning place in the whole complex; and 3) it gets you into the palace (where you can then take this self-guided tour) without standing in line quite so long.

The disadvantages: 1) it costs more; 2) it takes 90 minutes, sometimes with a boring guide; and 3) you see pretty much the same kinds of things covered in this tour. If you do it, do it first to get into the palace quicker. For true Versailles-o-philes, two more guided tours feature the queen's apartments and the royal opera and chapel.
• *Locate the entrances. The self-guided tour we'll take starts at door "A," located on the right side of the courtyard—where the line is. The guided tour (door C) is ahead on the left, in an alleyway. Remember, those with a museum pass can crowd ahead and enter door B. (If the lines are long, get in line now, but orient yourself from the statue.)*

The central palace, the part we'll tour, forms a U around the courtyard in front of you. The right half (King's Wing) is separated from the left half (Queen's Wing) by the Hall of Mirrors ahead of you. Then two long wings shoot out to the right and left (north and south) of this U. In this tour, we'll walk counterclockwise through the U-shaped part on the middle floor.

The Original Château

The part of the palace directly behind the horse in the statue, at the far end of the courtyard, is the original château. Louis XIV's dad used to come out to the forests of Versailles to escape the worries of kingship. Here he built this small hunting lodge. His son spent the happiest times of his boyhood at the lodge, hunting and riding. Louis XIV's three arched bedroom windows (beneath the clock) overlooked the courtyard. Naturally, it faced the rising sun. The palace and grounds are laid out on an east-west axis.

When he became king, Louis XIV spent more and more time here, away from the hubbub of Paris. He expanded the lodge, planted gardens, and entertained guests. The reputation spread about this "Enchanted Island," a kind of Disneyworld for dukes and duchesses. As visitors flocked here, Louis expanded around the original hunting château, attaching wings to create the present U shape. Then, the long north and south wings were built. The total cost of the project has been guesstimated to be half of France's entire GNP for one year.

Think how busy this courtyard must have been 300 years ago. There were as many as 5,000 nobles here at any one time, each with an entourage. They'd buzz from games to parties to amorous rendezvous in sedan-chair taxis. Servants ran about delivering secret messages and roast legs of lamb. Horse-drawn carriages arrived at the fancy gate with their finely dressed passengers, having driven up the broad boulevard that ran direct from Paris. (You can still see the horse stables lining the boulevard.) Incredible as it seems, both the grounds and most of the palace were public territory where even the lowliest peasant could come to gawk. Of course, this meant that there were, then as now, hordes of tourists, pickpockets, and dark-skinned men selling wind-up children's toys.

• *Enter at Entrance A1 (or at B if you have a museum pass) and buy your ticket. After showing your ticket, you first pass through the 21 rooms of the history museum, with paintings on the background of Versailles and its kings.*

Our tour starts upstairs, in the room that overlooks the lavish Royal Chapel. If you took the guided tour, you may spill out here, looking at the upper level of the Royal Chapel.

The State Apartments

Royal Chapel: In the vast pagan "temple" that is Versailles, built to glorify one man, Louis XIV—the Sun King and Apollo on earth—this Royal Chapel is a paltry tip of the hat to that "other" god, the Christian one. It's virtually the first, last, and only hint of Christianity you'll see in the entire complex. Versailles celebrates Man, not God, by raising Louis to almost godlike status, the personification of all good human qualities. In a way, Versailles is the last great flowering of Renaissance humanism and revival of the classical world.

Louis attended mass here every morning. While he sat on the upper level, the lowly nobles below would turn their backs to the altar and look up—worshiping Louis worshiping God. Important religious ceremonies took place here, including the marriage of young Louis XVI to Marie Antoinette.

• *Take a seat in the next room, a large room with a fireplace and a colorful painting on the ceiling.*

Hercules Drawing Room: Pleasure ruled. The main suppers, balls, and receptions were held in this room. Picture elegant party-goers in fine silks, wigs, rouge, and lipstick (and that's just the men) dancing to the strains of Mozart played by a string quartet.

On the wall opposite the fireplace is an appropriate painting, showing Christ in the middle of a Venetian party. The work by Veronese, a gift from the Republic of Venice, was one of Louis' favorites, so they decorated the room around it.

The ceiling painting of Hercules being crowned a god gives the room its name. Hercules (with his club) rides up to heaven on a chariot, where the king of the gods is ready to give him his daughter in marriage. Louis XIV built the room for his own daughter's wedding reception.

• *The following rooms are listed in order. The names of the rooms generally come from the paintings on the ceilings. From here on it's a one-way tour—getting lost is not allowed. Follow the crowds into the small green room with a goddess in pink on the ceiling.*

The King's Wing

Cornucopia Room: If the party in the Hercules Room got too intense, you could always step in here for some refreshments. Silver trays were loaded up with liqueurs, coffee, juice, chocolates, and, on really special occasions, three-bean salad.

The ceiling painting shows the cornucopia of riches poured down on invited guests. Around the edges of the ceiling are painted versions of the king's actual dinnerware and treasures.

Louis himself might be here. He was a gracious host who enjoyed letting his hair down at night. If he took a liking to you, he might sneak you through those doors there (in the middle of the wall), into his own private study, where he'd show off his collection of dishes, medals, jewels, or . . . the *Mona Lisa*, which hung on his wall.

Venus Room: Love ruled at Versailles. In this room, couples would cavort beneath a canopy of golden garlands (on the ceiling) sent down to Earth by the goddess of love to ensnare mortals in love. Notice how a painted garland goes "out" the bottom of the central painting, becomes a gilded wood garland held by a satyr, then back to a painting again—Baroque artists loved to mix their media to fool the eye. Another illusion is in the paintings at both ends of the room, which extend this grand room into mythical courtyards.

Don't let the statue of a confident Louis as a Roman emperor fool you. He started out as a poor little rich kid with a chip on his shoulder. His father had died before he was old enough to rule, and, during the regency period, the French Parliament treated little Louis and his mother like trash. They were virtual prisoners, humiliated in their home (the Louvre), surviving on bland meals, hand-me-down leotards, and pointed shoes. Once he attained power and wealth, there was one topic you never discussed in Louis' presence—poverty. Maybe Versailles was his way of saying, "Living well is the best revenge."

Diana Room: This was the billiards room. Men played on a table that stood in the center of the room, while ladies sat surrounding them on Persian-carpet cushions.

The famous bust of Louis by Bernini (now in the center) shows a handsome, dashing, 27-year-old play-boy-king. His gaze is steady amid his wind-blown cloak and hair. Young Louis loved life. He hunted by day (notice Diana the Huntress on the ceiling) and partied by night.

Games were actually an important part of Louis' political strategy known as "the domestication of the nobility." By distracting the nobles with the pleasures of courtly life, he was free to run the government his way. Billiards, dancing, and concerts were popular, but the biggest distraction was gambling, usually a card game similar to "21." Louis lent money to the losers, making them even more indebted to him. The good life was an addiction, and Louis kept the medicine cabinet well stocked.

Mars Room: Decorated with a military flair, this was the room for Louis' Swiss bodyguards. On the ceiling there's Mars, the Greek god of war, in a chariot pulled by wolves. The bronze cupids in the corners are escalating from love arrows to heavier artillery. Notice the fat walls that hid thin servants who were to be at their master's constant call—but out of sight when not needed. Don't miss the view of the sculpted gardens out the window.

Mercury Room: Louis' life was a work of art, and Versailles was the display case. Everything he did was a public event designed to show his subjects how it should be done. This room served as Louis' official bedroom, where the Sun King would ritually rise each morning to warm his subjects.

The tapestry on the wall shows how this ceremony might have looked. From a canopied bed, Louis would rise, dress, and take a seat for morning prayer. Meanwhile, the nobles (on the left) stand behind a balustrade, in awe of his piety, nobility, and clean socks. When Louis went to bed at night, the nobles would fight over who got to hold the candle while he slipped into his royal jammies. Bedtime, wake-up, and meals were all public rituals.

The two chests that furnish the room, with their curved legs, gilding, and heavy animal feet, are done in the "Louis the XIVth" style. Later furniture found in other rooms is lighter, straighter, and less ornamented. The clock dates from Louis' time. When the cocks crowed at the top of the hour and the temple doors opened, guess who popped out?

Apollo Room: This was the grand throne room. Louis held court from a 10-foot silver-canopied throne on a raised platform placed in the center of the room. (Notice the four metal bolts in the ceiling that once supported the canopy.)

Everything in here reminds us that Louis was not just any ruler, but the Sun King who lights the whole world with his presence. The ceiling shows Apollo in his chariot, dragging the sun across the heavens every day. Notice the ceiling's beautifully gilded frame and Goldfinger maidens.

In the corners are the four corners of the world—all, of course, warmed by the sun. Counterclockwise from above the exit door are 1) Europe, with a sword; 2) Asia, with a lion; 3) Africa, with an elephant; and 4) good old America, an Indian maiden with a crocodile.

The famous portrait by Rigaud over the fireplace gives a more human look at Louis. He's shown in a dancer's pose, displaying the legs that made him one of the all-time dancing fools of kingery. At night, they often held parties in this room, actually dancing around the throne.

Louis (who was 63 when this was painted) had more than 300 wigs like this one, changing them many times a day. This fashion "first" started when his hairline began to recede, then sprouted all over Europe, spreading even to the American colonies in the time of George Washington.

Louis may have been treated like a god, but he was not an overly arrogant man. His subjects adored him because he was a symbol of everything a man could be, the fullest expression of the Renaissance Man.

The War Room: Versailles was good propaganda. It showed the rest of the world how rich and powerful Louis was. One look at this eye-saturating view of the gardens sent visitors reeling.

But France's success also made other countries jealous and nervous. The semicircles on the ceiling show Germany (with the double eagle), Holland (with its ships), and Spain (with a red flag and roaring lion) ganging up on Louis. Two guesses who won. Of course, these mere mortals were no match for the Sun King. The stucco relief on the wall shows Louis on horseback triumphing over his fallen enemies.

But Louis' greatest triumph may be the next room, the one that everybody wrote home about.

The Hall of Mirrors: No one had ever seen anything like this hall when it was opened. Mirrors were still a great luxury at the time, and the number and size of these monsters were astounding. The hall is almost 250 feet long. There are 17 arched mirrors matched by 17 windows with that breathtaking view of the gardens. Lining the hall are 24 gilded candelabras, eight busts of Roman emperors, and eight classical-style statues (seven of them ancient). The ceiling decoration chronicles Louis' military accomplishments, topped off by Louis himself in the central panel (with cupids playing cards at his divine feet), doing what he did best—triumphing.

This was where the grandest festivities were held for the most important ambassadors and guests. The throne could be moved from the Apollo Room and set up at the far end of the hall. Imagine this place filled with guests dressed in silks and powdered wigs, lit by the flames of thousands of candles. The mirrors are a . . . reflection of an age when beautiful people loved to look at themselves. It was no longer a sin to be proud of good looks or fine clothes or to enjoy the good things in life: laughing, dancing, eating, drinking, flirting, and enjoying the view.

From the center of the Hall, you can fully appreciate the epic scale of Versailles. The huge palace (by architect Le Vau), the fantasy interior (Le Brun), and the endless gardens (Le Notre) made Versailles *le* best.

In more recent times, the Hall of Mirrors is where the Treaty of Versailles was signed, ending World War I (and, some say, starting World War II).

• *Enter the small Peace Room and grab a bench.*

The Peace Room: "Louis Quatorze was addicted to wars . . . " but by the end of his life, he was tired of fighting. In this sequel to

the War Room, peace is
granted to Germany, Holland,
and Spain as cupids play with
the discarded cannons, armor,
and swords.

The oval painting above
the fireplace shows 19-year-old
Louis bestowing an olive
branch on Europe. Beside him
is his wife, Marie Therese, cradling their two-year-old twin
daughters. If being a father at 17 seems a bit young, remember
that Louis was married when he was…four.

The Peace Room marks the beginning of the queen's half of
the palace. On Sundays the queen held chamber music concerts
here for family and friends.

• *Enter the first room of the Queen's Wing, with its canopied bed.*

The Queen's Wing

The Queen's Bedchamber: This was the queen's official bedroom. It was here that she rendezvoused with her husband. Two
queens died here. This is where 19 princes were born. The chande-
lier is where two of them were conceived. Just kidding.

True, Louis was not the most faithful husband. There was no
attempt to hide the fact that the Sun King warmed more than one
bed, for he was above the rules of mere mortals. Adultery became
acceptable—even fashionable—in court circles. The secret-looking
doors on either side of the bed were for Louis' late-night liaisons—
they lead straight to his rooms.

Some of Louis' mistresses became more famous and powerful
than his rather quiet queen, but he was faithful to the show of
marriage and had genuine affection for his wife. Their private
apartments were connected, and Louis made a point of sleeping
with the queen as often as possible, regardless of whose tiara he
tickled earlier in the evening.

This room looks like it did in the days of the last queen,
Marie-Antoinette. That's her bust over the fireplace, and the
double eagle of her native Austria in the corners. The big chest to
the left of the bed held her jewels.

The queen's canopied bed is a reconstruction. The bed, chair,
and wall coverings switched with the seasons. This was the cheery
summer pattern.

Drawing Room of the Nobles: The queen's circle of friends
met here, seated on the stools. Discussions ranged from politics to

gossip, food to literature, fashion to philosophy. The Versailles kings considered themselves enlightened monarchs who promoted the arts and new ideas. Folks like Voltaire—a political radical—and the playwright Molière participated in the Versailles court. Ironically, these discussions planted the seeds of liberal thought that would grow into the Revolution.

Queen's Antechamber: This is where the Royal Family dined publicly while servants and nobles fluttered around them, admiring their table manners and laughing at the king's jokes like courtly Paul Shaeffers. A typical dinner consisted of four different soups, two whole birds stuffed with truffles, plus mutton, ham slices, fruit, pastry, compotes, and preserves.

The portrait in the center is of luxury-loving, "Let-them-eat-cake" Marie-Antoinette, who became a symbol of decadence to the French peasants. The portrait at the far end is a P.R. attempt to soften her image, showing her with three of her nine children.

Queen's Guard Room: On October 6, 1789, a mob of revolutionaries—appalled by their queen's taste in wallpaper—stormed the palace. They were fed up with the life of luxury led by the ruling class in the countryside while they were starving in the grimy streets of Paris.

The king and queen locked themselves in. Some of the revolutionaries got access to this upper floor. They burst into this room, where Marie-Antoinette had taken refuge, then killed three of her bodyguards and dragged her and her husband off. (Some claim that, as they carried her away, she sang "Louis, Louis, oh-oh...we gotta go now".)

The enraged peasants then proceeded to ransack the place, taking revenge for the years of poverty and oppression they'd suffered. Marie-Antoinette and Louis XVI were later taken to the place de la Concorde in Paris, where they knelt under the guillotine and were made a foot shorter at the top.

Did the king and queen deserve it? Were the revolutionaries destroying civilization or clearing the decks for a new and better one? Was Versailles progress or decadence?

Coronation Room: No sooner did they throw out a king than they got an emperor. The Revolution established democracy, but it was shaky in a country that wasn't used to it. In the midst of the confusion, the upstart general Napoleon Bonaparte took control and soon held dictatorial powers. This room captures the glory of the Napoleon years, when he conquered most of Europe. In the huge canvas on the left-hand wall, we see him crowning himself emperor of a new, revived "Roman" Empire. (This is a lesser quality copy of a version hanging in the Louvre.)

Catch the portrait of a dashing, young, charismatic Napoleon by the window on the right. This shows him in 1796, when he was just a general in command of the Revolution's army in Italy. Compare this with the portrait next to it from 10 years later—looking less like a revolutionary and more like a Louis. Above the young Napoleon is a portrait of Josephine, his wife and France's empress. In David's *Distribution of Eagles* (opposite the *Coronation*), the victorious general (in imperial garb) passes out emblems of victory to his loyal troops. In *The Battle of Aboukir* (opposite the window), Napoleon looks rather bored as he slashes through a tangle of dark-skinned warriors. His horse, though, has a look of "What are we doing in this mob?! Let's get out of here!" Let's.

• *Pass through a couple of rooms to the exit staircase on your left. The long Battle Gallery ahead of you shows 130 yards of scenes from famous French battles, arranged chronologically clockwise around the gallery. The exit staircase puts you outside on the left (south) side of the palace.*

The Gardens— Controlling Nature

Louis was a divine-right ruler. One way he proved it was by controlling nature like a god. These lavish grounds, so elaborately planned out, pruned, and decorated, showed everyone that Louis was in total command.

• *Exiting the palace into the gardens, veer to the left toward the concrete railing about 75 yards away. You'll pass through flowers and cookie-cutter patterns of shrubs and green cones. Stand at the railing overlooking the courtyard below and the Louis-made lake in the distance.*

The Orangerie: The warmth from the Sun King was so great that he could even grow orange trees in chilly France. Louis had a thousand of these to amaze his visitors. In winter they were kept in the greenhouses (beneath your feet) that surround the courtyard. On sunny days they were wheeled out in their silver planters and scattered around the grounds.

• *From the stone railing, turn about-face and walk back toward the palace, veering left toward the two large pools of water. Sit on the top stair and look away from the palace.*

View down the Royal Drive: This, to me, is the most impressive spot in all of Versailles. In one direction, the palace. Stretching out in the other, the endless grounds. Versailles was laid out along an eight-mile axis that included the grounds, the palace, and the town of Versailles itself, one of the first instances of urban planning since Roman times and a model for future capitals like Washington, D.C., and Brasilia.

Looking down the Royal Drive (also known as "The Green Carpet"), you see the round Apollo fountain way in the distance. Just beyond that is the Grand Canal. The groves on either side of the Royal Drive were planted with trees from all over, laid out in an elaborate grid and dotted with statues and fountains. Of the original 1,500 fountains, 300 remain.

Looking back at the palace, you can see the Hall of Mirrors—it's the middle story, with the arched windows.

• *Stroll down the steps to get a good look at the frogs and lizards that fill the round Latona Basin.*

The Latona Basin: The theme of Versailles is Apollo, the god of the sun, associated with Louis. This round fountain tells the story of the birth of Apollo and his sister Diana. On top of the fountain are Apollo and Diana as little kids with their mother, Latona (they're facing toward the Apollo fountain). Latona, an unwed mother, was insulted by the local peasants. She called on the king of the gods, Zeus (the children's father), to avenge the insult. Zeus swooped down and turned all the peasants into the frogs and lizards that ring the fountain.

• *As you walk down past the basin toward the Royal Drive, you'll pass by "ancient" statues done by 17th-century French sculptors. The Colonnade is hidden in the woods on the left-hand side of the Royal Drive, about three-fourths of the way to the Apollo Basin.*

The Colonnade: Versailles had no prestigious ancient ruins, so they built their own. This prefab Roman ruin is a 100-foot circle of 64 marble columns supporting arches. Beneath the arches are small birdbath fountains. Nobles would picnic in the shade to the tunes of a string quartet, pretending they were the enlightened citizens of the ancient world.

The Apollo Basin: The fountains of Versailles were its most famous attraction, a marvel of both art and engineering. This one was the centerpiece, showing the Sun God—Louis—in his sunny chariot starting his journey across the sky. The horses are half submerged, giving the impression, when the fountains play, of the sun rising out of the mists of dawn. Most of the fountains were only turned on when the king walked by, but this one played constantly for the benefit of those watching from the palace.

All the fountains are gravity powered. They work on the same principle as when you block a hose with your finger to make it squirt. Underground streams feed into smaller pipes at the fountains that shoot the water high into the air.

Looking back at the palace from here, realize that the distance you just walked is only a fraction of this vast complex of buildings, gardens, and waterways. Be glad you don't have to mow the lawn.

The Grand Canal: Why visit Venice when you can just build your own? In an era before virtual reality, this was the next best thing to an actual trip. Couples in gondolas would pole along the waters accompanied by barges with orchestras playing *O Sole Mio.* The Canal is actually cross-shaped, this being the long arm, a mile from end to end. Of course, this too is a man-made body of water with no function other than pleasing.

The Trianon Area—Retreat from Reality
Versailles began as an escape from the pressures of kingship. In a short time, the palace was as busy as Paris ever was. Louis needed an escape from his escape and built a smaller palace out in the tules. Later, his successors retreated still farther into the garden, building a fantasy world of simple pleasures from which to ignore the real world, which was crumbling all around them.
• *You can rent a bike or catch the tourist tram (5/hr, 4 stops), but the walk is half the fun. It's about a 30-minute walk from here to the end of the tour, plus another 30 minutes to walk back to the palace.*

Grand Trianon: This was the king's private residence away from the main palace. Louis usually spent a couple nights a week here, but the two later Louis spent more and more time retreating.

The facade of this one-story building is a charming combination of pink, yellow, and white, a cheery contrast to the imposing Baroque facade of the main palace. Ahead you can see the gardens through the columns. The king's apartments were to the left of the columns.

The flower gardens were changed daily for the king's pleasure—for new color combinations and new "nasal cocktails."

Walk around the palace (to the right) if you'd like, for a view of the gardens and rear facade.
• *Facing the front, do an about-face. The Summer House is not down the driveway but about 200 yards away, along the smaller pathway at about 10 o'clock.*

The Summer House of the French Garden: This small white building with four rooms fanning out from the center was one more step away from the modern world. Here the queen spent summer evenings with family and a few friends, listening to music or playing parlor games. All avenues of *la douceur de vivre*—"the sweetness of living"—were explored. To the left are the buildings of the Menagerie, where cows, goats, chickens, and ducks were bred.

• *Continue frolicking along the path until you run into . . .*

The Petit Trianon: Louis XV developed an interest in botany. He wanted to spend more time near the French Gardens, but the Summer House just wasn't big enough. He built the Petit Trianon

(the "small" Trianon), a masterpiece of neoclassical architecture. This grey, cubical building has four distinct facades, each a perfect and harmonious combination of Greek-style columns, windows, and railings. Walk around it and find your favorite.

Louis XVI and his wife, Marie Antoinette, made this their home base. Marie Antoinette was a sweet girl from Vienna who never quite fit in with the fast, sophisticated crowd at Versailles. Here at the Petit Trianon she could get away and recreate the simple home life she remembered from her childhood. On the lawn outside she installed a merry-go-round.

• *Five minutes more will bring you to . . .*

The Temple of Love: A circle of 12 marble Corinthian columns supporting a dome decorates a path where lovers would stroll. Underneath, there's a statue of Cupid making a bow (to shoot arrows of love) out of the club of Hercules. It's a delightful monument to a society whose rich could afford that ultimate luxury, romantic love. When the Revolution came, I bet they wished they'd kept the club.

• *And finally you'll reach . . .*

Le Hameau—The Hamlet: Marie Antoinette longed for the simple life of a peasant. Not the hard labor of real peasants—who sweated and starved around her—but the fairy-tale world of simple country pleasures. She built this complex of 12 buildings as her own private village.

This was an actual working farm with a dairy, a waterwheel

mill, and domestic animals. The harvest was served at Marie's table. Marie didn't do much work herself, but she "supervised," dressed in a plain white muslin dress and a straw hat.

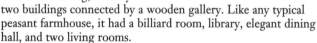

The Queen's House is the main building, actually two buildings connected by a wooden gallery. Like any typical peasant farmhouse, it had a billiard room, library, elegant dining hall, and two living rooms.

Nearby was the small theater. Here Marie and her friends acted out plays far from the rude intrusions of the real world....

• *The real world and the main palace are a 30-minute walk to the southeast. Along the way, stop at the Neptune Basin near the palace, an impressive minilake with fountains, and indulge your own favorite fantasy.*

DAY TRIPS
FROM PARIS

Grand Châteaus • Chartres •
Giverny • Disneyland Paris

GRAND CHÂTEAUS NEAR PARIS

The region around Paris (the Île de France) is dotted with sumptuous palaces. Paris's booming upper class made this the heartland of European château building in the 16th and 17th centuries. Most of these châteaus were lavish hunting lodges—getaways from the big city. The only thing they defended were noble and royal egos.

Consider four very different châteaus:

▲▲▲ **Versailles** - for its history, grandeur, and accessibility (closed Tue)

▲▲▲ **Vaux-le-Vicomte** - for sheer beauty and intimacy (open daily)

▲▲ **Fontainebleau** - for its history and fine interior (closed Tue)

▲ **Chantilly** - for its serene setting (closed Tue)

If you only have time for one château, choose between and Vaux-le-Vicomte and Versailles (see tour on page 142). Except for Versailles, these châteaus are quiet on weekdays. Versailles and Chantilly are covered by the Paris Museum Pass.

Vaux-le-Vicomte

While Versailles is most travelers' first choice for its sheer historic weight, Vaux-le-Vicomte (voh-luh-vee-komt) offers a more lavish interior and a far better sense of 17th-century château life. Sitting in a huge forest with magnificent gardens and no urban sprawl in sight, Vaux-le-Vicomte gave me just a twinge of palace envy.

Vaux-le-Vicomte was the architectural inspiration of Versailles and set the standard for European châteaus to come. The proud owner, Nicolas Fouquet (Louis XIV's finance minister), threw a château-warming party. Louis was so jealous that he arrested his host; took his architect (Le Vau), artist (Le Brun), and

— DAY TRIPS FROM PARIS —

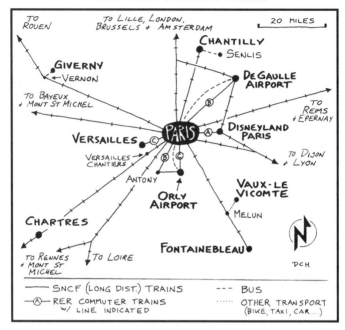

landscaper (Le Notre); and proceeded with the construction of the bigger and costlier (but not necessarily more splendid) palace of Versailles. Monsieur Fouquet is thought to be Alexandre Dumas' man in *The Man in the Iron Mask*, which was recently filmed here.

Vaux-le-Vicomte is expensive to get to (because of cab fare) but a joy to tour. While the gift shop's 25F souvenir booklet has helpful information, the château's rooms have English explanations. Start with the fine horse carriages exhibit (*equipages*) in the old stables. Wax figures and an evocative soundtrack get you in the proper mood. Next, stroll like a wide-eyed peasant across the drawbridge and up the front steps into the château. You'll notice candles. Over 1,300 flicker for candlelit night visits.

As you wander through Fouquet's dream home, you'll understand Louis' jealousy. Versailles was a rather simple hunting lodge when this was built. The furniture is not original— Louis confiscated it from other palaces in the area. You'll see cozy bedrooms upstairs and grand living rooms (billiards room, library, card room, and dining room) downstairs. The kitchen and wine cellar are in the basement. Climb the cupola for a great view.

Survey the garden from
the back steps of the palace.
This was the landscaper Le
Notre's first claim to fame.
This garden was the cutting
edge of sculpted French gardens. He integrated ponds,
shrubbery, flowers, and trees in
a style that would be copied in
palaces all over Europe. Take

the 30-minute walk (one way) to the Hercules viewpoint atop the
grassy hill way in the distance. Rentable golf carts (Club Cars,
80F/45 minutes) make the trip easier. Picnics are not allowed. (A
good indoor/outdoor café-restaurant, offering reasonable prices
and good salads, is inside the first courtyard.)

Cost and Hours: Steep 59F admission. Open daily 10:00–
13:00, 14:00–18:00 (gardens don't close midday) Mar–Oct, less
in winter, tel. 01 64 14 41 90. The impressive fountains run
15:00–18:00 the second and last Sat of each month (Apr–Oct).

Candlelit Visits: These *visites aux chandelles* are worth the
80F entry, but remember, it doesn't get dark until 22:00 in late
May, June, and early July (open 20:30–24:00 on Thu and Sat
May–Oct and holidays except July 14—call to ask about any
upcoming holidays—there are many in May; the last train to Paris
leaves Melun at about 22:00).

Getting to Vaux-le-Vicomte: To reach Vaux-le-Vicomte
by car or by a train and taxi combination, head for the city of
Melun. RER trains run to Melun from Paris' Gare du Nord and
Chatelet stations. Faster Banlieue trains leave from Paris' Gare
de Lyon (43F one way, hrly, 35 min). Taxis make the 10-minute
drive from Melun's station to Vaux-le-Vicomte (85F weekdays,
100F eves and Sun, taxi phone number posted above taxi stand).
Ask a staff person at the château to call a cab for your return or
schedule a pickup time with your driver. In either direction, split
the fare with other travelers. Melun's tourist office is a block
from the train station, past the ugly concrete building (Tue–Sat
10:00–12:00, 14:00–18:00, closed Sun–Mon, 2 avenue Gallieni,
tel. 01 64 37 11 31).

Adding Fontainebleau: Vaux-le-Vicomte and Fontainebleau
can be combined into a full, though manageable, day trip by car or
train from Paris (except on Tue, when Fontainbeau is closed).
Fontainebleau is 12 minutes by train from Melun.

Sleeping near Vaux-le-Vicomte: The modern but handy
IBIS Hotel is between Melun and the château (Db-300F, less on
weekends, tel. 01 60 68 42 45, fax 01 64 09 62 00).

Château of Fontainebleau

Fontainebleau's history rivals Versailles'. Another glamorous hunting lodge, many French kings have called this home. Napoleon welcomed the Pope here during his coronation celebration, and it was here that he abdicated his rule when exiled to Elba in 1814. General Patton set up headquarters at this château on his way to Berlin.

While Vaux-le-Vicomte and Versailles are French designed, Fontainebleau (fohn-ten-bloh) was built a century earlier by an Italian. The palace you see today is largely the work of Renaissance King Francois I. Inspired by his travels through Renaissance Italy, he hired Italian artists to build his palace.

Orient with a quick visit to the château information room, with its huge model of the château (first door on your right in the grand courtyard). The palace entry is next door. Your ticket provides access to the Chinese rooms and the main rooms of the château. Napoleon buffs will enjoy the little museum of Napoleonic history, which requires an additional ticket and a guided tour (16F; ask about tour times at the ticket window). While 20F guidebooklets give excellent room-by-room descriptions, you'll find adequate English explanations posted throughout.

Start downstairs with the small but impressive Chinese collection of the Empress of Napoleon III, then climb to the main rooms of the palace. Highlights include the stunning Renaissance hall of Francois I, the opulent dance hall with piped-in music (Salle de bal), Napoleon's throne room, and the Trinity chapel. The idyllic gardens, designed a century later by the landscaper Le Notre, are worth a stroll. Rent a rowboat in the *étang des carpes* (carp pond), or walk its path for a good view of the château complex.

Cost and Hours: 35F, Wed–Mon 9:30–18:00, closed Tue, Wed–Mon 9:30–12:30, 14:00–17:00 Nov–May, last entry 45 minutes before closing.

Getting to Fontainebleau: Catch a train from Paris' Gare de Lyon in the direction of Montereau (about 50F one way, 40 min) to the Fontainebleau-Avon station, where a bus goes to the château (Cars Verts, 4/hrly, 10F, pay on board; schedules posted in English). Taxis to the château cost about 40F, and to Vaux-le-Vicomte about 200F.

Town of Fontainebleau: The helpful tourist office has hiking maps, bike rental information, and hotel listings (daily

9:30–17:30, at the bus stop a block from château, tel. 01 60 74 99 99). You can rent a bike at the station, the tourist office, or, best, at La Petite Reine (95F/day, 60F/half day, 32 rue des Sablons, tel. 01 64 74 57 57).

Sleeping in Fontainebleau: One block from the château gardens, **Hotel Legris et Parc***** is a quiet, dreamy getaway with a courtyard and an elegant restaurant (Db-460–570F, CC:VMA, 36 rue Paul Seramy, tel. 01 64 22 24 24, fax 01 64 22 22 05). **Hotel a la Carpe d'Or**** is simpler (Db-250–320F, 7 rue d'Aven, tel. 01 64 22 28 64, fax 01 64 22 39 95).

Château of Chantilly

Chantilly (shan-tee-yee), 35 minutes north of Paris, floats serenely on a reflecting pond amid grand gardens. Unfortunately, the château interior is disappointing. Its best rooms are visitable only on a boring French-only guided tour, and the fine works of art in the picture galleries are poorly displayed. Still, Chantilly can be a pleasant experience if approached in the right way. Allow most of a day for Chantilly.

This extravagant hunting palace was destroyed during the Revolution. Today's château was largely rebuilt during the 19th century. It's divided into two parts: the painting gallery (with paintings by Raphael, Titian, Poussin, Delacroix, and others) and the private apartments (requiring a French-language tour). The highlight of the otherwise dull apartments is the first stop, the Prince's library, lined with more than 13,000 books and beautiful copies of pages from *Les Tres Riches Heures du Duc du Berry*, a much-admired 15th-century illuminated manuscript.

The gardens immediately behind the château are formal and austere. With your back to the château, follow the signs to the right to *le Hameau*. This little hamlet was the prototype for the more famous *hameau* at Versailles (and has a delightful garden café). Just beyond is a small kiosk, offering a tethered hot-air balloon ride (45F, great view) and electric-boat trips along the canals (35F, tel. 03 44 57 35 35).

Cost and Hours: 39F (included with museum pass), 17F for gardens only, Wed–Mon 10:00–18:00, closed Tue, off-season 10:30–12:45, 14:00–17:00, tel. 01 44 57 08 00.

Live Horse Stables (*Les Ecuries Vivant*): The Prince de Conde believed he'd be reincarnated as a horse, so he built this opulent horse château for his next go round. You'd have to have similar beliefs to pay the 50F entry for this albeit impressive and thorough horse museum, featuring 40 live horses in their stables and a daily demonstration, generally at 15:30, more often in summer (Wed–Mon 10:30–17:30 Apr–Oct , also open Tue in summer; Mon, Wed–Fri 14:00–17:30, Sat–Sun 10:30–17:30 Nov–Mar, tel. 03 44 57 13 13).

Getting to Chantilly: Leave from Paris' Gare du Nord for Chantilly-Gouvieux. The RER, Banlieue, and main train lines all leave from different tracks (about 45F one way, nearly hrly, 35 min; ask at info booth near track 18 for next departure). Upon arrival in Chantilly, confirm your return times (fewer trips on weekends). The tourist office is a block in front of the station. To get to the château, it's a 40F taxi ride, a free bus ride on a rare city bus (ask at the station), or a 30-minute walk (follow signs, stay on path, turn right before BP gas station, cross grass field, "château" in distance is stables, château is beyond that).

The well-preserved medieval town of Senlis is a 30-minute bus ride (110F taxi) from the Chantilly station.

MORE DAY TRIPS FROM PARIS

▲▲▲**Chartres**—In 1194 a terrible fire destroyed the church at Chartres with the much-venerated veil of Mary. With almost unbelievably good fortune, the monks found the veil miraculously preserved in the ashes. Money poured in for the building of a bigger and better cathedral decorated with 2,000 carved figures and some of France's best stained glass. The cathedral feels too large for the city because it was designed to accommodate huge crowds of pilgrims. One of those pilgrims, an impressed Napoleon, declared after a visit in 1811: "Chartres is no place for an atheist." Rodin called it "the Acropolis of France." British Francophile Malcolm Miller calls it home and gives superb "Appreciation of Gothic" tours Monday through Saturday, usually at noon and 14:45 (verify times in advance, no tours off-season, occasionally his assistant gives the tour, call tourist office at tel. 02 37 18 26 26). Each 40F tour is different; many stay for both tours. Tours begin at the gift shop inside the church (daily 7:00–19:00).

Explore Chartres' pleasant city center and discover the picnic-friendly park behind the cathedral. The helpful tourist office, next to the cathedral, has a map with a self-guided tour of Chartres (daily 9:30–18:45). Chartres is a one-hour train trip from Gare Montparnasse (about 75F one way, 10/day, last train on Sat departs at about 19:00). Upon arrival, confirm your return schedule to avoid an unplanned night in Chartres.

▲**Giverny**—From 1883 to 1926, Monet spent 43 of his most

creative years at Giverny (zhee-vayr-nee), the Camp David of Impressionism. Monet's gardens and home are split by a busy road. Buy your ticket, walk through the gardens, and take the underpass into the artist's famous lily-pad land. The path leads you over the Japanese Bridge, under weeping willows, and past countless scenes that leave artists aching for an easel. For Monet fans, it's strangely nostalgic. Back on the other side, continue your visit with a wander through his more robust and structured garden and his mildly interesting home. The jammed gift shop at the exit is the actual skylit studio where Monet painted his water lily masterpieces.

While lines may be long and tour groups may trample the flowers, true fans still find magic in those lily pads. Avoid crowds by arriving after 15:00 (35F, 25F for gardens only, Tue–Sun 10:00–18:00 Apr–Oct, closed Mon and off-season, tel. 02 32 51 94 65).

Take the Rouen-bound train from Paris' Gare St. Lazare station to Vernon (about 140F round-trip, long gaps in service, know schedule before you go). To get from the Vernon train station to Monet's garden (4 km away), take the Vernon-Giverny bus (5/day, scheduled to meet most trains), hitch, taxi (60F), or rent a bike at the station (60F, busy road). Get return bus times from the ticket office in Giverny or ask them to call a taxi. Big tour companies do a Giverny day trip from Paris for around $60.

The new **American Impressionist Art Museum** (100 yards from Monet's place, toward Vernon) is devoted to American artists who followed Claude to Giverny (same price and hours as Monet's home).

▲▲**Disneyland Paris**—Europe's Disneyland is a remake of California's, with most of the same rides and smiles. The main difference is that Mickey Mouse speaks French (and you can buy wine with your lunch). My kids went ducky. It's worth a day if Paris is handier than Florida or California. Crowds are a problem (tel. 01 64 74 30 00 for the latest). If possible, avoid Saturday, Sunday, Wednesday, school holidays, and July and August. After dinner, crowds are gone. Food is fun but expensive. I smuggle in a picnic.

Disney brochures are in every Paris hotel. The RER (about 43F each way, hrly, direct from downtown Paris to Marne-la-Vallee in 30 minutes) drops you right into the park. The last train back into Paris leaves shortly after midnight. (220F for adults, 170F for kids 3–11, 25F less in spring and fall. Daily 9:00–23:00 late Jun–early Sept and Sat–Sun off-season, shoulder-season Mon–Fri 9:00–19:00, off-season 10:00–18:00, tel. 01 60 30 60 30, fax 01 60 30 60 65 for park and hotel reservations.)

To sleep reasonably near the park, try Hotel Sante Fe (780F family rooms, less off-season; ask about hotel-and-park deal).

SLEEPING
IN PARIS

I've focused on three safe, handy, and colorful neighborhoods: rue
Cler, Marais, and Contrescarpe. For each, I list good hotels, helpful hints, and restaurants (see Eating in Paris). At the end of the
chapter, you'll find accommodations listed for Versailles, as well as
apartments in Paris for longer stays.

Reserve ahead for Paris, the sooner the better. Conventions
clog Paris in September (worst), October, May, and June. In
August, when Paris is quiet, some hotels offer lower rates to fill
their rooms (if you're planning to visit Paris in the summer, the
extra expense of an air-conditioned room can be money well
spent). Most hotels accept telephone reservations, require prepay-
ment with a credit-card number, and prefer a faxed follow-up to
be sure everything is in order. For more information, see "Making
Reservations" in this book's introduction.

French hotels are rated by stars (indicated in this book by an *).
One star is simple, two has most of the comforts, and three is, for
this book, plush. If you need maximum comfort, go for the three-
star places.

Old, characteristic, budget Parisian hotels have always been
cramped. Retrofitted with elevators, toilets, and private showers (as
most are today), they are even more cramped. Even three-star hotel
rooms are small and often not worth the extra expense in Paris.
Some hotels include the hotel tax (*taxe de sejour*, about 5F per
person per day), though most will add this to your bill. Two- and
three-star hotels are required to have an English-speaking staff.
Nearly all hotels listed will have someone who speaks English.

Quad rooms usually have two double beds. Recommended
hotels have an elevator unless otherwise noted. Because rooms
with double beds and showers are cheaper than rooms with twin
beds and baths, room prices vary within each hotel.

You can save as much as 100F by finding the increasingly rare room without a private shower, though some hotels charge for down-the-hall showers. Breakfasts cost 20F to 50F extra. Café or picnic breakfasts are cheaper, but hotels usually give unlimited coffee. Singles (except for the rare closet-type rooms that fit only one twin bed) are simply doubles used by one person. They rent for only a little less than a double.

Get advice for safe parking from your hotel (consider long-term parking at Orly airport and taxi in). Meters are free in August. Garages are plentiful (90–140F per day, with special rates through some hotels). Self-serve Laundromats are common; ask your hotelier for the nearest one (*Où est un laverie automatique?*; ooh ay uh lah-vay-ree auto-mah-teek).

Sleep Code

S = Single, **D** = Double/Twin, **T** = Triple, **Q** = Quad, **b** = bathroom, **t** = toilet only, **s** = shower only, **CC** = Credit Card (**V** = Visa, **M** = MasterCard, **A** = Amex), * = French hotel rating system (0–4 stars). **Exchange rate:** 6F = about $1

Sleeping in the Rue Cler Neighborhood

(7th *arrondissement*, Mo: École Militaire, zip code: 75007)
Rue Cler, a villagelike pedestrian street, is safe, tidy, and makes me feel like I must have been a poodle in a previous life. How such coziness lodged itself between the high-powered government/business district and the expensive Eiffel Tower and Invalides areas, I'll never know. Living here ranks with the top museums as one of the city's great experiences. (But if you're into nightlife, consider one of the other two neighborhoods I list.)

Rue Cler is the glue that holds this pleasant neighborhood together. From here you can walk to the Eiffel Tower, Napoleon's Tomb, the Seine, and the Orsay and Rodin Museums. The first six hotels listed below are within Camembert-smelling distance of rue Cler; the others are within a 5- to 10-minute stroll. Warning: The first two hotels are popular with my readers.

Hôtel Leveque** is ideally located, with an air-conditioned lobby (with ice machine), helpful staff, and a singing maid. Its well-designed and comfortable rooms have ceiling fans, cable TV, hair dryers, direct phone lines, safes, and French modem outlets (S-300F, Db-400–470F, Tb-580F, breakfast-40F, 1st breakfast free for readers of this book, CC:VMA, 29 rue Cler, tel. 01 47 05 49 15, fax 01 45 50 49 36, www.hotel-leveque.com, e-mail: info@hotelleveque.com).

RUE CLER HOTELS

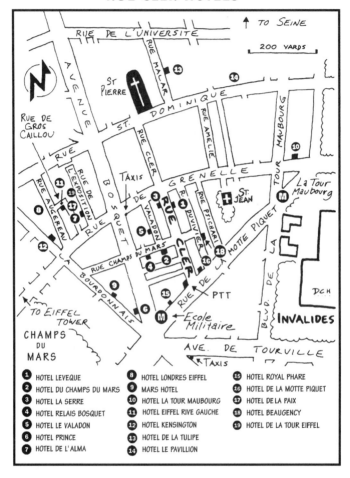

1. HOTEL LEVEQUE
2. HOTEL DU CHAMPS DU MARS
3. HOTEL LA SERRE
4. HOTEL RELAIS BOSQUET
5. HOTEL LE VALADON
6. HOTEL PRINCE
7. HOTEL DE L'ALMA
8. HOTEL LONDRES EIFFEL
9. MARS HOTEL
10. HOTEL LA TOUR MAUBOURG
11. HOTEL EIFFEL RIVE GAUCHE
12. HOTEL KENSINGTON
13. HOTEL DE LA TULIPE
14. HOTEL LE PAVILLION
15. HOTEL ROYAL PHARE
16. HOTEL DE LA MOTTE PIQUET
17. HOTEL DE LA PAIX
18. HOTEL BEAUGENCY
19. HOTEL DE LA TOUR EIFFEL

Hôtel du Champ de Mars**, with charming, pastel rooms and helpful English-speaking owners Françoise and Stephane, is an even cosier rue Cler option. The hotel has a Provence-style small-town feel from top to bottom. Rooms are comfortable and a very good value. Single rooms can work as tiny doubles (Sb-390F, Db-430–460F, Tb-550F, CC:VMA, cable TV, hair dryers, etc., 30 yards off rue Cler at 7 rue du Champ de Mars, tel. 01 45 51 52 30, fax 01 45 51 64 36, www: adx.fr/hotel-du-champ-de-mars, e-mail: stg@club-internet.fr).

Hôtel la Serre*, across the street from Hôtel Leveque, is a simple hotel with basic rooms, thin walls, tattered hallways, and a charming location. Beware: you'll likely be asked to pay before seeing the room, and refunds are rarely given (D-280F, Db-280–450F, Tb-550F, CC:VM, cable TV in some rooms, 24 rue Cler, tel. 01 47 05 52 33, fax 01 40 62 95 66, e-mail: laserre@easynet.fr).

Hôtel Relais Bosquet*** is bright, spacious, and a bit upscale, with sharp, comfortable rooms (Sb-600–800F, Db-650–1,000F, most at 850F, more expensive rooms with air-con, CC:VMA, 19 rue de Champ de Mars, tel. 01 47 05 25 45, fax 01 45 55 08 24, www.relaisbosquet.com).

Hotel Beaugency*** offers basic three-star comfort for less (Sb-680F, Db-730F, Tb-830F, includes buffet breakfast, 21 rue Duvivier, tel. 01 47 05 01 63, fax 01 45 51 04 96).

Hôtel Le Valadon**, on a quiet street with spacious, tired rooms, has a shy, Parisian cuteness (Db-410–530F, Tb-560F, CC:VMA, 16 rue Valadon, tel. 01 47 53 89 85, fax 01 44 18 90 56).

The following listings are a 5- to 10-minute walk west of rue Cler and are listed in order of proximity.

Hotel Prince**, just across avenue Bosquet from the École Militaire Métro stop, has fair-value rooms, many overlooking a busy street (Db-450–510F, CC:VMA, 66 avenue Bosquet, tel. 01 47 05 40 90, fax 01 47 53 06 62).

Hotel le Tourville**** is the most classy and expensive of my Paris listings. This four-star gem is surprisingly intimate and friendly, from its welcoming lobby to its air-conditioned pink-pastel rooms (small standard Db-690–900F, superior Db-800–1,150F, Db with private terrace-1,450F, 16 avenue de Tourville, Mo: École Militaire, tel. 01 47 05 62 62, fax 01 47 05 43 90, e-mail: hotel@tourville.com).

Hotel de Turenne**, with small air-conditioned rooms, is a good value when it's hot (Sb-360F, Db-430–500F, Tb-590F, extra bed-60F, CC:VM, 20 avenue de Tourville, tel. 01 47 05 99 92, fax 01 45 56 06 04, e-mail: hotel.turenne.paris7@wanadoo.fr).

Hôtel de l'Alma*** is another good value, with 32 small but pleasant look-alike rooms, all with cable TV and minibar (Sb-450F, Db-500F, includes breakfast, no triples but a kid's bed can be moved in for free, CC:VMA, 32 rue de l'Exposition, tel. 01 47 05 45 70, fax 01 45 51 84 47).

Hotel Londres Eiffel*** is just renovated with cheerful attention to detail and a melt-in-your-chair breakfast room. Its cozy rooms are thoughtfully appointed, and the owners seem eager to please (Sb-545F, Db-645F, Tb-825F, extra bed-70F, CC:VMA, 40 percent deposit required to reserve, 1 rue Augerau, tel. 01 45 51 63 02, fax 01 47 05 28 96, www.Londres-Eiffel.com).

Mars Hôtel** is a great, truly Old World value, with formal owners, a richly decorated lobby, spacious rooms and bathrooms, and a beam-me-up-Maurice, coffin-sized elevator. Front rooms are noisier but have views of the Eiffel Tower (large Sb-320F, Db-380F, Twin/b-480F, CC:VM, 117 avenue de la Bourdonnais, tel. 01 47 05 42 30, fax 01 47 05 45 91).

Hôtel Kensington** has just been renovated into a reasonable value with rude staff (Sb-315F, Db-400–500F, extra bed-80F, CC:VMA, 79 avenue de La Bourdonnais, tel. 01 47 05 74 00, fax 01 47 05 25 81).

Hotel de la Bourdonnais***, more famous for its highly respected restaurant, is a superb three-star hotel. This perfectly Parisian place mixes Old World elegance with top-notch service, comfortable and spacious rooms, and pleasant public spaces (Sb-630F, Db-720F, Tb-780F, Qb-830F, CC:VMA, cable TV, 111 aveune de la Bourdonnais, tel. 01 47 05 45 42, fax 01 45 55 75 54, e-mail: labourdonnais@adi.fr).

Hôtel de la Tulipe**, two blocks from rue Cler toward the river, charges top franc for its tastefully done rooms surrounding a wood-beamed lounge and a leafy courtyard (Db-650–680F, no elevator, 33 rue Malar, tel. 01 45 51 67 21, fax 01 47 53 96 37, www.hoteldelatulipe.com).

Hôtel La Tour Maubourg*** lies alone five minutes east of rue Cler, just off the Esplanade des Invalides, and feels like a slightly faded, elegant manor house with spaciously comfortable Old World rooms. It overlooks a cheery green lawn within sight of Napoleon's tomb (Sb-700F, Db-800–900F, suites for up to four 1,100F–1,800F, includes breakfast with freshly squeezed juice, prices reduced from mid-Jul–mid-Aug, CC:VM, immediately at La Tour Maubourg Métro stop, 150 rue de Grenelle, tel. 01 47 05 16 16, fax 01 47 05 16 14, e-mail: victor@worldnet.fr).

These places are lesser values but, in this fine area, acceptable last choices: **Hôtel de la Tour Eiffel**** (Sb-350F, Db-400F, Tb-520F, CC:VMA, 17 rue de l'Exposition, tel. 01 47 05 14 75, fax 01 47 53 99 46, Muriel speaks English); the quiet but tired **Hotel le Pavillon**, with a small courtyard (Db-460F, family suites-575F, 54 rue St. Dominique, tel. 01 45 51 42 87, fax 01 45 51 32 79); **Hôtel Royal Phare**** (Db-310–410F, CC:VMA facing École Militaire Métro stop, 40 avenue de la Motte Piquet, tel. 01 47 05 57 30, fax 01 45 51 64 41); **Hôtel la Motte Piquet**** (Db-370–470F, duplex suites-650–760F, CC:VM, 30 avenue de la Motte Piquet, tel. 01 47 05 09 57, fax 01 47 05 74 36); and simple, quiet **Hôtel de la Paix**, run agreeably by English-speaking Noël (S-180F, Ds-330F, Db-350F, Tb-480F, no elevator, 19 rue du Gros-Caillou, tel. 01 45 51 86 17, fax 01 45 55 93 28).

Rue Cler Orientation

✪ See the Rue Cler Walk, page 68, for more information on this area. Become a local at a rue Cler café for breakfast or join the afternoon crowd for *une bière pression* (a draft beer). On rue Cler you can eat and browse your way through a street full of tart shops, delis, cheeseries, and colorful outdoor produce stalls. (For cafés and restaurants, see Eating in Paris.) For an after-dinner cruise on the Seine, it's just a short walk to the river to the Bâteaux Mouches (see "Organized Tours" in the Orientation chapter).

Your neighborhood tourist office is at the Eiffel Tower (daily 11:00–18:00 May–Sept, tel. 01 45 51 22 15). The Métro station (École Militaire) and a post office are at the end of rue Cler, on avenue de la Motte Piquet, and there's a handy SNCF office under the *Aerogare* at Invalides Métro, where you can get information, buy tickets, and make seat reservations. Michelle runs the Laundromat Pressing Laverie with panache (daily 7:00–22:00, 16 rue Cler) or try Lav Club at 27 rue Augereau (same hours). The nearest Internet access is at Cyber Cube (5 rue Mignon, tel. 01 53 10 30 50). Taxi stands are on avenue de Tourville at avenue la Motte Piquet (near Métro stop) and on avenue Bosquet at rue St. Dominique. The Banque Populaire (across from Hôtel Leveque) changes money and has an ATM. Rue St. Dominique is the area's boutique-browsing street. The Epicerie de la Tour grocery shop is open until midnight at 197 rue de Grenelle.

The American Church and College is the community center for Americans living in Paris (65 quai d'Orsay, tel. 01 40 62 05 00). The interdenominational service at 11:00 on Sunday, the coffee hour after church, and the free Sunday concerts (18:00) are a great way to make some friends and get a taste of émigré life in Paris. Stop by and pick up copies of the *Free Voice*, for a monthly review of Paris entertainment, and *France-U.S.A. Contacts*, for information on housing and employment through the community of 30,000 Americans living in Paris.

Afternoon *boules* (lawn bowling) on the esplanade des Invalides is a relaxing spectator sport. Look for the dirt area to the upper right as you face the Invalides.

Helpful bus routes: Line 69 runs along rue St. Dominique and serves Les Invalides, Orsay, Louvre, Marais, and Père-Lachaise cemetery. Line 92 runs along avenue Bosquet and serves the Arc de Triomphe and Champs-Élysées in one direction and the Montparnasse tower in the other. Line 49 runs on boulevard La Tour Maubourg and serves St. Lazare and Gare du Nord stations.

MARAIS HOTELS

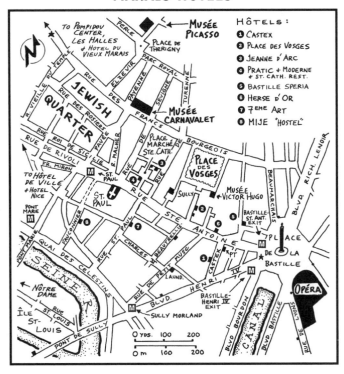

Sleeping in the Marais Neighborhood

(4th *arrondissement*, Mo: St. Paul or Bastille, zip code: 75004)
Those interested in a more Soho/Greenwich Village, gentrified, urban-jungle locale should make the Marais their Parisian home. The Marais is a more happening area than rue Cler. It's narrow medieval Paris at its finest, where elegant stone mansions sit side by side with trendy bars and antique shops. Only 15 years ago it was a forgotten Parisian backwater, but now the Marais is one of Paris' most popular residential and shopping areas. For us, the Marais runs from Hôtel de Ville to the Bastille (a 15-minute walk), with most hotels located a few blocks north of the main east-west drag, rue de Rivoli/St. Antoine. It's about 15 minutes on foot from any hotel in this area to Notre-Dame, Île St. Louis, and the Latin Quarter. The St. Paul Métro stop puts you right in the heart of the Marais, while the Hôtel de Ville stop serves its western end and the Bastille stop serves its eastern limit.

Hôtel Castex** This clean and cheery place is a great value, with comfortable rooms, many stairs, and a good location on a relatively quiet street. Reserve by phone and leave your credit-card number. The security code marked on your key opens the front door after hours (Ss-240F, Sb-260–290F, Ds-320–340F, Db-340–360F, Tb-460F, CC:VM, no elevator, 5 rue Castex, just off place de la Bastille and rue St. Antoine, Mo: Bastille, tel. 01 42 72 31 52, fax 01 42 72 57 91, e-mail: info@castexhotel.com). The owners have another good-value hotel two Métro stops away in a less appealing location that often has rooms when others don't: **Hotel de la Republique**** (Db-380F, elevator, cable TV, 31 rue Albert Thomas, 75010, Mo: Republique, tel. 01 42 39 19 03, fax 01 42 39 22 66).

Grand Hôtel Jeanne d'Arc**, a cozy, welcoming place with thoughtfully appointed rooms, is ideally located for connoisseurs of the Marais. Rooms on the street are noisy until the bars close. Sixth-floor rooms have a view. Corner rooms are wonderfully bright in the city of light (small Db-310F, Db-425–500F, Tb-540F, Qb-600F, extra bed-75F, CC:VM, 3 rue Jarente, Mo: St. Paul, tel. 01 48 87 62 11, fax 01 48 87 37 31).

Hotel Bastille Speria*** feels family run while offering a serious business-type service. Its spacious lobby and 45 newly redecorated rooms are modern, cheery, and pastel, and it's English-language friendly, from the *Herald Tribune*s in the lobby to the history of the Bastille in the elevator (Sb-540–580F, Db-600–680F, Tb-790F, extra bed-110F, CC:VMA, 1 rue de la Bastille, Mo: Bastille, tel. 01 42 72 04 01, fax 01 42 72 56 38, e-mail: speria@micronet.fr).

Hotel Lyon-Mulhouse**, on a busy street just off place de la Bastille, is a good value, with pleasantly renovated rooms and helpful owners (Sb-355–425F, Db-360–530F, Tb-545–575F, Qb-600–640F, CC:VM, elevator, 8 boulevard Beaumarchais, tel. 01 47 00 91 50, fax 01 47 00 06 31).

Hôtel de la Place des Vosges**, quasi-classy with a linoleum/antique feel, is ideally located on a quiet street (Sb-385F, Db-560–610F, CC:VMA, 12 rue de Biraque, just off the elegant place des Vosges and just as snooty, Mo: St. Paul, tel. 01 42 72 60 46, fax 01 42 72 02 64).

Hotel des Chevaliers***, one block northwest of place des Vosges, offers small but pleasant and comfortable rooms, with all the comforts from hair dryers to cable TV. Rooms off the street are quiet (Db-640–830F, CC:VMA, skip overpriced breakfast, 30 rue de Turenne, Mo: St. Paul, tel. 01 42 72 73 47, fax 01 42 72 54 10).

Hotel de la Herse D'Or is industrial-strength, three-coats-of-paint simple, with a good location, tortured floor plan, and hard-to-beat prices for its relatively comfortable rooms (S-170F,

D-210F, Db-290F, showers-10F, no elevator, 20 rue St. Antoine, Mo: Bastille, tel. 01 48 87 84 09, fax 01 48 87 94 01).

Hotel Sévigné** provides basic and cramped two-star comfort at fair prices with the cheapest breakfast in Paris—20F (Sb-355F, Db-375–470F, CC:VM, 2 rue Malher, Mo: St. Paul, tel. 01 42 72 76 17, fax 01 42 78 68 26).

Hôtel Pratic* has a slightly Arabic feel in its cramped lobby. The tidy, just-renovated rooms are simple but not confined, stairs are many, and it's right on a great, people-friendly square. Single rooms are tiny (S-230F, D-280F, Ds-310F, Db-400F, no elevator, 9 rue d'Ormesson, Mo: St. Paul, tel. 01 48 87 80 47, fax 01 48 87 40 04).

The bare-bones and dumpy **Hôtel Moderne**, next to Hôtel Pratic, might be better than a youth hostel if you need privacy. The only thing *moderne* about it is the name, which is illegible on the broken sign (S-150, D-190F, Db-320F, 3 rue Caron, Mo: St. Paul, tel. 01 48 87 97 05).

Hôtel de 7ème Art**, two blocks south of rue St. Antoine, is a Hollywood nostalgia place, run by young, friendly Marais types, with a full service café/bar and Charlie Chaplin murals. Most rooms are average, but the few large double rooms at 670F are very nice (Sb-300F, Db-420–490F, extra bed-100F, CC:VMA, 20 rue St. Paul, Mo: St. Paul, tel. 01 44 54 85 00, fax 01 42 77 69 10).

Grand Hotel du Loiret**, just north of rue de Rivoli, is a fair enough value, has laid-back management, and is popular with American students (S-190F, D-220F, Db-310–410F, Tb-400F, Qb-500F, CC:VMA, 8 rue des Garcons Mauvais, Mo: Hôtel de Ville, tel. 01 48 87 77 00, fax 01 48 04 96 56).

Hôtel de Nice** is a cozy "Marie Antoinette does tie-dye" place with lots of thoughtful touches on the Marais' busy main drag. Twin rooms, which cost the same as doubles, are roomier but on the street side (effective double-pane windows) (Sb-380F, Db-500F, Tb-630F, CC:VM, 42 bis rue de Rivoli, Mo: Hôtel de Ville, tel. 01 42 78 55 29, fax 01 42 78 36 07).

Hotel de la Bretonnerie***, three blocks north and east of the Hotel de Ville, is my favorite Marais splurge. It has elegant decor, tastefully decorated and spacious rooms with an antique, open-beam coziness, and an efficient, helpful staff (standard Db-650F, Db with character-795F, the standard Db has enough character for me, fine family-friendly suites-990F, CC:VMA, between rue du Vielle du Temple and rue des Archives at 22 rue Sainte Croix de la Bretonnerie, Mo: Hôtel de Ville, tel. 01 48 87 77 63, fax 01 42 77 26 78, www.HoteldelaBretonnerie.com).

Hotel Caron de Beaumarchais***, an 18th-century Marais manor house, charges top prices for its charming and comfortable rooms (Db-730–810F, CC:VMA, air-con, 12 rue Vielle du Temple, Mo: Hôtel de Ville, tel. 01 42 72 34 12, fax 01 42 72 34 63).

Hotel de Vieux Marais**, tucked away on a quiet street two blocks east of the Pompidou Center, offers spotless and fairly spacious rooms with air-conditioning, pleasing decor, and we-try-harder owners (Db-660–690F, extra bed-100F, CC:VM, just off rue des Archives at 8 rue du Platre, Mo: Hôtel de Ville, tel. 01 42 78 47 22, fax 01 42 78 34 32).

MIJE Youth Hostels: The *Maison Internationale de la Jeunesse des Étudiants* (MIJE) runs three classy old residences clustered a few blocks south of rue St. Antoine. Each offers simple, clean, single-sex, one- to four-bed rooms for families and travelers under the age of 30. Prices are per person; you can pay more to have your own room or be roomed with as many as three others (Sb-220, Db-170F, Tb-150F, Qb-140F, includes breakfast but not towels—which you can get from a machine, rooms are locked from 12:00–15:00 and at 01:00). MIJE Fourcy (cheap dinners, 6 rue de Fourcy, just south of the rue Rivoli), MIJE Fauconnier (11 rue Fauconnier), and the best, MIJE Maubisson (12 rue des Barres), share the same number (tel. 01 42 74 23 45, fax 01 40 27 81 64, e-mail: MIJE@wanadoo.fr) and Métro stop (St. Paul). Reservations are accepted.

Marais Orientation

✪ See the Marais Walk, page 64, for more information on this area. The nearest tourist offices are in the Louvre and Gare de Lyon (arrival level, daily 8:00–20:00, tel. 01 43 43 33 24). The Banque de France changes money, offering good rates and sometimes long lines (Mon–Fri 9:00–11:45, 13:30–15:30, at the corner where rue St. Antoine hits place de la Bastille). Most banks and other services are on the main drag, rue de Rivoli/St. Antoine. You'll find one taxi stand on the north side of rue St. Antoine, where it meets rue Castex, and another on the south side of St. Antoine, in front of the St. Paul church.

The new Bastille opera house, Promenade Plantée Park, place des Vosges (Paris' oldest square), the Jewish Quarter (rue des Rosiers), and the Pompidou Center are all nearby. Be sure to stroll into place des Vosges after dark. The massive budget department store is BHV, next to Hôtel de Ville. Marais post offices are on rue Castex and on the corner of rues Pavée and Francs Bourgeois.

Helpful bus routes: Line 69 on rue St. Antoine takes you to the Louvre, Orsay, Rodin, and Napoleon's Tomb and ends at the Eiffel Tower. Line 86 runs down boulevard Henri IV, crossing Île St. Louis and serving the Latin Quarter along boulevard St. Germain. Line 96 runs on rues Turenne and Francois Miron and serves the Louvre and boulevard St. Germain (near Luxembourg Gardens). Line 65 serves the train stations Austerlitz, Est, and Nord from place de la Bastille.

Sleeping in the Contrescarpe Neighborhood
(5th *arrondissement*, Mo: place Monge, zip code: 75005)
This lively, colorful neighborhood reminds me of Montmartre without all the tourists. It's just over the hill from the Latin Quarter, behind the Panthéon, and is a 15-minute walk from Notre-Dame, Île de la Cité, Île St. Louis, Luxembourg Gardens, and the grand boulevards St. Germain and St. Michel. Most of our hotels are on or very near rue Mouffetard, the spine of this area, running from the perfectly Parisian place Contrescarpe south to rue Bazelles. Rue Mouffetard is a market street by day and touristy restaurant row by night. Fewer tourists sleep here, and I find the hotel values generally better than in most other neighborhoods. These hotels are listed in order of proximity to the Seine river (and Notre-Dame).

The low-energy, bare-bones **Hôtel du Commerce** is run by Monsieur Mattuzzi, who must be a pirate gone good. This 300-year-old place (with vinyl that looks it) is a great rock-bottom deal and as safe as any dive next to a police station can be. In the morning, the landlady will knock and chirp, *"Restez-vous?"* (Are you staying tonight?) (S-130F, D-150F, Ds-170F, Ts-220F, Qs-280F, showers-15F, no elevator, takes no reservations, call at 10:00 and he'll say *"oui"* or *"non,"* 14 rue de La Montagne Ste. Geneviève, Mo: Maubert-Mutualité, tel. 01 43 54 89 69).

Hôtel Central* is unpretentious, with a charming location, a steep and slippery castlelike stairway, simple rooms (all with showers, though toilets are down the hall), so-so beds, and plenty of smiles. It's a fine budget value (Ss-165–190F, Ds-240–270F, no elevator, 6 rue Descartes, Mo: Cardinal Lemoine, tel. 01 46 33 57 93).

Hôtel des Grandes Écoles*** is simply idyllic. A short alley leads to three buildings protecting a flowering garden courtyard, preserving a tranquility rare in a city this size. This romantic place is deservedly popular, so call well in advance (Db-530–690F, Tb-630–780F, Qb-680–890F, extra bed-100F, 75 rue de Cardinal Lemoine, Mo: Cardinal Lemoine, tel. 01 43 26 79 23, fax 01 43 25 28 15, www.hotel-grandes-ecoles.com, mellow Marie speaks English).

The hotels listed below lie on or at the bottom of the rue Mouffetard and may have rooms when others don't.

Y&H Hostel offers a great location, easygoing English-speaking management, and basic but acceptable hostel-like conditions (110F-beds in four-bed rooms, 130F-beds in double rooms, 15F for sheets, rooms closed 11:00–17:00, though reception stays

CONTRESCARPE HOTELS

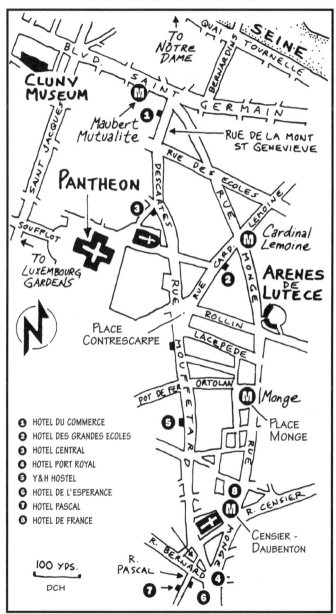

- **1** HOTEL DU COMMERCE
- **2** HOTEL DES GRANDES ECOLES
- **3** HOTEL CENTRAL
- **4** HOTEL PORT ROYAL
- **5** Y&H HOSTEL
- **6** HOTEL DE L'ESPERANCE
- **7** HOTEL PASCAL
- **8** HOTEL DE FRANCE

open, curfew at 02:00, reservations must be paid in advance, 80 rue Mouffetard, Mo: Cardinal Lemoine, tel. 01 45 35 09 53, fax 01 47 07 22 24).

Hotel de l'Esperance**, located at the bottom of rue Mouffetard, gives you nearly three stars for the price of two. It's quiet, fluffy, and comfortable, with thoughtfully appointed rooms complete with canopy beds, hair dryers, cable TV, and a flamboyant owner (Sb-440F, Db-450–520F, Tb-600F, CC:VM, 15 rue Pascal, Mo: Censier-Daubenton, tel. 01 47 07 10 99, fax 01 43 37 56 19).

Hotel Pascal*, across from Hotel Esperance, is a fair value, with a Byzantine floor plan, simple rooms, small double beds, and miniscule bathrooms. It won't win any cleanliness awards (S-205F, Db-305F, Tb-455F, Qb-605–705F, funky studio lofts with kitchenettes-460F, CC:VMA, 20 rue Pascal, Mo: Censier-Daubenton, tel. 01 47 07 41 92, fax 01 47 07 43 80, e-mail: hotpascal@mail .opsion.fr).

Hotel de France**, on a busy street, has fine, modern rooms and hardworking, helpful owners. The best and quietest rooms are *sur le cour* (on the courtyard) (Sb-380F, Db-410–440F, CC:VM, 108 rue Monge, Mo: Censier-Daubenton, tel. 01 47 07 19 04, fax 01 43 36 62 34, e-mail: hotel.de.fce@wanadoo.fr).

Hotel Port Royal* is well run, with a small, pleasant courtyard and incredibly clean, comfortable rooms at very fair prices. Ask for a room off the street (S-195–240F, D-245F, Db-365–450F, 8 boulevard de Port Royal, Mo: Gobelins, climb the stairs from rue Pascal to the busy boulevard Port Royal, tel. 01 43 31 70 06, fax 01 43 31 33 67).

Contrescarpe Orientation

The nearest tourist office is at the Louvre Museum. The post office (PTT) is between rue Mouffetard and rue Monge at 10 rue de l'Épée du Bois. Place Monge hosts a colorful outdoor market on Wednesday, Friday, and Sunday until 13:00. The street market at the bottom of rue Mouffetard bustles daily except Monday (Tue–Sat 8:00–12:00, 15:30–19:00, Sun 8:00–12:00, 5 blocks south of place Contrescarpe), and the lively place Contrescarpe hops in the afternoon and evening until the wee hours.

The flowery Jardin des Plantes park is close by and great for afternoon walks, as are Luxembourg Gardens, which easily justify the 15-minute walk. The doorway at 49 rue Monge leads to a hidden Roman arena (Arènes de Lutèce). Today, *boules* players occupy the stage while couples cuddle on the seats. Walk to the Panthéon, admire it from the outside (it's not worth paying to go in), and go into the wildly beautiful St. Étienne-du-Mont church.

Sleeping near Paris, in Versailles
(zip code: 78000)

For a laid-back alternative to Paris within easy reach of the big city by RER train (5/hrly, 30 min), with easy, safe parking, Versailles can be a good overnight stop.

Hôtel Le Cheval Rouge**, built in 1676 as Louis XIV's stables, now houses tourists comfortably. It's a block behind place du Marché in a quaint corner of town on a large quiet courtyard (Ds-290F, Db-350–400F, extra bed-90F, CC:VMA, 18 rue Andre Chenier, tel. 01 39 50 03 03, fax 01 39 50 61 27).

Ibis Versailles**, a slick business-class place, offers all the comfort with none of the character (Db-420F, CC:VMA, across from RER station, 4 avenue du Gen. de Gaulle, tel. 01 39 53 03 30, fax 01 39 50 06 31).

Hotel du Palais, facing the RER station, has cheap and handy beds; ask for a quiet room off the street. It's a pink and funky place, dumpy enough to lack even one star but proud enough to put candy on the beds (D-180F, Ds-220F, Db-250F, extra person-30F, miles of stairs, 6 place Lyautey, tel. 01 39 50 39 29, fax 01 39 50 80 41).

Hotel d'Angleterre** is a peaceful, well-worn old place near the palace; first-floor rooms are best (Db-300, 350, and 450F, extra bed-100F, CC:VMA, 2 rue de Fontenay, tel. 01 39 51 43 50, fax 01 39 51 45 63).

For Longer Stays

Staying a week or longer? Consider the advantage of renting a furnished apartment. Complete with a small, equipped kitchen and living room, this option is family friendly. Among the many English-speaking organizations ready to help, the following have proven most reliable; their Web sites are generally excellent and essential to understanding your options.

Paris Appartements Services rents studios and one-bedroom apartments in the Opéra, Louvre, and Marais neighborhoods (2 rue d'Argout, 75002 Paris, tel. 01 40 28 01 28, fax 01 40 28 92 01, www.paris-appartements-services.fr).

Apalachee Bay is British owned and offers an extensive range of carefully selected, furnished apartments (21 rue de Madrid, 75008 Paris, tel. 01 42 94 13 13, fax 01 42 94 83 01, www.apalachee.com).

Locaflat offers accommodations ranging from studios to five-room apartments (tel. 01 43 06 78 79, fax 01 40 56 99 69, http://locaflat.com).

EATING
IN PARIS

Paris is France's wine and cuisine melting pot. While it lacks a style of its own, it draws from the best of France. Paris could hold a gourmet's Olympics and import nothing.

Picnic or go to bakeries for quick take-out lunches, or stop at a café for a lunch salad or *plat du jour*, but linger longer over dinner. You can eat well, restaurant style, for 100F to 140F. Your hotel can usually recommend nearby restaurants in the 70F to 100F range. Remember, cafés and simple small restaurants are happy to serve a *plat du jour* (garnished plate of the day, about 60F) or a cheflike salad (45–60F) day or night. Famous places are often overpriced, overcrowded, and overrated. Find a quiet neighborhood and wander, or follow a local recommendation. Restaurants open for dinner around 19:00, and small local favorites get crowded after 21:00. To save piles of francs, review the budget eating tips in this book's introduction. Our recommendations are centered around the same three great neighborhoods for which we list hotels so that you can come home exhausted after a busy day of sight-seeing and have a good selection of restaurants right around the corner. And evening is a fine time to explore any of these delightful neighborhoods even if you're sleeping elsewhere.

Carve time out of your busy day to relax at a Parisian café. Sound good? See "Les Grand Cafés de Paris," at the end of this chapter.

Restaurants

The Parisian eating scene is kept at a rolling boil. Entire books (and lives) are dedicated to the subject. If you are traveling outside of Paris, save your splurges for the countryside, where you'll enjoy better cooking for less money. I've listed places that conveniently fit a busy sightseeing schedule and places near recommended hotels. If you'd like to visit a district specifically to eat, consider the many romantic restaurants that line the cozy Île St. Louis' main street and the colorful, touristic-but-fun string of eateries along rue Mouffetard behind the Panthéon (in the Contrescarpe neighborhood). Beware: Many restaurants close Sunday and Monday.

Cafeterias and Picnics

Many Parisian department stores have huge supermarkets hiding in the basement and top-floor cafeterias offering not really cheap but low-risk, low-stress, what-you-see-is-what-you-get meals.

For lunch and dinner picnics, you'll find handy little groceries (*épiceries*) and delis (*charcuteries*) all over town but rarely near famous sights. Good picnic fixings include roasted chicken, drinkable yogurt, fresh bakery goods, melons, and exotic pâtés and cheeses. Great take-out deli-type foods like gourmet salads and quiches abound. *Boulangeries* make good, cheap miniquiches and sandwiches. While wine is taboo in public places in the United States, it's *pas de problème* in France.

Romantic Picnic Spots: My favorite dinner-picnic places are the pedestrian bridge (Pont des Arts) across from the Louvre, with unmatched views and plentiful benches; the Champ de Mars park under the Eiffel Tower; and the western tip of Île St. Louis, overlooking Île de la Cité. Bring your own dinner feast and watch the riverboats or the Eiffel Tower light up the city for you. The Palais Royal (across the street from the Louvre) is a good spot for a peaceful, royal picnic, as is the little triangular Henry IV Park on the west tip of Île de la Cité. For lunch picnics with great people watching, try the Pompidou Center (by the *Homage to Stravinsky* fountain), the elegant place des Vosges (closes at dusk), the gardens at the Rodin Museum, and Luxembourg Gardens.

Eating in the Rue Cler Neighborhood

Restaurants: The rue Cler neighborhood isn't famous for its restaurants. That's why I enjoy eating here. Several small family-run places serve great dinner menus for 100F and *plats du jour* for 60F to 80F. My first three recommendations are easygoing cafés, ideal if what you want is a light dinner (good dinner salads) or more substantial but simple meals.

Café du Marché, with the best seats, coffee, and prices on rue Cler, serves hearty salads and good 60F *plats du jour* for lunch or dinner to a trendy, mainly French crowd. Arrive before 19:30 or wait at the bar. A chalkboard listing the plates of the day—each a meal—will momentarily be hung in front of you (at the corner of rue Cler and rue Champ de Mars). You'll find the same menu and prices with better indoor seating at their other restaurant,

Le Comptoir du Septième, at the École Militaire Métro stop (39 avenue de la Motte Piquet, tel. 01 45 55 90 20).

Café La Roussillon also offers relaxed, good bistro fare at reasonable prices with fewer crowds; their *La Planche* is a board of cheese, meats, pâtés, and some salad (at the corner of rue de Grenelle and rue Cler).

Café le Bosquet is owned by the nicest guy in Paris. Jean Francois will make you feel welcome at his classic Parisian café (many good choices, including French onion soup, 98F menu, 46 avenue Bosquet, tel. 01 45 51 38 13).

Leo le Lion, run by Mimi for 20 years, is an easygoing place. A warm, charming souvenir of old Paris, it's popular with locals. The 115F menu comes with a first course that could feed two for an entire meal (but no splitting) and a fully garnished main course (closed Sun, 23 rue Duvivier, tel. 01 45 51 41 77).

Vegetarians will appreciate the Mediterranean cuisine at **7ème Sud**, (closed Sun, at the corner of rue de Grenelle and rue Duvivier).

Thoumieux, the neighborhood's classy, traditional Parisian brasserie, is deservedly popular (basic 82F and fine 160F menu, complete *à la carte*, 79 rue St. Dominique, tel. 01 47 05 49 75).

For a special dinner, survey the handful of fine places that line rue de l'Exposition one block west of avenue Bosquet between rue St. Dominique and rue de Grenelle: **Restaurant La Serre**, at #29, has fun ambience, usually great food, but an unpredictable staff (*plats* 50–70F, daily from 19:00, often a wait after 21:00, good onion soup and duck specialties, tel. 01 45 55 20 96, Marie-Alice and intense Philippe speak English). **Le P'tit Troquet**, across the street at #28, is delightfully Parisian, popular with locals, and ideal for a last-night splurge—allow 160F per person for dinner (closed Sun–Mon, tel. 01 47 05 80 39). The quieter **La Maison de Cosima** at #20 offers refined, creative French cuisine and excellent 100F and 150F menus that include a vegetarian option (closed Sun, tel. 01 45 51 37 71, run by friendly Helene). The softly lit tables and red velvet chairs of **Auberge du Champ de Mars**, at #18, draw a romantic crowd (closed Mon). For top *à la carte*-only cuisine, locals reserve early for the charmingly situated **La Fontaine de Mars** (allow 250F per person with wine, 129 rue St Dominique, tel. 01 47 05 46 44). Around the corner, just off rue de Grenelle, the friendly and unpretentious **La Varanque** is a good budget bet, with 60F *plats* and an 80F menu (27 rue Augereau, tel. 01 47 05 51 22).

Ambassade du Sud-Ouest, a wine and food boutique/restaurant, specializes in southwestern French cuisine such as *daubes de canard*—duck meatballs (46 avenue de la Bourdonnais, tel. 01 45 55 59 59). **L'Ami de Jean** is a lively place to sample Basque cuisine (closed Sun, 27 rue Malar, tel. 01 47 05 86 89).

Picnicking: The rue Cler is a moveable feast that gives "fast food" a good name. The entire street is clogged with connoisseurs of good eating. Only the health-food store goes unnoticed. A festival of food, the street is lined with people whose lives seem to be devoted to their specialty: stacking polished produce, rotisserie chicken, crêpes, or cheese squares.

For a magical picnic dinner at the Eiffel Tower, assemble it in no fewer than six shops on rue Cler and lounge on the best grass in Paris (the police don't mind after dusk), with the dogs, Frisbees, a floodlit Tower, and a cool breeze in the Parc du Champ de Mars.

The **crêpe stand** next to Café du Marché does a wonderful top-end dinner crêpe for 25F. An Asian deli, **Traiteur Asie** (across from Hôtel Leveque, another across from Hôtel du Champ de Mars), has tasty low-stress, low-price take-out treats. Its two tables offer the cheapest place to sit, eat, and enjoy the rue Cler ambience. For quiche, cheese pie, or a pear/chocolate tart, try **Tarte Julie's** (takeout or stools, 28 rue Cler). The elegant **Flo Prestige** *charcuterie* (at the École Militaire Métro stop) is open until 23:00 and offers mouthwatering meals to go. **Real McCoy** is a little shop selling American food and sandwiches (194 rue de Grenelle). A good, small late-night grocery is at 197 rue de Grenelle.

The bakery (*boulangerie*) on the corner of rue Cler and rue de Champ de Mars is the place for a fresh baguette, sandwich, tiny quiche, or *pain au chocolat*, but the almond croissants at the *boulangerie* on rue de Grenelle at rue Cler make my day. The bakery at 112 rue St. Dominique is in a league by itself and worth the detour, with classic decor and tables to enjoy your café au lait and croissant.

Cafés and Bars: If you want to linger over coffee or a drink at a sidewalk café, try **Café du Marché** (see above), **Petite Brasserie PTT** (opposite #53 rue Cler, local workers eat here), or **Café le Bosquet** (46 avenue Bosquet, tel. 01 45 51 38 13). **Café La Roussillon**, peopled and decorated belle epoche, also offers a quintessential café experience (see above, corner of rue de Grenelle and rue Cler). **Le Sancerre** wine bar/café is wood-beam warm and ideal for a light lunch or dinner (great omelettes), or just for a glass of wine after a long day of sightseeing, served by the owner, whose cheeks are the same color as his wine (open until 21:30, 22 avenue Rapp, tel. 01 45 51 75 91). **Maison Altmayer** is a hole-in-the-wall place for a quiet drink (9:00–19:30, 6 rue du Gros Caillou, next to Hôtel Eiffel Rive Gauche). Cafés like this originated (and this one still functions) as a place where locals enjoyed a drink while their heating wood, coal, or gas was prepared for delivery.

Nightlife: This sleepy neighborhood is not the place for night owls, but there are four notable exceptions: **Café du Marché** and its brother, **Le Comptoir du Septième** (both listed above), hop with a Franco-American crowd until about midnight. **O'Brien's Pub** is a relaxed, Parisian rendition of an Irish pub (77 St. Dominique). **Café Thoumieux** is a sophisticated place with big screen sports and a trendy young crowd (4 rue de la Comete, Mo: Latour Maubourg).

Eating in the Marais Neighborhood

The windows of the Marais are filled with munching sophisticates and crowd-pleasing eateries. And with Île St. Louis a short walk away (see below), those sleeping in the Marais have a great selection of good-value restaurants.

You'll find several good places at place du Marché Ste. Catherine, a tiny square just off rue St. Antoine between the St. Paul Métro stop and place des Vosges. **Le Marais Ste. Catherine** is a good value (110F menu, daily from 19:00, nonsmoking, extra seating in candlelit cellar, 5 rue Caron, tel. 01 42 72 39 94), but if it's warm, I prefer the outdoor tables at **Le Marché** (2 place Marché Ste. Catherine, tel. 01 42 77 34 88). Just off the square, **L'Auberge de Jarente** offers a well-respected and traditional cuisine (120F menu, closed Sun–Mon, 7 rue Jarente, tel. 01 42 77 49 35).

Dinners under the candlelit arches of the place des Vosges are *très* romantic: **Nectarine**, at #16, serves fine salads, quiches, and reasonable *plats du jour* daily and nightly, while **Ma Bourgogne** is where locals go for a splurge (open daily, at northwest corner, no CC, reserve dinner ahead, tel. 01 42 78 44 64).

For a fast, cheap change of pace, eat at (or take out from) the Chinese/Japanese **Delice House**. Two can split 200 grams of chicken curry (or whatever, 28F) and rice (20F). There's lots of seating, with pitchers of water at the ground-floor tables and a roomier upstairs (81 rue St. Antoine, open until 21:00).

The Crêperie, near Hôtel Castex, serves a 60F menu, and the cozy restaurant **de la Poste** (13 rue Castex) offers inexpensive, light meals (both closed Sun). I like **La Bastoche**'s warm ambience and good 100F menu (7 rue St. Antoine, tel. 01 48 04 74 34). Across the street, **Le Paradis de Fruit** serves salads and organic foods to a young local crowd (on the small square at rues Tournelle and St. Antoine).

Near Hôtel du 7ème Art, try the romantic and traditional **L'Excuse** for a worthwhile splurge (190F menu, closed Sun, 14 rue Charles V, call ahead, tel. 01 42 77 98 97). Across the street, **L'Énoteca** (wine bar) has lively and reasonable Italian cuisine in a relaxed, open setting (closed Sun, 20 rue St. Paul, tel. 01 42 78 91 44).

Wine lovers shouldn't miss the superb Burgundy wines and exquisite, though limited, menu selection at **Au Bourguignon du Marais** (closed Sat–Sun, 52 rue Francois Miron, call by 19:00 to reserve, tel. 01 48 87 15 40).

Vegetarians appreciate the excellent cuisine at the popular **Picolo Teatro** (closed Mon, 6 rue des Ecouffes, tel. 01 42 72 17 79) and **L'As du Falafel**, serving the best falafel on rue Rosier at #34.

Le Petit Gavroche, closer to Hôtel de Ville at 15 Ste. Croix de la Bretonniere, attracts a local crowd in search of a simple, good-value meal (tel. 01 48 87 74 26).

Picnicking: Picnic at the peaceful place des Vosges (closes at dusk). Hobos stretch their francs at the supermarket in the basement of the **Monoprix** department store (close to place des Vosges on rue St. Antoine), and connoisseurs prefer the gourmet take-out places all along rue St. Antoine, such as **Flo Prestige** (open until 23:00, on the tiny square where rue Tournelle and rue St. Antoine meet). A few small grocery shops are open until 23:00 on rue St. Antoine (near intersection with rue Castex). An open-air market, held Sunday morning, is just off place de la Bastille on boulevard Richard Lenoir.

For a cheap breakfast, try the tiny *boulangerie/pâtisserie* where the hotels buy their croissants (coffee machine, 3F; 10F baby quiches, 5F *pain au chocolat*, one block off place de la Bastille, corner of rue St. Antoine and rue de Lesdiguieres).

Cafés and Bars: The trendiest cafés and bars are clustered on the rues Vielle du Temple, Archives, and Ste. Croix de la Bretonniere (open generally till 02:00), and are popular with gay men. **Hamman** is an ethnically hip cybercafé (4 rue des Rosiers, on place du Marché Ste. Catherine.) The *très* local wine bar at **Au Temps des Cerises** is amiably run and a welcoming if smoky place (rue du Petit Musc and rue de Cerisaie, around the corner from Hôtel Castex).

Nightlife: Le Vieux Comptoir is tiny, lively, and not too hip (just off place des Vosges at 8 rue Biraque). **La Perla** is trendy with Parisian yuppies in search of the perfect margarita (26 rue Francois Miron). **The Quiet Man** is a traditional Irish pub with happy hour from 16:00 to 20:00 (5 rue des Haudriettes).

Eating in the Contrescarpe Neighborhood

The rue Mouffetard and rue du Pot-de-Fer are lined with inexpensive, lively, and forgettable restaurants. Study the many menus, compare crowds, then dive in. **Le Jardin d'Artemis** is one of the better values on rue Mouffetard at #34 (89F menu). **Restaurant l'Epoque**, a fine neighborhood restaurant, has excellent menus at 78F and 118F (one block off place

Contrescarpe at 81 rue Cardinal Lemoine, tel. 01 46 34 15 84).
Savannah Café's creative Mediterranean cuisine attracts a loyal,
artsy crowd (27 rue Descartes, tel. 01 43 29 45 77). **Le Jardin
des Pates** is popular with vegetarians. They serve pastas and
salads at fair prices (4 rue Lacepede, near Jardins des Plantes,
tel. 01 43 31 50 71). **Le Villaret** serves excellent cuisine from
France's southwest (menus from 110F, closed Sun, near recommended Hotel Central at 44 rue Montagne Ste. Genevieve,
tel. 01 46 34 26 46).

Cafés: Brasserie La Chope, a classic Parisian brasserie right
on the place Contrescarpe, is popular until the wee hours. Sit
indoors or outdoors for good people watching. **Café Le Mouffetard** is in the thick of the street market hustle and bustle (at the corner of rue Mouffetard and rue de l'Arbalete). The outdoor tables at
Cave de la Bourgogne (at the bottom of rue Mouffetard, on rue
Bazelles) are picture-perfect. At **Café de la Mosque** you'll feel like
you've been beamed to Morocco. In this purely Arab café, order a
mint tea, pour in the sugar, and enjoy the authentic interior and
peaceful outdoor terrace (2 rue Daubenton, behind mosque).

Eating in the Latin Quarter
La Petite Bouclerie is a cozy place with classy family cooking
(70F menu, closed Mon, 33 rue de la Harpe, center of touristy
Latin Quarter, tel. 01 43 54 18 03). The popular **Restaurant
Polidor** is an old turn-of-the-century-style place, with *cuisine
bourgeois*, a vigorous local crowd, and a historic toilet. Arrive at
19:00 to get a seat in the restaurant (65F *plat du jour*, 100F menus,
41 rue Monsieur le Prince, midway between Odéon and Luxembourg Métro stops, tel. 01 43 26 95 34).

Eating on Île St. Louis
Cruise the island's main street for a variety of good options, from
cozy *crêperies* to romantic restaurants. Sample Paris' best sorbet
and ice cream at any place advertising *les glaces Berthillon*; the
original Berthillon shop is at 31 rue St. Louis en l'Île.

All listings below are on rue St. Louis en l'Île and listed from
the Île de la Cité end. **Café Med**, at #73, serves inexpensive salads,
crêpes, and lighter menus in a cheery setting. **La Castafiore**, at
#51–53, serves fine Italian dishes in a cozy setting (160F menu).
Farther down lie two fine romantic splurges: **Le Tastevin** (150F
and 220F menus, #46, tel. 01 43 54 17 31) and, next door, **Au
Gourmet de l'Isle** (150F and 185F menus, closed Mon–Tue).

For crazy, touristy cellar atmosphere and hearty, fun food,
feast at **La Taverne du Sergeant Recruiter**. The "Sergeant
Recruiter" used to get young Parisians drunk and stuffed here,

then sign them into the army. It's all-you-can-eat, including wine and service, for 190F (daily from 19:00, #41, tel. 01 43 54 75 42). There's a near-food-fight clone next door at **Nos Ancêtres Les Gaulois** ("Our Ancestors the Gauls," 190F, daily at 19:00, tel. 01 46 33 66 07).

Elegant Dining on the Seine
La Plage Parisienne is a nearly dress-up riverfront place popular with locals, serving elegant, healthy meals at good prices (Port de Javel-Haut, Mo: Javel, tel. 01 40 59 41 00).

LES GRANDS CAFÉS DE PARIS
Please see "Café Culture" in this book's introduction for help in approaching Parisian cafés.

History of Cafés in Paris
The first café in the Western world was in Paris—established in 1686 at Le Procope (still a restaurant today). Coffee had just been discovered by the French. And at about the same time, La Comedie Française theater was inaugurated, creating the necessary artsy, coffee-sipping crowds. France's robust economy was growing a population of pleasure seekers and thinkers looking for places to be seen, to exchange ideas, and to plot revolutions political and philosophical. By the year 1700, over 300 cafés had opened their doors, and at the time of the Revolution there were over 1,800 cafés in Paris. Revolutionaries from Marat to Napoleon to Dalí enjoyed the spirit of free thinking that the cafés engendered.

Café society took off in the early 1900s. Life was changing rapidly with the Industrial Revolution and wars on a global scale. Many retreated to Parisian cafés to try to make sense out of the confusion. Vladimir Lenin, Leon Trotsky, Igor Stravinsky, Ernest Hemingway, Scott Fitzgerald, James Joyce, Albert Einstein, Jean Paul Sartre, Gene Openshaw, and Albert Camus were among the devoted café society. Some virtually lived at their favorite café, keeping their business calendars, entertaining friends, and having every meal. Parisian apartments were small, walls were thin (still often the case), and heating (particularly during war times) was minimal, making the warmth of cafés all the harder to leave.

There are over 12,000 cafés in Paris today. They're still used for business meetings, encounter sessions, and political discussions. Most Parisians are loyal to their favorites and know their waiter's children's names. And with the recently approved 35-hour workweek, most will have even more time to linger longer over their *café crème*.

Here's a short list of grand Parisian cafés, worth the detour only if you're not in a hurry and don't mind paying outrageous prices for a shot of espresso. Think of these cafés as museums. Try to understand why they matter today as much as yesterday.

Grand Cafés by Neighborhood

St. Germain

Where the boulevard St. Germain meets rue Bonaparte (Mo: St. Germain-des-Près), you'll find two famous cafés. **Les Deux Magots** offers great outdoor seating and a warm, wood-paneled interior. Once a favorite of Ernest Hemingway (in the *Sun Also Rises*, Jake met Brett here) and of Jean Paul Sartre (he and Simone de Beauvoir met here), today's café is filled with tourists. **Le Café de Flore**, right next door, feels more local, hip, and literary—wear your black turtleneck. Picasso was a regular here while painting *Guernica*. The smoky interior is European popular.

For great outdoor seating at almost half the price, skip these places and set up at **Café Bonaparte** (one block down rue Bonaparte toward the river from Les Deux Magots). You're farther from the large boulevards and exhaust fumes here but still in the thick of this pleasant café-sitting area. Skip the inside tables.

Boulevard Montparnasse

An eclectic assortment of historic cafés gather along the boulevard Montparnasse, just a few blocks from Luxembourg Gardens at the intersection with boulevard Raspail (Mo: Vavin).

La Coupole, built in the 1920s, was decorated by aspiring artists (Leger, Brancusi, and Chagall, among others) in return for free meals. This cavernous place feels like a classy train station, with grand chandeliers, red velvet booths, brass decor, and waiters by the dozen. Bring your friends and make noise. The food is fine but not the reason you came (102 boulevard Montparnasse, tel. 01 43 26 70 50).

Le Dome sits right at the intersection of Raspail and Montparnasse and forms a dramatic contrast to the party atmosphere of La Coupole. Smaller, more elegant, and refined in every way, this place makes me want to dress up and look better than I do. The sumptuous decor is pure 1920s, and the best tables are just inside, facing the sidewalk. While La Coupole is not known for its cuisine, Le Dome is. Come here for a splurge dinner (figure 250F per person, tel. 01 43 35 25 81).

Le Select was popular with the more rebellious types—Leon Trotsky, Jean Cocteau, and Pablo Picasso loved it. It feels more conformist today, with good salads from 50F to 60F, outdoor seating, and pleasant tables just inside the door (99 boulevard Montparnasse, across from La Coupole).

Champs-Élysées
Le Fouquet's, which opened in 1899, served as James Joyce's dining room. Today it's known as the film stars' place to go. Those golden plaques at the entry are from winners of France's version of our Oscar awards, the Cesars. While the intimidating interior is impressive, the outdoor setting is Champs-Élysées great—and you can buy the most expensive shot of espresso I found in Paris (29F). Fouquet's was recently saved from foreign purchase and eventual destruction when the government declared it a historic monument (99 Avenue du Champs-Élysées, Mo: George V)

Near the Louvre
Within a short walk of the Louvre, you'll find two melt-in-your-chair cafés (Mo: Palais Royal/Musée du Louvre).

The staunchly Parisian **Café Le Nemours** is tucked into the corner of Palais Royal adjacent to Comedie Francaise. Brass-and-art-deco elegant, with outdoor tables under an arcade two minutes from the pyramid, this place makes a great post-Louvre retreat (2 place Colette).

Café de l'Epoque, inside a classy pedestrian minimall, is softly lit and elegantly appointed, a tranquil escape from city street noise (2 rue du Bouloi).

On Place de la Concorde
Hotel de Crillon's four-star elegance can be yours for an afternoon. Considered the most exclusive hotel in Paris (and the last of the great hotels to be French owned), this is the place to experience château life. Wear the best clothes you packed, arrive after 15:00, let the bellhop spin the door, and settle into the royal blue chairs in the *salon du thé* (45F for a pot of tea or double café au lait, 155F for high tea). You'll be serenaded by a harpist and surrounded by famous people you won't recognize.

PARIS WITH CHILDREN

Paris is surprisingly kid friendly. With so many parks, squares, and pedestrians and such a variety of kid-friendly sights, your children may want to return to Paris before you do. Consider these tips:

- Hotel selection is critical. Stay in a kid-friendly area near a park. The rue Cler neighborhood is ideal. If you're staying a week or more, rent an apartment (see "For Longer Stays," page 179).
- Eat dinner early (19:30 at restaurants, earlier at cafés). Skip famous places. Try relaxed cafés (or fast-food restaurants), where kids can move around without bothering others. Picnics work well.
- Follow this book's crowd-beating tips to a tee. Kids (and parents) don't like to stand in long lines.
- Get your kids in the spirit (rent or read Madeleine stories, *The Hunchback of Notre-Dame*, or *The Man in the Iron Mask*).
- The best and cheapest toy selection is in the large department stores, such as Bon Marché (see the Shopping chapter).
- French marionette shows, called *guignols*, are fun for the entire family. They take place in several locations in Paris, mostly in big parks. See *Pariscope* or *L'Officiel des Spectacles* under "Marionettes" for times and places. The plots, while in French, are easy to follow. Arrive 20 minutes early for good seats.

TEN TOP KIDS' SPOTS IN PARIS

1. Luxembourg Gardens: This is my favorite place to mix kid business with pleasure. This perfectly Parisian park has it all—from an extensive big-toys play area with imaginative slides, swings, and jungle gyms (open daily, kids-15F, adults-9F, good for all day, many parents watch from chairs outside the play area) to pedal go-karts, a fun merry-go-round, pony rides, toy sailboats in the main pond (18F/hr, daily in summer, otherwise Wed, Sat–Sun), and big open areas perfect for kicking a ball. Near the main building is a toddler wading pool and sandpit (free). Adults and kids enjoy the terrific puppet shows (*guignols*) held in the afternoons (Mo: St. Sulpice, Odéon, or Notre-Dame-des-Champs; tel. 01 43 26 46 47).

2. Jardin des Plantes: These pleasant, colorful gardens are short on grass but have a zoo, a maze made of plants, and several kid-friendly natural-science museums (closed Tue). Kids go bug-eyed at the Insect Museum (Galerie d'Entomologie, kids-10F, adults-15F, Wed–Mon 13:00–17:00) and love the dinosaur exhibit (Galerie d'Anatomie Comparée et de Paléontologie, kids-20F, adults-30F, Wed–Mon 10:00–17:00; includes Musée de Mineralogie). From the main entrance on place Valhubert, the museums line the left side of the park (Mo: Gare d'Austerlitz or Jussieu).

3. Eiffel Tower, Trocadero, and Champ de Mars Park: All ages enjoy the view from Trocadero across the river to the Eiffel Tower, especially after dark (Mo: Trocadero). Roller bladers and skateboarders make Trocadero a teenage scene, particularly in afternoons and evenings. A ride up the tower is a hit day or night. See the video on the first floor. The vast Champ de Mars park stretches out from the tower's base; near the southwestern corner of the park (about halfway between the tower and the military school) are grassy play areas (bring your own ball, play after dusk), childrens' big toys, pony rides, and picnic-perfect benches (Mo: École Militaire). For more information on the tower, see page 31.

4. Notre-Dame, Towers, and Crypt: Paris' famous Gothic cathedral doesn't have to be dry and dull. Replay Quasimodo's stunt and climb the tower. Kids love being on such a lofty perch with an in-your-face look at a gargoyle. The crypt on the square in front of Notre-Dame is manageable and fun. Kids can push buttons to highlight remains of Roman Paris and leave with a better understanding of how different civilizations build on top of each other. The small but beautiful park along the river and behind Notre-Dame has sandboxes, picnic benches, and space to run (Mo: Cité). ✪ See Historic Paris Walk on page 39.

5. Seine River Boat Rides: A variety of boats offer one-hour Seine cruises on huge glass boats, with departures until 23:00. Or hop on a Bateau-Bus, a river bus connecting six stops along the river: Eiffel Tower, Orsay/place de la Concorde, Louvre, Notre-Dame, Hôtel de Ville, and St. Germain-des-Près. Use the Bateau-Bus by day, and take a twilight cruise on a Bateau-Mouche. See page 26.

6. Arc de Triomphe and Champs-Élysées: Watching the crazy traffic rush around the Arc de Triomphe provides endless entertainment. Then stroll the Champs-Élysées with its car dealerships (particularly Renault's, with its antique car museum), Virgin Megastore, Disney Store, and the river of humanity that flows along its broad sidewalks. Take your teenager to see a movie on the Champs-Élysées ("v.o." next to the show time means original-version language). ✪ See Champs-Élysées Walk on page 57.

7. Versailles: This huge complex of palaces, gardens, fountains, and forest is a great Parisian family getaway. My kids even enjoy the 30-minute train ride to Versailles. Rent a bike for the gardens or a rowboat for the canal. Come on Sunday, when the fountains are flowing. The Hameau has barnyard animals nearby. Visit the palace at the end of the day and you can do cartwheels in an empty Hall of Mirrors. ✪ See Versailles Tour on page 142.

8. Pompidou Center: The Pompidou Center appeals more to teens with its crazy outdoor entertainers, throngs of young people and happening cafés, and fun fountains next door. Inside, the temporary exhibits on the main floor are visually impressive, and the *Star Wars* escalator to the top is fun for all ages (Mo: Rambuteau).

9. The Cité des Sciences in the Parc de la Vilette: This is like a city of its own, filled with hands-on science museums (closed Mon). It's brilliantly organized with something for all ages and provides helpful information in English for most exhibits. Walk up from the Métro Porte de la Vilette into the huge metal building and stop at the information desk to understand your options. Pick up the essential brochure ("The Keys to the Cité") explaining the exhibits, which include discovery/play areas for kids 3 to 5 years, kids 5 to 11 years, and a *Technocité* for 12+ years (each 25F); the most important Explora museum (50F, helpful English audioguide available for 25F); an aquarium (35F); a Geode (a giant spherical movie screen, 45F); and a planetarium (35F). Whew, you could go broke if you don't focus—the Explora museum and the Geode are the most famous exhibits. Most of these areas have alloted times when you can enter, which are generally limited to 90 minutes per area (Tue–Sat 10:00–18:00, Sun until 19:00, closed Mon, tel. 01 40 05 12 12).

10. La Butte Chaumont Park: Rather than manicured gardens, this is a big park where your kids can explore hills, lakes, trails, and a waterfall. Baron Haussmann designed this converted city dump into a remarkable mix of cafés and outdoor fun (Mo: Buttes-Chaumont).

LE SHOPPING
IN PARIS

Consider three ways to shop in Paris:
1) If you just need souvenirs, hit a souvenir shop.
2) For more elaborate purchasing plans, the city's large department stores offer relatively painless one-stop shopping in elegant surroundings.
3) Neighborhood boutiques offer the greatest reward at the highest risk. While clerks and prices can be intimidating, the selection is generally more original and the experience totally Parisian.

Tips

Before you enter a Parisian store, remember:
• The customer is not always right. In fact, figure the clerk is doing you a favor by waiting on you.
• Except for department stores, it's not normal for the customer to handle clothing. Ask first if you can look at an item.
• Forget returns (and don't count on exchanges).
• Saturdays are busiest.
• Observe French shoppers. Then imitate.

Souvenir Shops

Avoid souvenir carts in front of famous monuments. Prices and selection are better in shops. Look under the arcades of rue de Rivoli (across from Tuileries Gardens), around the Pompidou Center, on the streets of Montmartre, and in department stores (see below). The riverfront stalls near Notre-Dame sell a variety of used books, magazines, and tourist paraphernalia in the most romantic setting.

Department Stores (*Les Grandes Surfaces*)

Like cafés, department stores were invented here (surprisingly, not in America). While the stores seem overwhelming at first, they

Key Phrases

Just looking. - *Je regards.* (zhuh ruh-gar)

How much is it? - *Combien?* (kohm-bee-en)

Too big/small/expensive. - *Trop grand/petit/cher.* (troh grahn/puh-tee/sher)

May I try it on? - *Je peut l'essayer?* (zhuh puh luh-say-yay)

Can I see more? - *Puis-je en voir d'autres?* (pweezh en vwahr doh-truh)

I'll think about it. - *Je vais y penser.* (zhuh vay ee pahn-say)

I'd like this. - *Je voudrais ça.* (zhuh voo-dray sah)

generally work like ours, and those listed here are accustomed to foreign shoppers. These stores are not only beautiful monuments to more elegant times but also a great lesson on how others live. Most have spectacular perfume sections, a good selection of souvenirs and toys at fair prices, great view terraces, reasonably priced restaurants, and helpful information desks (near the front door). Stores are generally open Monday through Saturday 10:00 to 19:00. Choose from these four great Parisian department stores:

Galleries Lafayette and Printemps

You'll find both Galeries Lafayette and Printemps (pran-tom) department stores in many Parisian neighborhoods. The most convenient and busiest are side by side behind the old Opéra (Mo: Chaussee d'Antin, Havre-Caumartin, or Opéra). Both Galeries Lafayette and Printemps sprawl over three buildings and consume entire city blocks. The selection is huge. Don't miss the belle epoque dome at Galeries Lafayette. Continue your shopping by walking from this area to the place Vendôme (see "Boutiques," below).

Samaritaine

Samaritaine (sah-mah-ree-ten) is Paris' most central department store (on the Seine at Pont Neuf, Mo: Pont Neuf, see Historic Paris Walk). Old World elegant yet not high priced, this is a handy place to take care of business and enjoy one of the best views of Paris. Review the history of the store in dioramas at the top of the elevator. Then climb to the panorama terrace on the 11th floor.

Bon Marché

Combine this fine department store with a great neighborhood shopping experience. Bon Marché, quieter and more relaxed than the others, is surrounded by pleasant shopping streets (see "Boutiques," below). Graze through the gourmet grocery store in the basement. (Mo: Sevres-Babylone.)

Boutiques

I enjoy window shopping on city streets, pausing at cafés, and observing the rhythm of neighborhood life. While the shops are more intimate, sales clerks can be in-your-face intimidating. Here are three very different areas to try:

Sevres-Babylone to St. Sulpice

Start at the elegant Bon Marché department store, described above (Mo: Sevres-Babylone), then shop the smart boutiques that line the streets between Bon Marché and St. Sulpice Church. The rue de Sevres (turns into rue du Four) is the spine of this upscale area. Explore rues du Dragon, Cherche Midi, Bonaparte, and Vieux Colombier. End your shopping stroll in the Luxembourg Gardens or at a grand café on the boulevard St. Germain (see "Les Grands Cafés de Paris" on page 187).

Le Marais

For more eclectic, avant-garde stores, peruse the shops between the Pompidou Center and place des Vosges. Stick to the east-west axis formed by rue des Francs Bourgeois, rue des Rosiers, and rue Ste. Croix de la Bretonniere. (These streets are part of the Marais Walk, on page 64.) On Sunday afternoons this trendy area pulses with shoppers and café crowds.

Place Vendôme

The ritzy streets connecting the Galeries Lafayette with place de la Concorde are a miracle mile of jewelry stores, four-star hotels, perfumeries, and exclusive clothing boutiques.

From place de l'Opéra (Mo: Opéra), walk down rue de la Paix to place Vendôme. The *très* elegant place Vendôme is home to the Ritz Hotel (Hemingway liberated the bar in World War II) and equally exclusive boutiques. The square was created by Louis XIV in the 17th century as a setting for a statue of himself. One hundred and fifty years later, Louis was replaced by a statue of Napoleon.

Continue on rue Castiglione, window-shopping the arcades, to rue de Rivoli. Turn right on Rivoli, passing Paris' largest English bookstore, W. H. Smith, at #248, to reach place de la Concorde.

Paris is brilliant after dark. Save energy from your day's sightseeing and get out at night. Whether it's a concert at Sainte Chapelle, a boat ride on the Seine, an elevator up the Arc de Triomphe, or a late-night café, experience the city of light lit. The *Pariscope* magazine (3F at any newsstand) offers a complete weekly listing of music, cinema, theater, opera, and other special events—we decipher this useful periodical for you below. The *Free Voice* newspaper, in English, has a monthly review of Paris entertainment (available at any English-language bookstore, French-American establishments, or the American Church).

A Tour of *Pariscope*

The weekly *Pariscope* (3F) or *L'Officiel des Spectacles* (2F) are both cheap and essential if you want to know what's happening. Pick one up and page through it. For a head start, *Pariscope* has a Web site: www.pariscope.fr.

Each begins with culture news. Skip the bulky "Theatres" and "Diners/Spectacles" sections and anything listed as "des environs" (outside of Paris). "Musique" or "Concerts Classiques" follow, listing each day's events (program, location, time, and price). Venues with phone numbers and addresses are listed in an "Adresses des Salles de Concerts" sidebar. Touristic venues (such as Sainte-Chapelle and Église de la Madeleine) are often featured in display ads. "Opéras, Musique Traditionelle, Ballet/Danse," and "Jazz/Rock" listings follow.

Half of these magazines are devoted to Cinema—a Paris forte. After the "Films Nouveaux" section trumpets new releases, the "Films en Exclusivite" pages list all the films playing in town. While a code marks films as "Historique, Karate, Erotisme," and so on, the key mark for tourists is "v.o.," which means *version original* (American films have their English soundtracks). Films are listed alphabetically, with theaters and their *arrondissements* at the end of each entry. Then films are listed by neighborhood ("Salles Paris") and by genre. First-runs are shown at cinemas on the Champs-Élysées and on place de l'Odeon; art films and older films are best found in the Latin Quarter. To find a showing near your hotel, simply match the *arrondissement*. (But don't hesitate to hop on the Métro for the film you want.) "Salles Périphérie" is out in the suburbs.

Pariscope has a small English "Time Out" section listing the week's events. The "Musées" sections ("Monuments," "Jardins," "Autres Curiosites," "Promenades," "Activites Sportives," "Piscines") give the latest hours of the sights, gardens, curiosities, boat tours, sports, swimming pools, and so on. "Clubs de Loisirs" are various athletic and social clubs. "Pour les Jeunes" is for young people (kids' films, animations/cartoons, marionettes, circuses, and amusement parks such as Asterix and Disney). Conferences are mostly lectures. For cancan mischief, look under "Paris la Nuit," "Cabarets," or the busty "Spectacles Erotiques."

Finally, you'll find a TV listing. Paris has four countrywide stations: TF1, France 2, France 3, and the new Arte station (a German/French cultural channel). M6 is filled with American series. Canal Plus (channel 4) is a cable channel that airs an American news show at 7:00 in the morning and an American sports event on Sunday evening.

Music

Jazz Clubs: With a lively mix of American, French, and international musicians, Paris has been an internationally acclaimed jazz capital since World War II. You'll pay from 30F to 130F to enter a jazz club (one drink may be included; if not, expect to pay 30–60F per drink; beer is cheapest). See *Pariscope* magazine under "Musique" for listings, or better, the American Church's *Free Voice* paper for a good monthly review (in English), or drop by the clubs to check out their calendars posted on the front door. Music starts after 22:00 in most clubs. Some offer dinner concerts from about 20:30 on. Here are a few good bets:

Caveau de la Huchette, a characteristic old jazz club for visitors, fills an ancient Latin Quarter cellar with live jazz and frenzied dancing every night (60F weekday, 75F weekend admission, 30F drinks, Tue–Sun 21:30–02:30 or later, closed Mon, 5 rue de la Huchette, recorded info tel. 01 43 26 65 05).

For a hotbed of late-night activity and jazz, go to the two-block-long rue des Lombards, at boulevard Sebastopol, midway between the river and Pompidou Center (Mo: Chatelet). **Au Duc**

des Lombards, right at the corner, is one of the most popular and respected jazz clubs in Paris (42 rue des Lombards, tel. 01 42 33 23 88, www:jazzvalley.com/duc). **Le Sunset**, a block west, offers more traditional jazz—Dixieland, big band—and fewer crowds (60 rue des Lombards, tel. 01 40 26 46 60).

All Jazz Club, more expensive than the rest, is a happening club in the heart of the St. Germain area, attracting a more mature crowd in search of recognizable names (7 rue St. Benoit, Mo: St. Germain-des-Près, tel. 01 42 61 53 53).

At the more down-to-earth and mellow **Le Cave du Franc Pinot**, you can enjoy a glass of Chardonnay at the main-floor wine bar, then drop downstairs for a cool jazz scene (good dinner values as well, 1 quai de Bourbon, located on Île St. Louis where Pont Marie meets the island, Mo: Pont Marie, tel. 01 46 33 60 64).

The **American Church** regularly plays host to fine jazz musicians for the best price in Paris (free, 65 quai d'Orsay, Mo: Invalides, RER-C: Pont de l'Alma, tel. 01 40 62 05 00).

Classical Concerts: For classical music on any night, consult *Pariscope* magazine; the "Musique" section under "Concerts Classique" lists concerts (free and fee). Look for posters at the churches. Churches that regularly host concerts include St. Sulpice, St. Germain-des-Près, Basilique de Madeleine, St. Eustache, and Sainte-Chapelle. It's worth the 100F to 150F entry for the pleasure of hearing Mozart surrounded by the stained glass of the tiny Sainte-Chapelle. Even the Galeries Lafayette department store offers concerts. Many are free (*entrée libre*), such as the Sunday Atelier concert sponsored by the American Church (18:00, 65 quai d'Orsay, Mo: Invalides, RER: Pont de l'Alma, tel. 01 47 05 07 99).

Opera: Paris is home to two well-respected operas. The Opéra Garnier, Paris' first opera house, hosts opera and ballet performances. Come here for less expensive tickets and grand belle-epoque decor (Mo: Opéra, tel. 01 44 73 13 99). The Opéra de la Bastille is the massive modern opera house that dominates place de la Bastille. Come here for state-of-the-art special effects and modern interpretations of classic ballets and operas (Mo: Bastille, tel. 01 43 43 96 96). For tickets, call 01 44 73 13 00, go to the opera ticket offices (open 11:00–18:00), or best, reserve on the Web: www.ticketavenue.com (for both operas).

Bus Tours

Paris Illumination Tours, run by Paris Vision, connect all the great illuminated sights of Paris with a 100-minute bus tour in 12 languages. Double-decker buses have huge windows, but

Moulin Rouge customers get the most desirable front seats. You'll stampede on with a United Nations of tourists, get a hand-held audio stick, and listen to a tape-recorded spiel (interesting but occasionally hard to hear). Uninspired as it is, this provides a fine first-night overview of the city at its floodlit scenic best. Left seats are marginally better. Visibility is fine in the rain. You're entirely on the bus except for one five-minute cigarette break at the Eiffel Tower viewpoint (150F-adult, 75F-ages 4–11, free-under 3, second adult pays only 100F on 20:30 tours, departures at 20:30 nightly all year and 22:00 Apr–Oct only, departs from Paris Vision office at 214 rue de Rivoli, across the street from Mo: Tuileries). These trips are sold through your hotel (brochures in lobby) or direct at the address listed above (tel. 01 42 60 30 01, fax 01 42 86 95 36, www.parisvision.com).

Seine River Cruises

The Bateaux-Mouches offer one-hour cruises on huge glass boats with departures (every 30 minutes from 10:00–23:00) from the pont de l'Alma, the centrally located pont Neuf, and right in front of the Eiffel Tower (see "Organized Tours of Paris" page 25).

Walks

Go for a walk to best appreciate the city of light. Break for ice cream, pause at a café, and enjoy the sidewalk entertainers as you join the post-dinner Parisian parade. Consider these walks:

Champs-Élysées and the Arc de Triomphe—✪ See Champs-Élysées Walk, on page 57. These are brilliant after dark. Start at the Arc de Triomphe then stroll down the lively Champs-Élysées. A right turn on avenue George V leads to the Bateaux-Mouches river cruises. A movie on the Champs-Élysées is a fun experience (weekly listings in *Pariscope* under "Cinema").

Trocadero and Eiffel Tower—These monuments glimmer at night. Take the Métro to the Trocadero stop and join the party on place de la Trocadero for a magnificent view of the glowing Eiffel Tower. It's a festival of gawkers, drummers, street acrobats, and entertainers. Pass the fountains and cross the river to the base of the tower, worth the effort even if you don't go up. See "Eiffel Tower," page 31.

From the Eiffel Tower, you can stroll through the Parc du Champ de Mars past Frisbees, soccer balls, and romantic couples and take the Métro home (École Militaire stop, across avenue de la Motte-Picquet from the far southeast corner of the park). Or, if you've had enough, there's a handy RER stop (Champ de Mars-Tour Eiffel) two blocks west (downriver) of the Eiffel Tower.

TRANSPORTATION
CONNECTIONS
(21)

paris

This chapter covers Paris' two airports, six train stations, and main bus station.

CHARLES DE GAULLE AIRPORT

Charles de Gaulle Airport is Paris' primary airport. It has three main terminals: T-1, T-2, and T-9. (Air France uses T-2; charters dominate T-9.) Terminals are connected every few minutes by a free *navette* (bus), and the RER (Paris subway) stops at T-1 and T-2 terminals. There is no bag storage at the airport.

Those flying to or from the U.S.A. will probably use T-1. Here you'll find an American Express cash machine, an automatic bill changer (at baggage claim 30), and an exchange window (at baggage claim 18). A bank (with barely acceptable rates) and an ATM are near gate 16. At the Meeting Point, you'll find the tourist office, which has free maps and information (daily 7:00–22:00), and Relais H, which sells *télécartes* (phone cards). Car rental offices are on the arrival level from gates 10 to 22; the SNCF (train) office is at gate 22. For flight information, call 01 48 62 22 80.

Transportation between Charles de Gaulle Airport and Paris: There are plenty of choices. Three efficient public transportation routes, taxis, and airport shuttle vans link the airport's T-1 and T-2 terminals with central Paris. At T-1 (where most will land), the free *navette* (bus) runs between gate 28 and the **RER Roissy Rail** station, where a train zips you into Paris' subway system in 30 minutes (49F, stops at Gare du Nord, Chatelet, St. Michel, and Luxembourg Gardens). The **Roissy Bus** runs every 15 minutes between gate 30 and the old Opéra Garnier (stop is on rue Scribe, in front of American Express), costs 45F (use the automatic ticket machine), and takes 40 minutes, but can be jammed. The **Air France Bus** leaves every 15 minutes from gate 34 and serves the Arc de Triomphe and Porte Maillot in about 40 minutes for 60F, and the Montparnasse Tower in 60 minutes for 75F (from any of these stops you can reach your hotel by taxi). For most people, the RER Roissy Rail works best. A **taxi** ride with luggage costs about 230F; a taxi stand is at gate 16. The **Disneyland Express bus** departs from gate 32. (The RER Roissy Rail, Roissy Bus, and Air France bus described above serve the T-2 terminal as efficiently and economically as T-1.)

For a stress-free trip between either of Paris' airports and downtown, consider an **airport shuttle minivan**, ideal for single travelers or families of four or more. Reserve from home and they'll meet you at the airport. Consider Airport Shuttle (allow 150F for one person, 89F per person for two, cheaper for larger groups and kids, plan on a 30-minute wait if you ask them to pick you up at the airport, tel. 01 45 38 55 72, fax 01 43 21 35 67, www.paris-anglo.com/clients/ashuttle.html, e-mail: ashuttle@club-internet.fr) or Paris Airport Services (tel. 01 49 62 78 78, fax 01 49 62 78 79, www.magic.fr/pas, e-mail: pas@magic.fr).

Sleeping at or near Charles de Gaulle Airport: Those with early flights can sleep in T-1 at Cocoon (60 cabins, Sb-250F, Db-300F, CC:VM, tel. 01 48 62 06 16, fax 01 48 62 56 97). Take the elevator down to "boutique level" or walk down from the departure level. You get 16 hours of silence buried under the check-in level with TV and toilet. Hôtel IBIS, at the Roissy Rail station, offers more normal accommodations (Db-420F, CC:VMA, free shuttle bus to either terminal takes two minutes, tel. 01 49 19 19 19, fax 01 49 19 19 21).

ORLY AIRPORT

This airport feels small. Orly has two terminals: Sud and Ouest. International flights arrive at Sud. After exiting baggage claim (near gate H), you'll be greeted by signs directing you to city transportation, car rental, and so on. Turn left to enter the main terminal area, and you'll find exchange offices with barely acceptable rates, an ATM machine, the ADP (a quasi–tourist office that offers free city maps and basic sight-seeing information), and an SNCF French rail desk (sells train tickets and even Eurailpasses). Downstairs is a sandwich bar, bank (lousy rates), newsstand (buy *télécarte* phone card), and post office (great rates for cash or American Express traveler's checks). For flight info on any airline serving Orly, call 01 49 75 15 15.

Transportation between Paris and Orly Airport: There are three efficient public-transportation routes, taxis, and a couple of airport shuttle services linking Orly and central Paris. The **Air France bus** (outside gate F) runs to Paris' Invalides Métro stop

(40F, 4/hrly, 30 min) and is best for those staying in or near the rue Cler neighborhood (from the Invalides terminal, take the Métro two stops to École Militaire to reach recommended hotels). The **Jetbus #285** (outside gate F, 24F, 4/hrly) is the quickest way to the Paris subway and the best way to the recommended hotels in the Marais and Contrescarpe neighborhoods (take Jetbus to Villejuif Métro stop, buy a carnet of 10 Métro tickets, then take the Métro to the Sully Morland stop for the Marais area or the Cardinal Lemoine stop for the Contrescarpe area). The **Orlybus** (outside gate H, 30F, 4/hr) takes you to the Denfert-Rochereau RER-B line and the Métro, offering subway access to central Paris. The **Orlyval trains** are overpriced (57F). Allow 150F for a **taxi** into central Paris.

Airport shuttle minivans are ideal for single travelers or families of four or more (see under "Charles de Gaulle Airport," above; from Orly, figure about 120F for 1 person, 80F per person for 2, less for larger groups and kids).

Sleeping near Orly Airport: The only reasonable airport hotel is the IBIS (Db-420F, CC:VMA, tel. 01 46 87 33 50, fax 01 46 87 29 92). The Hilton offers more comfort for a price (Db-680F, tel 01 45 12 45 12, fax 01 45 12 45 00). Both offer free shuttle service to the terminal.

PARIS' TRAIN STATIONS

Paris is Europe's rail hub, with six major train stations, each serving different regions: Gare de l'Est (east-bound trains), Gare du Nord (northern Europe), Gare St. Lazare (northwestern France), Gare d'Austerlitz (southwest Europe), Gare du Lyon (southern Europe), and Gare Montparnasse (northwestern France and TGV service to France's southwest). Any train station can give you schedule information, make reservations, and sell tickets for any destination. Buying tickets is handier from an SNCF neighborhood office (e.g., Louvre, Invalides, Orsay, Versailles, airports) or at your neighborhood travel agency—worth their small fee (SNCF signs in their window indicate they sell train tickets). For schedule information, call 08 36 35 35 35 (3F/minute, English sometimes available).

All six train stations are connected by Métro, bus, and taxi. All have banks or change offices, information desks, telephones, cafés, lockers (*consigne automatique*), newsstands, and clever pickpockets. Each station offers two types of rail service: long distance to other cities, called *Grandes Lignes* (major lines); and suburban service to outlying areas, called *Banlieue* or RER. Both *Banlieue* and RER serve outlying areas and the airports; the only difference is that *Banlieue* lines are operated by SNCF (France's train system) and RER lines are operated by RATP (Paris' Métro and bus system). Paris train

Key Train Phrases

accueil (ah-coy) = information assistance
billets (bee-yay) = tickets
départs (day-par) = departures
arrivées (ah-ree-vay) = arrivals
aller simple (ah-lay sam-pluh) = one way
aller-retour (ah-lay ruh-toor) = round-trip
voyageurs munis de billets = travelers with tickets
Grandes Lignes (grahnd leen) = major domestic and
     international lines
RER (air-ay-air) = suburban lines
Banlieue (bahn-lee-yuh) = suburban lines
quai (kay) = platform
voie (vwah) = track
retard (ruh-tar) = delay
salle d'attente (sahl dah-tahnt) = waiting room
consigne automatique (kohn-seen auto-mah-teek) =
     storage lockers
première classe (pruhm-yair klahs) = first class
deuxième classe (duhz-yehm klahs) = second class

stations can be intimidating, but if you slow down, take a deep breath, and ask for help, you'll find them helpful and efficient. Bring a pad of paper for clear communication at ticket/info windows.

Station Overview

Here's an overview of Paris' major train stations. Métro, RER, buses (BUS), and taxis are well signed at every station. When arriving by Métro, follow signs for *Grandes Lignes*-SNCF to find the main tracks and look for helpful *accueil* (information) booths.

Gare du Nord: Serves cities in northern France and international destinations to the north of Paris (including London). This is one of Paris' largest stations, offering the most services and confusion. A train information booth is opposite track 18, and information booths for Eurostar and Thalys trains are opposite track 8. Passengers departing on the Eurostar (London via the Chunnel) must check in on the second level, opposite tracks 4 through 6. (Note: Britain's time zone is one hour earlier than the Continent's; times listed on Eurostar tickets are local times.) A peaceful waiting area is provided on the upper level overlooking the tracks. Storage lockers and baggage check are at the far end, just past track 3.
     Key destinations served by Gare du Nord *Grandes Lignes*:

Brussels (10/day, 1.5 hrs), **Amsterdam** (10/day, 4 hrs), **Copenhagen** (3/day, 16 hrs), **Koblenz** (3/day, 7 hrs), **London** via Eurostar Chunnel (12/day, 3 hrs). By *Banlieue*/RER lines: **Chantilly-Gouvieux** (hrly, fewer on weekends, 35 min), **Charles de Gaulle airport** (2/hrly, 30 min, from 5:30–23:00).

Gare de l'Est: Serves eastern France and European points to the east of Paris. Much smaller than the Gare du Nord, this single-floor station (with underground Métro) is a snap. Train information booths are at tracks 1 and 26; ticket windows and the main exit to buses and Paris is opposite track 8; luggage storage is opposite track 12.

Key destinations served by Gare de l'Est: **Colmar** (6/day, 5.5 hrs, transfer in Strasbourg or Mulhouse), **Strasbourg** (10/day, 4.5 hrs), **Reims** (8/day, 2 hrs), **Verdun** (5/day, 3 hrs), **Munich** (4/day, 8.5 hrs), **Vienna** (3/day, 13 hrs), **Zurich** (10/day, 7 hrs), **Prague** (2/day, 15 hrs).

Gare Montparnasse: This big modern station covers three floors, serves Lower Normandy and Brittany, and offers TGV service to the Loire Valley and southwestern France. At street level you'll find a bank and *Banlieue* trains (serving Chartres); ticket windows are just to the right of the turnstiles in the center of this floor. (You can also reach the *Banlieue* trains from the second level). Lockers (*consigne automatique*) are on the mezzanine level between levels 1 and 2. Most services are provided on the second level, where the *Grandes Lignes* arrive and depart (ticket windows are to your left as you exit the escalators). An information booth is near track 10; *Banlieue* trains depart from tracks 10 through 19. The main rail information office is opposite track 15.

Key destinations served by Gare Montparnasse: **Chartres** (10/day, 1 hr), **Mont St. Michel** (2/day, 4.5 hrs, via Rennes), **Dinan** (7/day, 3 hrs, via Rennes and Dol), **Bordeaux** (14/day, 3.5 hrs), **Sarlat** (5/day, 6 hrs, transfer in Bordeaux), **Toulouse** (7/day, 5 hrs, possible transfer in Bordeaux), **Albi** (6.5 hrs, via Toulouse), **Carcassonne** (6.5 hrs, via Toulouse), **Tours** (14/day, 1 hr).

Gare du Lyon: This huge and confusing station offers TGV and regular service to southeastern France, Italy, and other international destinations. *Banlieue* trains serve Melun (near Vaux-le-Vicomte) and Fontainebleau. All trains arrive and depart from one level but are divided into two areas (tracks A–N and 5–23); they are connected by the long platform along tracks A and 5 and by the hallway adjacent to track A and opposite track 9. This hallway has all the services, ticket windows, banks, and shops. *Banlieue* ticket windows are just inside the hall adjacent to track A. *Grandes Lignes* (main lines) and *Banlieue* (suburban) lines share the same tracks. A Paris tourist information office and the main train information office are at track L. From the RER or Métro, follow signs for *Grandes Lignes Arivées* and take the escalator up to reach the platforms. Train information booths (*accueil*) are opposite tracks G and 13.

Key destinations served by Gare de Lyon: **Melun** (hrly/30 min), **Fontainebleau** (nearly hrly, 45 min), **Beaune** (8/day, 2.5 hrs), **Dijon** (13/day, 1.5 hrs), **Chamonix** (3/day, 9 hrs, transfer in Lyon and St. Gervais, one direct night train), **Annecy** (8/day, 4–7 hrs), **Lyon** (16/day, 2.5 hrs), **Avignon** (10/day, 4 hrs), **Arles** (10/day, 5 hrs), **Nice** (8/day, 7 hrs), **Venice** (5/day, 11 hrs), **Rome** (3/day, 15 hrs), **Bern** (5/day, 5 hrs).

Gare St. Lazare: This relatively small station serves Upper Normandy, including Rouen and Giverny. All trains arrive and depart one floor above street level. Follow signs to *Grandes Lignes* from the Métro to reach the tracks. You'll pass a minimall. Ticket windows and a Thomas Cook exchange are in the first hall on the second floor. The tracks are through the small hallways (lined with storage lockers). *Grandes Lignes* (main lines) depart from tracks 17 through 27; *Banlieue* suburban trains depart from 1 through 16. The train information office (*accueil*) is opposite track 15; the reservation office is opposite track 16. Baggage consignment and the post office are along track 27, and WCs are opposite track 19.

Key destinations served by Gare St. Lazare: **Giverny** (train to Vernon, 5/day, 45 min; then bus or taxi 10 minutes to Giverny), **Rouen** (15/day, 75 min), **Honfleur** (6/day, 3 hrs, via Lisieux, then bus), **Bayeux** (9/day, 2.5 hrs), **Caen** (12/day, 2 hrs).

Gare d'Austerlitz: This small station provides non-TGV service to the Loire Valley, southwestern France, and Spain. All tracks are at street level. The information booth is opposite track 17, and a Thomas Cook exchange is in the hall opposite track 10. Baggage consignment is at Porte 27 (along the side, opposite track 21).

Key destinations served by Gare d'Austerlitz: **Amboise** (8/day, 2.5 hrs), **Cahors** (5/day, 7 hrs), **Barcelona** (3/day, 13 hrs), **Madrid** (5/day, 16 hrs), **Lisbon** (1/day, 24 hrs).

BUSES

Buses provide cheaper, if less comfortable and less flexible, transportation to major European cities. The main bus station is Gare Routière du Paris-Gallieni (avenue du General de Gaulle, in suburb of Bagnolet, Mo: Gallieni, tel. 01 49 72 51 51). Eurolines buses depart from here.

APPENDIX

French (and Parisian) History

Celts and Romans (52 B.C.–A.D. 500)
Julius Caesar conquered the Parisii, turning Paris from a tribal fishing village into a European city. The mix of Latin (southern) and Celtic (northern) cultures, with Paris right in the middle, defined the French character.

Paris Sites: Cluny Museum (Roman baths), Louvre (Roman antiquities), and Archeological Crypt near Notre-Dame.

Dark Ages (500–1000)
Roman Paris fell to German pirates (the "Franks" = France) and later to the Vikings ("Norsemen" = Normans). During this turbulent time, Paris was just another island state ("Île de France") in the midst of many warring kingdoms. The lone bright spot was the reign of Charlemagne (A.D. 800) who briefly united the Franks, giving a glimpse of the modern nation-state of France.

Paris Sites: Cluny Museum artifacts and statue of Charlemagne near Notre-Dame.

Border Wars with England (1066–1500)
In 1066, the Norman king William (the Conqueror) invaded and conquered England. This united England, Normandy, and much of what is today western France, sparking centuries of border wars and French-speaking kings of England. In 1328, a Norman-English king declared war on the king of France, leading to more than 100 years of Franco-Anglo wars (called the Hundred Years' War). Rallied by the teenage visionary Joan of Arc, the French finally united north and south, driving the English across the Channel in 1453. Modern France was born, with Paris as its capital.

Paris Sites: Notre-Dame, Sainte-Chapelle, Cluny Museum tapestries, Carnavalet Museum, Sorbonne, and the Latin Quarter.

Renaissance and Religious Wars (1500s)

A strong centralized France emerged, with French kings setting Europe's standard. Francois I made Paris a cultural capital, inviting Leonardo and *Mona Lisa* to visit. Catholics and Protestants fought openly, with 2,000 Parisians slaughtered in the St. Bartholomew's Day Massacre.

Paris Sites: Louvre (palace and Renaissance art), pont Neuf, place des Vosges, and Fontainebleau.

Louis XIV, the Absolute Monarch (1600s)

Louis XIV centralized power in himself, neutered the nobility, and moved the capital to Versailles, which also became the center of European culture. France's wealth sparked new Enlightened ideas. With these came the seeds of democracy.

Paris Sites: Versailles, Vaux-le-Vicomte, Les Invalides, paintings by Poussin and Lorraine.

Decadence and Revolution (1700s)

A financial crunch from wars and royal excess drove the French people to revolt. On July 14, 1789, they stormed the Bastille. Later, they kidnapped and beheaded the king and queen. Thousands lost their heads—guillotined if suspected of hindering progress. A charismatic commoner rose amid the chaos, promising stability—Napoleon Bonaparte. Along with Napoleon, this was the age of Louis XV, Louis XVI, Marie Antoinette, Voltaire, Rousseau, and Robespierre.

Paris Sites: Versailles, place de la Concorde, place de la Bastille, Conciergerie, and paintings by Watteau, Boucher, Fragonard, and David.

Elected Emperors and Constitutional Kings (1800s)

Napoleon conquered Europe, crowned himself emperor, invaded Russia, and ended up defeated on the battlefields of Waterloo. The monarchy was restored, but a series of popular uprisings (1830, 1848, 1870) forced rulers to toe the democratic line. Napoleon's nephew, Napoleon III, presided over a wealthy, middle-class nation with a colonial empire in slow decline. France's political clout was fading even as Paris remained the world's cultural center during the "belle epoque," or beautiful age.

Paris Sites: Arc de Triomphe, Haussman's wide boulevards, Eiffel Tower, Les Invalides and Napoleon's Tomb, pont Alexandre, Grand and Petit Palais, Montmartre, Opéra Garnier, paintings of Ingres and Delacroix at the Louvre, and Impressionist and Postimpressionist paintings (Manet, Monet, Renoir, Degas, Toulouse-Lautrec, Cézanne, and so on) at the Orsay, Marmottan, and L'Orangerie (closed for renovation).

War and Depression (1900–1950)

France began the turn of the century as top dog, but the two World Wars with Germany (and the earlier Franco-Prussian War of 1870) wasted the country. France lost millions of men in World War I, sank into a depression, and was easily overrun by Hitler in World War II. Paris, now dirt cheap, attracted foreign writers and artists.

This was the age of Picasso, Ravel, Debussy, Satie, Stravinsky, Nijinsky, Hemingway, Fitzgerald, Stein, Pound, Sartre, Edith Piaf, and Maurice Chevalier.

Paris Sites: Picasso Museum, Deportation Memorial, Pompidou Center.

Postwar France (1950–Present)

Wartime hero Charles de Gaulle reestablished a democratic Republic. France's colonial empire dissolved after bitter wars in Algeria and Vietnam. Immigrants from former colonies flooded Paris. The turbulent '60s, progressive '70s, socialist-turned-conservative '80s, and the middle-of-the-road '90s bring us to the *début de siècle* (beginning of the century).

Paris Sites: Montparnasse Tower, La Defense, Louvre's Pyramid, and Pompidou Center.

Contemporary Politics in France

The key political issues in France today are high unemployment (about 12 percent), a steadily increasing percentage of ethnic minorities, and a recognized need to compete in a global marketplace. The challenge is to address these issues while maintaining the social benefits the French expect from their government. As a result, national policies seem to conflict with each other (e.g., France supports the lean economic policies of the European Union but has recently reduced the French work week to 35 hours).

The unification of Europe has been powered by France and Germany. The 15-member European Union, which is well on its way to becoming a "United States of Europe," is dissolving borders, freeing up trade, and establishing an all-European currency called the Euro. Some stores already have prices marked in francs and Euros (though Euros won't appear as bills and coins until 2002).

French national politics are fascinating. While only two parties dominate American politics, France has five major parties. From left to right, these include the reformed Communists

(PCF-Parti Communiste Francaise), the moderate Socialists (PS-Parti Socialiste), the aristocratically conservative UDF (Union pour la Democratie Francaise), the center-right RPR (Rassemblement pour la République), and the racist Front National. In general the UDF and RPR split the conservative middle ground and the Socialists dominate the liberal middle ground. But in France (unlike the U.S.A.), coalitions are generally necessary for any party to "rule." At the fringes you'll read about the racist Front National party, led by Jean-Marie Le Pen. Le Pen's "France for the French" platform calls for the expulsion of ethnic minorities and broader police powers. As unemployment has gone up, so has the popularity of this far right party. Garnering 15 percent of a recent national vote, Le Pen has been able to force center-right parties farther in his direction. On the far left, the reformed Communists, still recovering from the fall of the Soviet Union, have had to work more flexibly with the less radical Socialists and the environmental parties.

While the French president is elected by popular vote every seven years, he is more of a figurehead than his American counterpart. The more powerful Prime Minister is elected by the parliament (every three years). With five major parties, a single majority is rare—it takes a coalition to elect a Prime Minister. Currently the left is working together better than the right, and France has a liberal Prime Minister (socialist Lionel Jospin) with a conservative president (Jacques Chirac). This "cohabitation," as it's called in French, is similar to an American president having to deal with a Congress controlled by an opposing party.

Let's Talk Telephones

Dialing Direct

Here are general instructions for making phone calls. (For information specific to France, see page 8). International access codes and country codes are listed below. Most European countries use area codes, but France is one of the exceptions (see "Europe's Exceptions," below).

Calling between Countries: Dial the international access code (of the country you're calling from), the country code (of the country you're calling), the area code (if it starts with zero, drop the zero), and the local number.

Calling Long Distance within a Country: First dial the area code (including its zero), then the local number.

Europe's Exceptions: Some countries, such as France, Italy, Spain, Portugal, Norway, and Denmark, do not use area codes. To make an international call to these countries, dial the international access code (usually 00 in Europe, 011 for the United States or

Canada), the country code (see chart below), then the local number in its entirety (okay, so there's one exception: for France, drop the initial zero of the local number). To make long-distance calls within any of these countries, simply dial the local number in its entirety.

International Access Codes

When dialing direct, first dial the international access code of the country you're calling from. For the U.S.A. and Canada, it's 011. Virtually all European countries use "00" as their international access code; the only exceptions are Finland (990), Estonia (800), and Lithuania (810).

Country Codes

After you've dialed the international access code, then dial the code of the country you're calling.

Austria—43	Finland—358	Norway—47
Belgium—32	France—33	Portugal—351
Britain—44	Germany—49	Spain—34
Canada—1	Greece—30	Sweden—46
Czech Repub.—420	Ireland—353	Switzerland—41
Denmark—45	Italy—39	U.S.A.—1
Estonia—372	Netherlands—31	

Handy Phone Numbers

Directory assistance for Paris and France: 12
Police: 17
Emergency medical assistance: 15

Calling Card Operators

AT&T: 0800 99 00 11
MCI: 0800 99 00 19
Sprint: 0800 99 00 87

Medical Needs

American Hospital: 63 boulevard Victor Hugo, in suburb of
    Neuilly, Mo: Porte Maillot, then bus 82, tel. 01 46 41 25 25
American Pharmacy: Mo: Opéra, tel. 01 47 42 49 40
Chiropractic Centers: tel. 01 43 54 26 25 or tel. 01 43 87 81 62

Consulates/Embassies

U.S.A.: Consulate, 2 rue St. Florentin, tel. 01 43 12 48 45;
    Embassy, 2 avenue Gabriel, tel. 01 43 12 22 22, same Métro
    stop (Concorde) for both
Canada: Consulate and Embassy, 35 avenue Montaigne, Mo:
    Franklin-Roosevelt, tel. 01 44 43 29 00

Tourist and Transportation Information

Paris Tourist Information: tel. 01 45 26 94 82, tel. 01 43 43 33 24, or tel. 01 49 52 53 54; recorded information for events: tel. 01 49 52 53 56

Île de France Tourist Information (Paris area): tel. 01 42 60 28 62

Train (SNCF) information: tel. 08 36 35 35 35

Bus and Métro (RATP) information: tel. 08 36 68 77 14

Travel Companies

The American Express Travel Company (11 rue Scribe, Mo: Opéra, tel. 01 47 77 77 07) is a popular hangout for American travelers, but you'll find cheaper flights at:

- Cash and Go (34 avenue Champs-Élysées, Mo: Franklin-Roosevelt, tel. 01 53 93 63 63)
- Voyageurs en Amerique du Nord (55 rue Sainte Anne, Mo: Pyramides, tel. 01 42 86 17 30)
- CTS Voyages (20 rue des Carmes, Mo: Maubert Mutualité, tel. 01 43 25 00 76)

Airports

Charles de Gaulle: tel. 01 48 62 22 80

Orly: tel. 01 49 75 15 15

Airlines

Air France: tel. 08 02 80 28 02 (fee call)

Air Canada: tel. 01 44 50 20 20

Air Lingus: tel. 01 47 42 95 00

Alitalia: tel. 01 44 94 44 00

American Airlines: tel. 08 01 87 28 72 (fee call)

British Airways: tel. 08 02 80 29 02 (fee call)

British Midlands: tel. 01 48 62 55 65

Continental: tel. 01 42 99 09 09

Delta: tel. 01 47 68 92 92

Iberia: tel. 01 40 47 80 90

KLM: tel. 01 44 56 18 18

Lufthansa: tel. 01 55 60 43 43

Northwest: tel. 01 42 66 90 00

Olympic: tel. 01 42 65 92 42

Sabena: tel. 08 36 67 88 00

SAS: tel. 01 53 43 25 25

Swissair: tel. 08 02 30 04 00 (fee call)

TWA: tel. 01 49 19 20 00

United: tel. 08 01 72 72 72 (fee call)

US Air: tel. 01 49 10 29 00

Classes

French-Language Classes

- American University of Paris (tel. 01 40 62 07 20, fax 01 40 62 07 17, www.aup.fr)
- France Ecole Langue (tel. 01 45 00 40 15, fax 01 45 00 53 41, www.france-langue.fr)

Cooking Schools
These have demonstration courses:
- Le Cordon Bleu (tel. 01 53 68 22 50, fax 01 48 56 03 96)
- Ritz Escoffier École de Gastronomie Française (tel. 01 43 16 30 50)
- La Cuisine de Marie Blanche (tel. 01 45 51 36 34, fax 01 45 51 90 19)

Wine Classes
- Maison de la Vigne (tel. 01 47 20 20 76)

Climate
First line is average daily low; second line is average daily high; third line, days of no rain.

J	F	M	A	M	J	J	A	S	O	N	D
34°	34°	39°	43°	49°	55°	58°	58°	53°	46°	40°	36°
43°	45°	54°	60°	68°	73°	76°	75°	70°	60°	50°	44°
16	15	16	16	18	19	19	19	19	17	15	14

Numbers and Stumblers
- Europeans write a few of their numbers differently than we do. 1 = 1 , 4 = 4 , 7 = 7 . Learn the difference or miss your train.
- In Europe, dates appear as day/month/year, so Christmas is 25/12/00.
- Commas are decimal points and decimals commas. A dollar and a half is 1,50, and there are 5.280 feet in a mile.
- When pointing, use your whole hand, palm downward.
- When counting with fingers, start with your thumb. If you hold up your first finger to request one item, you'll probably get two.
- What we Americans call the second floor of a building is the first floor in Europe.
- Europeans keep the left "lane" open for passing on escalators and moving sidewalks. Keep to the right.

Metric Conversion (approximate)
1 inch = 25 millimeters	32 degrees F = 0 degrees C
1 foot = 0.3 meter	82 degrees F = about 28 degrees C
1 yard = 0.9 meter	1 ounce = 28 grams
1 mile = 1.6 kilometers	1 kilogram = 2.2 pounds
1 centimeter = 0.4 inch	1 quart = 0.95 liter
1 meter = 39.4 inches	1 square yard = 0.8 square meter
1 kilometer = .62 mile	1 acre = 0.4 hectare

Basic French Survival Phrases

Hello (good day).	**Bonjour.**	bohn-zhoor
Do you speak English?	**Parlez-vous anglais?**	par-lay-voo ahn-glay
Yes. / No.	**Oui. / Non.**	wee / nohn
I'm sorry.	**Désolé.**	day-zoh-lay
Please.	**S'il vous plaît.**	see voo play
Thank you.	**Merci.**	mehr-see
Goodbye.	**Au revoir.**	oh vwahr
Where is...?	**Où est...?**	oo ay
...a hotel	**...un hôtel**	uhn oh-tehl
...a youth hostel	**...une auberge**	ewn oh-behrzh
	de jeunesse	duh zhuh-nehss
...a restaurant	**...un restaurant**	uhn rehs-toh-rahn
...a grocery store	**...une épicerie**	ewn ay-pee-suh-ree
...the train station	**...la gare**	lah gar
...the tourist info office	**...l'office du tourisme**	loh-fees dew too-reez-muh
Where are the toilets?	**Où sont les toilettes?**	oo sohn lay twah-leht
men / women	**hommes / dames**	ohm / dahm
How much is it?	**Combien?**	kohn-bee-an
Cheaper.	**Moins cher.**	mwan shehr
Included?	**Inclus?**	an-klew
Do you have...?	**Avez-vous...?**	ah-vay-voo
I would like...	**Je voudrais...**	zhuh voo-dray
...a ticket.	**...un billet.**	uhn bee-yay
...a room.	**...une chambre.**	ewn shahn-bruh
...the bill.	**...l'addition.**	lah-dee-see-ohn
one	**un**	uhn
two	**deux**	duh
three	**trois**	twah
four	**quatre**	kah-truh
five	**cinq**	sank
six	**six**	sees
seven	**sept**	seht
eight	**huit**	weet
nine	**neuf**	nuhf
ten	**dix**	dees
At what time?	**À quelle heure?**	ah kehl ur
Just a moment.	**Un moment.**	uhn moh-mahn
Now.	**Maintenant.**	man-tuh-nahn
today / tomorrow	**aujourd'hui / demain**	oh-zhoor-dwee / duh-man

For more user-friendly French phrases, check out *Rick Steves'
French Phrase Book and Dictionary* or *Rick Steves' French, Italian &
German Phrase Book and Dictionary*.

Road Scholar Feedback for Paris 2000

We're all in the same travelers' school of hard knocks. Your feedback helps us improve this guidebook for future travelers. Please fill this out (or use the on-line version at www.ricksteves.com/feedback), include more info or any tips/favorite discoveries if you like, and send it to us. As thanks for your help, we'll send you our quarterly travel newsletter free for one year. Thanks! **Rick**

Of the recommended accommodations/restaurants used, which was:

Best _____

    Why? _____

Worst _____

    Why? _____

Of the sights/experiences/destinations recommended by this book, which was:

Most overrated _____

    Why? _____

Most underrated _____

    Why? _____

Best ways to improve this book:

_____

I'd like a free newsletter subscription:

_____ Yes   _____ No   _____ Already on list

_____
Name

_____
Address

_____
City, State, Zip

_____
E-mail Address

Please send to: ETBD, Box 2009, Edmonds, WA 98020

Jubilee 2000—Let's Celebrate the Millennium by Forgiving Third World Debt

Let's ring in the millennium by convincing our government to forgive the debt owed to us by the world's poorest countries. Imagine spending over half your income on interest payments alone. You and I are creditors, and poor countries owe us more than they can pay.

Jubilee 2000 is a worldwide movement of concerned people and groups—religious and secular—working to cancel the international debts of the poorest countries by the year 2000.

Debt ruins people: In the poorest countries, money needed for health care, education, and other vital services is diverted to interest payments.

Mozambique, with a per capita income of $90 and life expectancy of 40, spends over half its national income on interest. This poverty brings social unrest, civil war, and often costly humanitarian intervention by the U.S.A. To chase export dollars, desperate countries ruin their environment. As deserts grow and rain forests shrink, the world suffers. Of course, the real suffering is among local people born long after some dictator borrowed (and squandered) that money. As interest is paid, entire populations go hungry.

Who owes what and why? Mozambique is one of 41 countries defined by the World Bank as "Heavily Indebted Poor Countries." In total, they owe $200 billion. Because these debts are unlikely to be paid, their market value is only a tenth of the face value (about $20 billion). The U.S.A.'s share is under $2 billion.

How can debt be canceled? This debt is owed mostly to the U.S.A., Japan, Germany, Britain, and France either directly or through the World Bank. We can forgive the debt owed directly to us and pay the market value (usually 10 percent) of the debts owed to the World Bank. We have the resources. (Norway, another wealthy creditor nation, just unilaterally forgave its Third World debt.) All America needs is the political will . . . people power.

While many of these poor nations are now democratic, corruption is still a concern. A key to Jubilee 2000 is making certain that debt relief reduces poverty in a way that benefits ordinary people: women, farmers, children, and so on.

Let's celebrate the new millennium by giving poor countries a break. For the sake of peace, fragile young democracies, the environment, and countless real people, forgiving this debt is the right thing for us in the rich world to do.

Tell Washington, D.C.: If our government knows this is what we want, it can happen. Learn more, write letters, lobby legislators, or even start a local Jubilee 2000 campaign. For details, contact Jubilee 2000 (tel. 202/783-3566, www.j2000usa.org). For information on lobbying Congress on J2000, contact Bread for the World (tel. 800/82-BREAD, www.bread.org).

Faxing Your Hotel Reservation

Faxing is more accurate and cheaper than telephoning. Use this handy form for your fax (or find it online at www.ricksteves.com /reservation). Photocopy and fax away.

One-Page Fax

To: _____ @ _____
            hotel   *fax*

From: _____ @ _____
             name   *fax*

Today's date: ____ /_____ /____
                      day   *month*   *year*

Dear Hotel _____,

Please make this reservation for me:

Name: _____

Total # of people: _____   # of rooms: _____   # of nights: _____

Arriving: ____ /_____ /____   My time of arrival (24-hr clock): _____
                 day   *month*   *year*   (I will telephone if I will be late)

Departing: ____ /_____ /____
                    day   *month*   *year*

Room(s):   Single___   Double___   Twin___   Triple___   Quad___

With: Toilet___   Shower___   Bath___   Sink only___

Special needs: View___   Quiet___   Cheapest Room___

Credit card: Visa___   MasterCard___   American Express___

Card #: _____

Expiration date:_____

Name on card: _____

You may charge me for the first night as a deposit. Please fax or mail me confirmation of my reservation, along with the type of room reserved, the price, and whether the price includes breakfast. Thank you.

_____
Signature

_____
Name

_____
Address

_____
City   *State*   *Zip Code*   *Country*

_____
E-mail Address

INDEX

Rick Steves' Phrase Books

Unlike other phrase books and dictionaries on the market, my well-tested phrases and key words cover every situation a traveler is likely to encounter. With these books you'll laugh with your cabby, disarm street thieves with insults, and charm new European friends.

Each book in the series is 4" x 6", with maps.

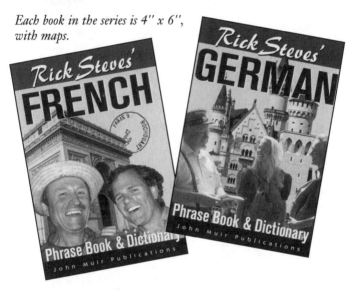

RICK STEVES' FRENCH PHRASE BOOK & DICTIONARY
U.S. $6.95/Canada $10.75

RICK STEVES' GERMAN PHRASE BOOK & DICTIONARY
U.S. $6.95/Canada $10.75

RICK STEVES' ITALIAN PHRASE BOOK & DICTIONARY
U.S. $6.95/Canada $10.75

RICK STEVES' SPANISH & PORTUGUESE PHRASE BOOK & DICTIONARY
U.S. $8.95/Canada $13.95

RICK STEVES' FRENCH, ITALIAN & GERMAN PHRASE BOOK & DICTIONARY
U.S. $8.95/Canada $13.95